MW00931016

THE SURVIVORS PROJECT

Telling the Truth About Life After Sexual Abuse

THIS BOOK IS DEDICATED TO EVERYONE WHOSE
LIFE HAS BEEN AFFECTED BY SEXUAL ABUSE.
THERE ARE TOO MANY OF YOU TO NAME.

THE SURVIVORS PROJECT:
Telling the Truth About Life After Sexual Abuse

For more information, contact *Philadelphia Weekly*:
1500 Sansom Street, Third Floor, Philadelphia, PA 19102
Email: books@philadelphiaweekly.com

First print publication: February 2013

ISBN: 978-1482549911

THE SURVIVORS PROJECT

Telling the Truth About Life After Sexual Abuse

edited by Nina and Joel Hoffmann

A special project of the *Philadelphia Weekly*
Review Publishing
Philadelphia

WARNING: PSYCHOLOGICAL TRIGGERS

You are about to read a collection of first-person
stories written by survivors of sexual abuse,
their loved ones, and advocates. Please take great care
in reading these essays, as many of them contain
graphic descriptions and other passages that may
trigger strong emotional responses.

TABLE OF CONTENTS

Introduction

I N THE WAKE of high-profile, institutional failures to protect children from sexual predators, news organizations across the U.S. have ramped up their reporting on child molestation and rape. They have shed light on a taboo issue that is difficult to comprehend, and they have made it easier for survivors of all kinds of sexual abuse to tell their stories.

But news coverage of sexual abuse has clung too often to the most sensational details while glossing over the long, turbulent recovery that survivors must endure in order to reclaim their lives.

A number of journalistic conventions and constraints have contributed to the way sexual abuse is reported. Libel and privacy laws limit what news organizations can publish about allegations of sexual abuse that have not been made public in court. Verifying the events that surround sexual abuse can be difficult because abusers often silence their victims. Only so many lengthy, complicated news stories will fit in print anymore, and online revenue models often depend on the number of users who click on content that elicits a strong response. We also have to account for compassion fatigue and information overload.

We have compiled this book of essays to fill the gap that exists in the popular dialogue about sexual abuse. *The Survivors Project* is more than just a public-service journalism project produced by an alternative-media company. We, the editors, are connected in a very real way to sexual abuse. It nearly destroyed our marriage.

Talking publicly about how our lives have been affected by sexual abuse didn't happen overnight. Using a pseudonymn, Joel first wrote about his experience as a sexual-abuse survivor in a special June 2011 issue of *Philadelphia Weekly*, in which the newspaper tackled some particularly damaging myths surrounding the culture of sexual violence. Then, when news of sexual-abuse allegations at Penn State broke, Nina wrote about how difficult it was, as the spouse of a survivor, to see how sensational the coverage had become. Nina purposefully omitted Joel's name, but anyone who knew him could figure it out. It was the best way we knew how to ensure Joel's comfort in coming forward. A little less than a year later, in April 2012, we spoke publicly at an event organized by Women Organized Against Rape (WOAR), a Philadelphia-based agency that provides counseling services to victims of all types of sexual violence. We had officially outed ourselves. The public response was overwhelming. We realized our work to bring the terrible effects of sexual abuse to light was just beginning.

On June 27, 2012, Nina, *Philadelphia Weekly*'s senior editor, penned an editorial calling for first-person stories from sexual-abuse survivors, their loved ones and advocates. We didn't know what kind of response to expect. But as word about the project spread to local and national organizations, we were eventually flooded with inquiries from male and female survivors of child sexual abuse, partner rape, incest, and many other forms of sexual violence. They were all ready to tell us—and the world—that they would no longer suffer in silence. They were all ready to share their stories of abuse, but more so, of healing, and what that process looked like.

What resulted was an anthology of personal essays, written largely by non-journalists and edited by journalists, all connected by pain and tragedy.

This is not a definitive account of the effects of sexual abuse. While this book features more than 55 essays from survivors of varying age, gender and background, it speaks for a small fraction of those who have been affected by sexual abuse. Many American communities are not represented here. We wish they were.

This is not a work of clinical psychology, though it is probably the result of it. Talk therapy and any number of chemical, homeopathic and cognitive coping tools have made it possible for survivors to tell you their stories.

This book is full of heartbreaking insights, but it will not be easy to apply the lessons learned by the contributors. The circumstances of and responses to sexual abuse vary widely because surviving it will always be a matter of trial and error.

This is not a self-help book. This is not a manual to follow.

Here's what this book is: It is a resource for those who are in any stage of the healing process. These stories, however tragic and graphic, are full of hope. If you are a survivor, know that so many others before you have endured the hell that is recovery. We hope you can find comfort in the fact that you're not alone.

The contributors understand full well that their essays have been fact-checked to the furthest extent possible, and they have assured us that their recollections are accurate to the best of their knowledge. While we have no reason to doubt them, we cannot authenticate their experience. Only they can do that.

Some contributors have provided legal documents that clearly affirm the horror they have suffered. Most of them had the support they needed to take their cases to court and see some resolution. But survivors of sex crimes have long been muted by shame and a lack of support. This does not make their experience any less real or debilitating.

Most of the contributors in this book have published their essays either under a pseudonym (where marked with an asterisk) or under their first name and last initial. We have taken this approach for legal reasons. Sexual abuse is secretive by nature and usually occurs out of public view. There are very real privacy concerns for the contributors, their families and the perpetrators.

We hope this book helps usher in a broad and honest discussion about what it takes to prevent and heal from sexual abuse. There are signs that the taboo that has stifled conversations about sex abuse is becoming less of an obstacle, but many survivors still feel that they have no one to talk to and nowhere to go for help. We have to create an environment in which survivors feel safe to disclose the abuse, seek support and ask for what they need in order to get better.

This will not be an easy book to read, nor should you expect it to be. But by reading this book, you're taking an important step with survivors and advocates. The more we talk about the effects of sexual abuse, the more we can prevent it. This is a public-health issue, a human-rights issue, as serious and significant as any we've rallied to address in the past.

Survivors need more opportunities to fight back against the culture of shame and secrecy that steals their voices. We can't let it stop here. We have to seize this moment and make sure that no one has to suffer in silence anymore.

Nina Hoffmann, senior editor, *Philadelphia Weekly*
Joel Hoffmann, co-editor, *The Survivors Project*

Trista

Gender: Female
Age: Late 30s
Race/ethnicity: White
Occupation: Self-employed
Location: Pacific Northwest
Age abuse occurred: 17

IT HAS TAKEN half my life to be able to say that I was sexually abused as a teenager and *not* feel that there was shame in that. There is still a remnant there that feels like it will *always* be there. But mostly I have come to believe that while this was a part of my story, it is only a *small* part.

I do not know where the story started. I am sure now that I was slowly groomed—probably as a young child.

I only remember being down in my bedroom around my 17th year, my stepdad starting with a massage under the guise of talking to me about my day. It would start innocently enough, but he would slowly edge toward my panties, eventually taking them off. (Perhaps this is why I never wear panties now.)

Beyond that, I don't remember much. I usually either pretended to be asleep or actually fell asleep. I took to reading my Bible all the time, as if that would somehow protect me when he came into my room.

I remember the night when my mother knocked on the locked door and my stepdad told her to go away. And she *did*.

There was a brief glimpse of hope while she paused at the door, waiting for him to unlock it. *Perhaps this will stop.* But she walked away upon command and he went right back to what he was doing.

And I remember that later, when my sister told my mom, and she confronted me, she became unhinged in a way I thought she would never recover from. And I knew then that she blamed *me* and wanted me to make it better for *her*.

And so I told her, "Fine. It never happened."

And then she became hysterical again. "How could you say that about *my* husband?"

And I said nothing.

And to this day, all I can think is, *Why do you suppose that door was locked, Mom?* Is there *ever* a reason for an adult man to be in a locked bedroom with a teenage girl?

I think that one thing that made it easy for my stepdad to groom me was that my dad was never able to give me a compliment. I know he loved me and he was a very stable father. But he kept his feelings to himself, and I suppose I have some resentment about that as well. Most of the "compliments" I received were from my stepfather.

I did not talk to my stepdad for nearly eight years after completely telling him off in a way that I am sure he never recovered from. His health has steadily gone downhill since then. He only recently met my children, and while I finally believe he is sorry, he will *never* be alone with them.

The hardest thing to come to terms with is that there is still a part of him that I love—and that I will always love. He was still—at least partially—my *dad*. I have happy memories, too—funny things that still make me smile. I have hated him, but there has always been love.

I think this is why it has been important for me to reconnect with him before he dies.

What is harder for me to grapple with is not the abuse, but my mother's betrayal. To this day, she cannot talk about it. She cannot *acknowledge* it. And if I broach the subject, it's like she has either completely forgotten about it or just really blocked it out to the point where she truly believes that it never happened.

And I know that that has not just affected me, it has affected her. Her weight has nearly doubled. Her thinking has become slurred and blurry from years of smoking pot. There is never a moment when the TV is not on at full blast in her home, as if one second of quiet time would be un-bearable. She even sleeps with the TV on.

It is a very sad thing to not be able to trust your own mother. For a long time, I didn't think that we could ever have a normal relationship. It's better than it was, but it will never be what I longed for as a little girl, as a young adult woman, or even now in my late 30s.

It took a long time for me to realize that my mom was not going to be able to acknowledge what happened to me. It took a long time to know that I did not need her to. It took longer for me to accept my mother, with her faults, and see who she is as a person.

You cannot heal yourself until you come to terms with your parents' lives as well. When you have children you begin to understand, a bit more, what their lives likely entailed. You begin to ask the questions you were numb to as a child.

My mother also suffered abuse. This contributed to her inability to fully parent me as a young woman. She has never healed. She still justifies her own abuse. Listening to her made me realize I needed to do something dif-ferent.

I knew almost instantly the first time I became pregnant that I had a boy coming. I almost willed it that way. I was *terrified* to have a daughter. There was still so much left unhealed in me, and I was horrified at the idea of having a girl.

After years of therapy, I felt ready for a girl three years later. This time, I knew I was having a girl and smiled at the fact that the promise I had made to myself at the age of 20 was finally coming to pass. It was then I picked her name, after the first woman I met in my life who was completely happy and at ease with herself.

I thought I was ready for her arrival but near the end of my pregnancy, the rage at my mother re-emerged. I wrote her a letter, telling her off. It was nearly six months before we came to some sort of terms, and I allowed her to be around my children again.

This was my half-sister's first awareness of what had happened to me. She was seven years younger and shielded from the initial drama. She was shocked, and had a really hard time with it. Our relationship has never fully recovered. I felt as though everyone was much more comfortable keeping it hidden so it would not hurt *them* so much. I felt like screaming, *How do you think this has been for me?*

My sister has a completely different relationship with her dad. He is fully her father. She adores him. Half of her is made from him, and that makes it hard. If he is the monster I claim him to be, what does that make *her*?

I have also had guilt about the possibility of him molesting someone else. There is a large family available to him. Somehow, I have felt that they would never believe me since I have always been an outsider. I would just be the wicked stepdaughter getting even. And then I wonder if I am only justifying myself.

Recently, an older mentor asked me how this has affected me sexually, and the floodgates opened. For a long time, I think it made me prude and embarrassed of my sexuality. I come from a family that is full of sexual energy on one side, and completely repressed on the other.

Over the years, I have had many partners. I do not have regrets about that. I know there is a theory that victims of sexual abuse often become promiscuous. For me, it was a way of reclaiming my sexuality on my own terms. What I have noticed is that I have often put up with more than I should in long-term relationships. This became dangerous for me. My children's father was an alcoholic, and our relationship was tumultuous at best. My therapist reminded me I was used to chaos. I didn't know what to do with "normal."

Perhaps growing up with addicts has prohibited me from being able to see things as they are. I never learned to trust my own reality. I never knew I was even entitled to one. My deepest fear now is for my daughter. I want to listen to her. I want to protect her.

I realized several years ago just how deep that fear seeped into me. I received a photo of her on my phone while she was visiting her father and showed it to my then-boyfriend. "Look at how pretty she is!" I said proudly. He smiled and replied, "She is beautiful! I think she's even prettier than you!" And that's when I lost it. I began to cry in a way he could not understand. Perplexed, he responded, "If I had a son and someone told me they were more handsome than me, I would be happy?"

After listening to him explaining himself for about half an hour, I realized it wasn't about that. It had been a light-hearted comment. It was about the way my stepdad always put my mom down by declaring how beautiful *I* was, as if she were not. I was *skinnier*. I was *younger*. I was *prettier*. He had pitted us against each other in a way that made her blame *me*.

I still sleep with my daughter, and I think part of that is my fear that someone will come into her room at night. When I hold her close to me, her innocence and vulnerability strike me. She is just a little girl, like I had been.

It has been the birth of both of my children that has inspired me to heal my life. I do not want to bring the patterns I have suffered into their worlds. I cannot change my past. But I can vow to always listen to my daughter, and to commit to my own healing. I am not there yet—at least all the way—but I do believe the day will come.

For me, stopping the cycle of abuse is about becoming conscious. Going to therapy; writing. Getting back in touch with my body through yoga and meditation. And for this last little bit that still remains, I have decided I need to learn belly dancing. I need to reconnect with the body that became rigid when I was abused. Something in me has known I needed this dance for a long time. I tried it when I was 19, but I was so stiff, the teacher laughed about my inability to shake my hips. Freer now and more in tune with my body, I have started some one-on-one lessons via Skype with a trusted friend. I envision myself now as I was meant to be. Less encumbered; finally happy and in love with a man who treats me well.

I have also finally learned that it is not my duty to the world to be "pretty." I have more important things to accomplish with my life. Pretty has often come at a high price.

We are the composite of what happens to us. But we are also strong, resilient and brave. I no longer see myself as a victim or a survivor. I am a person, no more and no less deserving of love and grace than anyone else.

Susan DiPronio

Gender: Female
Race/ethnicity: White
Occupation: Food broker
Location: Philadelphia, Pa.
Age abuse occurred: 18, 20, 21

WRITING THIS IS the most difficult thing I have ever done. There were nauseating hours of trying to figure out the sequence, remember what happened. Twisting, blurring memories. Confessing to myself that it was me. As words hit the page, forming a sentence, I panic and feel sick and drained and shaking and have to walk away to catch myself, wondering if it's real. My hope is that this sheds some light on the constant emotional pain endured by a victim of rape. It's not a one-time horror—it's a lifetime of night terrors. It damages not only a body, but it steals a life. Yet, like a pair of old worn shoes, this dark place is a comfort, self-punishment for "letting it happen." I don't expect anyone to understand it. Holding the emotional memories, but not the actual ones.

I can't say the words in relation to me: sexual assault. My brain does not accept them. It spits them out. After years of not remembering, a convenient denial devised by the brain to save my sanity, a bit of trauma leaks out and rationally I know it was me. A cement door blocks that part of my life. When the door is triggered open, hell rushes in and crushes me into pieces. Then, I rebuild and come back. Living with trauma is like the movie *Groundhog Day*, in which you relive it over and over. Except there is no happy ending. It takes work to keep from vomiting the memories at inappropriate times.

An essay about healing from sexual assault? There is no immediate healing. Being a victim is a chronic disease. You're in constant crisis. Stuck, like a buoy, thrashing on a turbulent sea. Not going anywhere. Trauma leaks out of your psyche and you go from fearless to fearful in an instant. It's toxic to hold it close. Sexual assault is a sterile, academic name for being brutally and repeatedly raped, sodomized, kidnapped, tortured, beaten and left for dead. Not once in my life—three times: The assaults were horrific, but the fact is that every single time, there were people near or watching it happen who never tried to help. I can't think of any excuse that would justify their inaction. Sometimes, I still feel that somehow it was my fault, but realize that what matters is that I save myself now and resolve the guilt I've held on to for so many years. I am a victim and I have to stop blaming myself. The world is doing enough "victim blaming."

The first time happened when I was around 18. I was walking down the street in daylight going home from a new job and was probably followed from the bus stop. Unsure of the neighborhood, I got turned around. He grabbed me from behind, his hand covering my mouth, a sharp point at my back, saying he had a knife and I'd better do what he said. He forced me into an empty building where he raped me, and choked me until I passed out. I remember a dirty mattress or something and coming to with a sore throat, my clothes ripped and scattered around. I don't remember how I got home, but I never told anyone. I felt stupid and dirty and ashamed. *Maybe I looked like I wanted it? Asked for it? I deserve this. They will blame me. It's my fault.* A few days or so later, I was at the same bus stop, and a lot of people were around me waiting. I was detached, leaning against a large store window and there he was, AGAIN. He grabbed me, picked me up and started slamming me into the window. People just WATCHED and did nothing. I vividly remember a woman cleaning her glasses. Somehow, I fought and broke free and ran down the street and never went back to that town, or that job.

A short while after, I began a meditation practice and was then lured into a cultish Buddhist sect. Meditation helped me to function without recycling the crime in my mind. The Buddhists gave me community, but they were controlling. So, the rape was still there like a cancer growing, a twisting ball of barbed wire inside me. I buried it deep and then started on a road of self-medication: alcohol, drugs and running away from everyone, everything. I totally shut down emotionally, went to San Francisco and became a Hari Krishna devotee for a minute. Then lived on the streets for years. At one point, having dropped too much acid, I ended up in a psychiatric hospital somewhere in Northern California. They released me with a bucket of pills. I guess they figured it was the acid, not me. I don't know how long I was there or how I got there. I guess I hitchhiked back to San Francisco.

Trying to clean up my life led me to move in with a group of supportive women. Although I never told them what had happened to me, they knew something was wrong and persuaded me to get into therapy. I would have severe panic attacks and get lost, not knowing where or who I was for hours, sometimes days. The talk therapy had stirred up the horrible feelings, escalated the terror. I couldn't deal with it and left them all.

The second time I was sexually assaulted was a couple years later in a different city. I had accepted a ride home from a co-worker's boyfriend, but instead he took me to his apartment saying he had to pick up something before he could take me home. He kept saying, "Why don't you come in for a minute?" I started to get a bad feeling and said no. He got out of the car and came around to my door, pulling a gun out of his pocket. I still refused to go in, but was too frozen to run or fight. He grabbed me and pushed the gun into my back and forced me into his place. I don't know why I didn't fight or scream, but still feel guilty, like it was my fault. A girl was coming down the steps and looked right at us. She did nothing. I know she knew and really thought she would call the police and I would be saved, but she didn't. He shoved me into his apartment. He raped, beat and brutally sodomized me. Devoured by a wild animal. Shredded. He dragged, pushed, shoved me back to his car and drove me somewhere, I don't remember where, and threw me out on the street—like trash. I never told anyone, not even the co-worker. She had bragged so much about him being this great new guy in her life. I said the bruises were from a fall. I could barely walk or eat for a long time. Every part of my body hurt to touch, and the shutting down went deeper. I still feel guilty for not telling the co-worker. I was ashamed and afraid that maybe she would think that I wanted it, had come on to him. I quit the job and moved on again.

How many showers does it take, how hard can I scrub my body with a coarse brush? Until it bleeds. Bathe in perfumed water for hours to get the lingering smell of them off me. Back to heavy self-medicating with alcohol and drugs. Living in a stupor, not sleeping for days, weeks of wandering until passing out somewhere. This time, I was pushed into electro-stimulation therapy (EST) by a former drug dealer of mine who had claimed to be saved by it. Not helpful; controlling and creepy.

The third time that I was assaulted was maybe a year later in a car. I had been living in a place where the buses ran sporadically and would walk the six or so miles to work. But this one morning, I was running late, had already walked halfway and it was pouring rain. It was the beginning of rush hour. I hesitated, and even though something in me said don't, I put my thumb out and instantly a car stopped. I got in and he turned the car in the opposite direction. He was exposed and I tried to get out, but he grabbed me by the hair and repeatedly bashed my head and face into the dashboard. He pulled over at the side of an intersection and reached for a gun shoving my face into his crotch with the gun pressed at the back of my head. As he pushed the gun into the back of my head, he came, screaming. In that moment I somehow kicked, fought free and jumped out of the car. I didn't care if he shot me. He had already told me how he was going to kill me and where he was going to bury my body. I figured I'd rather be killed right there. Where someone would know what happened to me. I felt like there was mud or blood oozing down my body. It was his cum running down my face. I wasn't sure if I was really shot at. I think it happened, but I'm not sure if I heard it or felt it. I think that I was hit in the head as I jumped from the moving car and fell in the mud. In the pouring rain, he tried to run me over. I remember banging on people's car windows, begging for help. Not one person rolled down their window. He kept coming at me over and over. I could hear car wheels spinning in the mud, drowning my screams. Dozens of cars were stopped at the intersection that day. No one tried to help me. Some looked away, others turned up their car radios. (Background music to rape and murder?) It seemed to go on forever. Then, when the light changed, they drove away. They just left me there! Why did they feel that my life was not worth saving? Collapsing into the mud, cum and blood dripping down my face, choking on my own blood, I wanted to die. I don't know why he gave up and left. Nor do I remember where I went after or how. This was the end for me and I turned off my life. People became unnecessary. Used sporadically, no commitments.

"It" stole a big part of who I was and could have been. My anger is deep, but the sadness is deeper, mourning the death of Me. Never to be the person I was meant to be. Instead, a woman of many boundaries. Living in a maze, darting down its paths, hoping one of them is the way out. I am a ghost in this world, a builder of fantasy places in which to hide. Daring others to try to find me.

I am always watching over my shoulder. When a shadow appears on a sidewalk looming from behind me, getting closer, in that instant, terror engulfs me and I automatically move to the side to let them pass. Breathe, breathe, breathe. I gather myself and continue. Can you imagine being trapped there, forever? In a place where shadows and strangers' smiles can bring absolute terror, your heart pounding, nausea filling your day? The thoughts recycle, replaying over and over and over until they settle. A window opens and fresh air comes rushing in, but it's short-lived.

Talk therapy, group therapy, art therapy, meds, eye movement desensitization and reprocessing (EMDR), hypnosis therapy, reiki, mindfulness meditation, guided healing imagery, acupuncture. I have tried it all. Everything helps, but "It" lingers in me. I changed after what I didn't believe would ever be the last attack—for the worse. My emotional numbness took over my physical body, my face sank on the left side. Eventually, I was diagnosed with Post Traumatic Stress Disorder and referred to a therapist who had experience with PTSD. After more than a year of talk therapy and into a state of high anxiety where I could no longer differentiate between reality—to the point of being terrified of going into a shower—she unsuccessfully tried hypnosis therapy on me. Then, honestly, said she could not help me. She recommended that I go to a psychiatrist and get on meds. I did not and instead with the help of my partner at the time, I found a psychologist who focused on hypnosis therapy. She slowly reintroduced the world to me. Allowing me to remember what I could in small pieces. At the same time, I started meeting with an art therapist, meditating and falling into a hypnotic dream state and upon his cue, awakening to paint on large pages of what I remembered. Ultimately, what has helped me more is writing, every day. The healing power of written words is the key for me. This is the first time I have written about the sexual assaults. It's been really hard to do, but it may be the most important step yet.

It's taken decades to be able to go forward, before I could feel a little, before I cried for the first time. Those first tears were so strange; foreign. I wiped my fingers across my face, gathering them to look at in disbelief, and tasted them. And then put them back on my face, proof I was like everyone else, treasuring my entry back, not being sure it would ever happen again.

Tonight I laughed along with other people and then the Muppet song, "The Rainbow Connection," made me cry. Yeah, sappy, not sure what the trigger is there, but it may be in the lyrics: "It's something that I'm supposed to be." Maybe there is a healing journey, a path, that I'm on and for me, it's just taking longer to save myself.

Meagan, Michael and Jere

* * *

Meagan H.D.

Gender: Female
Age: 34
Race/ethnicity: White/Caucasian
Occupation: Nonprofit program director
Location: Philadelphia, Pa. The abuse happened in New Jersey.
Age abuse occurred: 7
Relationship to survivor: Survivor and daughter of a survivor
Note: *So you are aware, I did not know that my father was also abused before reading his essay. My mother has thanked me for asking them to write about my abuse, as this is only the second time that he has ever discussed it, and the first time was the night of my abuse. I probably would never have known if it was not for PW's request for stories. Obvious to say that my mom feels that sharing it has helped with some of his healing. Writing these pieces has opened up a dialogue between my parents and I that never would have occurred otherwise. While it is quite emotional, I feel strongly that it has been very helpful to understanding each other and fostering personal healing.*

I WANT TO STATE for the record that I am very lucky, and while what happened to me was terrible, I think it was overall good that it occurred because it stopped a lifetime of abuse and hatred for others. Gaps in my memory have spared me many specifics of what happened, but the story as a whole will stay with me forever, and has influenced who I am today. As this is an account of my story, all names have been changed. I truly hope that with time, the other people involved are able to share their story enough to heal.

One typical day, I believe I was 7 years old, I walked down to my friend's house. Shelly and I grew up in a low-income neighborhood surrounded by woods that led to hours of running around outside. I think there may be two pictures from my childhood in which there was not dirt smeared on my face. On this day however, Shelly asked if I wanted to play "Doctor."

Shelly and I went upstairs to her brother's bedroom, where her two brothers sat on one of the beds. Her younger brother seemed nice but I didn't have much interaction with him. However, her other brother, Greg, was a year older and I just didn't like him. There was nothing I could put my finger on, but he just seemed cruel. Again, it was just a gut reaction.

The bedroom was the "waiting room" that we would sit in until it was time to see Shelly's 20-year-old brother, Tom, the "doctor." I don't remember if Shelly went in first or I did. And I remember her looking at me sadly, almost apologetically, but that may be how I want to remember her face.

When it was my turn, I walked into the "doctor's office," and both bedroom doors were closed behind me. Yet due to poor construction, the large gaps above the doors allowed you to see the ceiling of the "waiting room" from behind the closed door of the "doctor's office." During my examination, Tom asked me if I felt OK, and when I replied that I was fine, he said that he still needed to check me out. Tom pulled down my pants and examined me with his mouth. He kept asking me if it hurt, and I could say nothing. I do not remember much else other than continuing to see Greg's head appear near the ceiling as he repeatedly jumped up to see through the gaps above the doors. When I walked out of the doctor's room, Greg sneered as he asked why I let it happen. Again, I said nothing.

That night, I must have been subdued because my parents wanted to know what was wrong. I couldn't tell them, but eventually they threatened not to let me play with Shelly anymore if I didn't tell them what happened.

The ensuing conversation is another piece of my story that I do not remember, but later that night, the police arrived and took my statement.

There was a little bit of time between that night and Tom confessing and going to jail. In that time, I found out that Shelly had been abused by her brother for years. We could not remain friends after what happened, but stayed friendly. I heard that she went to counseling and her mother moved Shelly and her brothers out of the house and away from some of the more toxic members of the family. I pray that she is well.

This terrible episode happened and was mainly forgotten. My family moved over an hour away and things were over. Then, when I was in middle school, I accidentally found a letter addressed to my mother. It was from Tom. He was writing because he was getting out of jail and wanted to thank my mother for all of her counseling.

I would love to write that the letter floated out of my hand as I sank to the floor, tasting the salt as it ran into my mouth. It would be lovely imagery. Yet this is another painful moment that has been wiped from my memory. I remember finding the letter in the wooden desk where various pieces of mail and junk would be thrown. I couldn't tell you why I took the letter out of the envelope or what I did after I read the letter.

It took several days before I could confront my mother. I learned that Tom had been abused by his father, and about the vicious cycle that often occurs when these horrible things happen, especially when they continue to happen to small children by those they should be able to trust. I also learned that Mom regularly went to visit Tom before and after sentencing. She told me that regardless of how evil Tom's act was, jail would not allow him to become mentally better. Therefore, she had petitioned the court to send him to counseling in an institution instead. Unfortunately, his family's dynamic was very unhealthy and not able to provide him with support and strength to recognize his problems and try to change them. So when he was sentenced to jail, Mom, a minister, took his treatment upon herself because Tom had no one else. All of these actions were decisions made by both my parents, because while my mother did most of the actions, she had my father's support.

Some may not be able to comprehend my parents' actions. What I cannot comprehend is how Mom found the forgiveness to go to this man who had so harmed her child and minister to him. He caused me so much pain. But Mom, who thinks of others' needs by nature, was able to go to Tom, listen to his story and try to help him to heal at the same time she was trying to help me heal. And just so you know, he felt terrible about what he did to Shelly and me. He knew it was wrong, yet he continued to do it.

I don't know if Mom was able to help Tom, but I do know that my parents love me very much, and I am the person I am because they are so kindhearted that they could want to heal this man who made a victim of me, and was a victim himself.

*   *   *

Michael H.D.

Gender: Male
Age: 64
Race/ethnicity: White
Occupation: Technical professional
Location: Southern N.J.
Relationship to survivor: Father/self

THIS IS ABOUT instances of sexual abuse at two different times and affecting two different lives. The first one is about what happened to me, but I now consider it of little consequence. The second concerns my daughter, and has caused me far greater anguish.

I was raised in a South Jersey suburb near Philadelphia. Our family might be seen as lower-middle class, as we had our share of financial struggles. My parents both worked, and believed that after high school you find a good company to work for, and live frugally while you save money for your own family.

I think I've driven many of the memories out of my mind, so I don't remember some of the details that well, but I believe it was the summer of my freshman year. During that summer, I worked at a theater as part of the stage crew. What I do remember is that when it was over, I blamed my own naiveté for allowing myself to be placed in a room where one of the bit actors stayed during the dates the play ran.

It started with a conversation after one of the final shows between the actor and I. We talked about having a beer as we walked around town. Looking back, it's hard to believe how gullible I must have been, but I ended up walking to the boarding house to meet him. In his room, we talked a little and he offered a small glass of gin and grapefruit juice (explaining he had forgotten the beer). He asked me what I thought of some pictures he had (men wrestling) and I made some comments but didn't spend much time looking at them. We talked about how tall I might grow and he said he could tell by feeling my muscle tone. He was probably in his late 30s or 40s, so his age made him more credible to me.

I remember him massaging my legs and later being on top of me. Before he had finished, I managed to gather the courage, clench my fists and say "No." At first, he told me it would be OK, but I was adamant and he got off me. As I pulled my clothes back on, he reminded me that when I had first arrived, I had promised not to tell anyone about being there. I thought the promise was about having a drink.

I walked home and changed and washed my clothes. I never told anyone, maybe because I had made the promise but more likely because I was too embarrassed. As time has moved on, I have forced myself not to think about it. There has never been a need of forgiveness or resolution because I mostly blamed myself. Eventually, I did tell my wife about the incident, but only after she and I found out that our 7-year-old daughter was sexually violated by the son of a neighboring family.

I didn't want to believe it, but knew it couldn't be avoided. I went down to his family's house and told his parents I needed to talk with him. I had thought about taking a bat with me, but if I had, perhaps it would not have ended well for anyone. He denied everything, which probably angered me even more. I wanted to believe that nothing happened, but I knew inside that he had lied. My wife and I contacted the police and the county prosecutor's office and issued a complaint. He was arrested and sent away as an offender. I never knew how to talk to my daughter about it, but thankfully, my wife did.

Eventually, the boy wrote a letter or two expressing how sorry he was. Still, I have never forgiven him, nor do I care to. I know in my mind that I couldn't possibly be with my daughter every moment to protect her from things such as this, but part of me still wants to punish him for what he did.

I have always had the feeling that my daughter never wanted to talk to me about it, and so I have never broached the topic. These are things that my wife is much better equipped to deal with. I know that I have rambled a bit, and yet writing down what I remember may have helped resolve some of my feelings. The most curious thing is that it was my daughter who sent us the announcement for this project, and now I find myself writing this only because of her.

* * *

Jere H.D.

Gender: Female
Age: 62
Race/ethnicity: Caucasian
Occupation: United Methodist minister
Location: Southern N.J.
Relationship to survivor: Mother/wife

THERE ARE DETAILS about the sexual molestation of our daughter that are vividly frozen in time like a photograph, while other aspects are blurred with obscurity. It was 27 years ago in 1985, late on a Sunday afternoon, the weekend prior to Halloween, when our 7-year-old daughter plopped down beside me while I was reading in bed. Her body position and her voice were unnatural and I instinctively knew something was wrong. As I prodded her to tell me, her reluctance felt like a mixture of confusion, shame and guilt. I put down my book, totally turned my attention to her and gently tried to encourage her to tell me what had happened while she was playing at our neighbor's house. She said that they had been playing "doctor" when her friend's reclusive older brother joined the game. He took her friend, and then her, into a separate room, pulled down her pants and underwear, and molested her.

The remainder of that evening is a hazy whirlwind of emotions and actions. I went next door and informed our church youth group I would not be there to supervise the Halloween party and to do whatever they needed to do. I told my husband. We inadequately tried to reassure our daughter. We were in shock. My husband and I started smoking again (a habit that took me another decade to break). He went to our neighbor's house, confronted them, and learned that the older son, although still a high school sophomore, was 18, an adult. We called the police without revealing the specifics of the crime. A patrolman came to our house, and we described a "what if" situation without any names or details. We were advised to file a report. My husband called work and took a family leave day off, a radical abnormality. I felt totally responsible and guilty for even allowing our daughter to play at our neighbor's house. I usually only let her friend come to our house because I knew she came from a dysfunctional, rough home. Our daughter went to bed while my husband and I stayed awake talking, anguishing, deciding what to do, and crying.

The next day, my husband and I went to the police station and reported the crime in detail to a very professional and caring detective. He briefly talked with our daughter while we were present and told us not to have any contact with our neighbor's family. The following day, all three of us went to the county prosecutor's office, where a female detective met privately with our daughter while we watched behind a mirrored window. She used dolls to assist in describing the crime. I cried and was secretly relieved that I could only watch and not hear what was being said to and by our daughter. The next day, when our daughter returned to school, a detective and a social worker called her friend out of class, went to the home, and confronted the family. That night, on Halloween, three days after our daughter was sexually assaulted, the older son was arrested.

The crime does not end there. It is woven into the very essence of who our daughter is. It shapes her life and her relationships, and that is her story to share. I have never felt I had the right to tell anyone about this because it is her choice to talk about it or not. I am writing this because she asked me to, and it is woven into our family relationships, our memories and our healing.

I am a United Methodist pastor and our church had ministered to our neighbor's family through some of their problems. That night after the arrest, his mother knocked on my door, crying that her son had been arrested and seeking solace. The only person she could turn to in her distress was her pastor, me, the mother of the victim who reported the crime. It felt sickeningly ironic and paradoxical. My husband took our daughter upstairs while I listened to her grief as she claimed her son's innocence. I tried to stress that our daughters were the victims and needed our support. This was the position I took in the months and years ahead while our church continued to assist the family and welcome the children in Sunday School throughout the years. Her daughter and ours continued to attend school together and remained distant friends.

Although conflicted as mother and pastor, I did contact the prosecutor's office and advocate that the defendant receive legal assistance and psychiatric help. Eventually, he pleaded guilty and was sent to state prison rather than the sexual offender prison, through a plea bargain arrangement. His mother asked me to visit him in county jail before he was sent to prison. I did. He asked for my forgiveness. At that moment, I felt a wall split me in half between mother and minister. We prayed. As minister, I offered him God's forgiveness for I believe he sincerely needed that grace and I said the words "I forgive you" although the other part of me was screaming in pain. He said he could not confess to his mother that he had molested our daughter and his half-sister.

I needed to resolve my broken and split selves. I needed to seek forgiveness for my guilt of allowing our daughter to play at the neighbor's house instead of being lazy and reading a book. Two years later, I sought solace from a clergy friend and spent time in confession and prayer, wavering between anger and forgiveness. God's grace and forgiveness was/is readily available but it took years for me to forgive myself. Over the decades, I have had to revisit that problem inside myself as other issues have arisen in our family, in our daughter's and in my life. It does not haunt me anymore, yet it is a part of who I am and how I choose to respond in difficult situations. Our daughter has had to learn more, experience more pain, and adjust to the reality of being a victim of sexual assault as she grew through adolescence, young adult and her own sexual maturity. I have vivid images of her tears when the enormous reality hit her in junior high.

After the son went to New Jersey state prison, he wrote to me several times as he seemed to come to grips with the consequences and devastation of his crime. I answered occasionally, reminding him that he needed to tell his mother the truth and to seek forgiveness from the victims. He became involved in the chaplain program in prison. After about eight years, he was approaching a parole hearing. He finally did confess his crime to his mother. He wrote a letter to me asking my husband and our daughter to forgive him. When I shared that letter with them, it opened the door for their own healing. Although he did ask, I never told him our new address after we moved to another congregation. I never tried to communicate with him after he was released in order to protect our daughter.

The letter is still somewhere in our house today in case any member of our family needs to revisit it or reconcile any issues. The violation of sexual abuse never disappears. I absolutely believe in redemption, but this offender would have to discover the help, counseling, therapy and transformation from others besides myself. I could, and did, offer him that opportunity through forgiveness. My connection is with the healing and health of our daughter, my husband and myself. I trust that openly talking about the crime, holding the abuser accountable through legal justice, and continuing to work through our emotional, practical and spiritual issues as the need arises has enabled us to experience wholeness. With time, there are memories that have faded, like the fact that I can no longer remember his last name, but there are other images such as our daughter's face that night, which will never diminish.

Anonymous

Gender: Female
Age: 24
Race/ethnicity: White
Occupation: Waitress and artist
Location: Philadelphia, Pa.
Age abuse occurred: 16

IF YOU TAKE the trolley west to 60th Street, make a right at the Chinese corner store and walk to the end of the block, you will find a house. The street ends at this house, and there is a large concrete partition covered in the fading pastel of old graffiti. I'm not sure what's behind it. It could be the train tracks or it could be the end of the world. But forgetting the wall, if you turn left and climb the steps to the front door of the house, you will see that there is only a hole where the doorknob should be. If you squat down and peer through the hole, you might see dirty brown carpet. You might smell its dank, mildew-y smell and think that it has not been vacuumed for a very, very long time. If you look further through the hole you might see a soggy old couch that is green and slouching against a wall covered in mirrors.

At this point, you have probably paused to look over your shoulder, craning your neck to see if anyone is watching you as you peer through this hole in this door at the end of this block. People say this is not a good neighborhood, and you know you don't belong here. You can feel the eyes watching you from behind curtains across the street. You have blindly followed my directions to some forgotten little corner of Philadelphia and you are not really sure where you are or when the next trolley comes and now the sun is beginning to slip lower in the sky. And this makes you nervous. But you still can't bring yourself to leave, not just yet. And so you turn back to the hole in the door.

From your position squatting on the front stoop and peering through the hole, you can see just a bit beyond the couch to what is most likely the dining room. Through the mirrors on the wall, you can catch just a glimpse of the stairs leading to the second floor. You wonder if anyone lives here, or whose home this used to be. But now your legs are beginning to go numb, and your eyes are starting to ache from the strain of peering through the hole. Your curiosity catches you and you stand up, legs full of pins and needles and you reach your fingers through the hole and pull open the door. You look over your shoulder and down the quiet street. The sun is almost gone and the corner store sign is glowing that toxic neon yellow. You step into the house.

As soon as you step inside, you can feel it. There is sadness, an emptiness that pervades. The air is thick with it; it seems to seep from the fibers of the dank carpeting, to rise from between the cushions of the couch. There are no photographs on the wall, no trinkets on mantle. *Hello? Hello?* You call out, just louder than a whisper is all you're able to muster. But no one answers. It's a house for ghosts. Don't look in the mirrors.

You walk from the living room into what would be the dining room; there is no furniture, no table, no chairs. To the left is the kitchen; beneath your feet, carpet becomes yellowed linoleum. White wooden cabinets lined with curling brown paper, a porcelain sink. A trash can full of nothing. There's not a dish in the house. You don't dare open the basement door.

It's dark now. You try a light switch but the power's off. Through the window in the kitchen trees cast the shadows of monsters across the floor in moonlight. You feel cold. Your heart is working faster now. Why have you come here, all alone? This is not safe. There is no one to help you, you know no one here. A stranger, a tourist, a sitting duck. This is what you are.

You open the back door and look into an abyss that begins just shy of the last concrete step. You grip the cold metal railing and wait for your eyes to adjust. The ground is littered with years of dead branches and rotting leaves from a thousand falls. Towering walls of prickers and vines choke the trunks of dying trees, their bodies twisted and leafless in the summer night. And that is when you see her: a ghost. Tall and skinny in a pink tank top and cut-offs, a girl of just barely 16. My ghost. The girl who was brought to this abandoned house eight years ago and raped.

This is the first time I've ever written about what happened to me eight years ago. Until very recently, I never spoke about my assault to anyone. I never went to the police, I never told my parents, my friends, my lovers or my doctor. I suppressed this incident with a thick layer of shame and the firm belief that I had brought this upon myself. It was my fault. I should never have gotten on the trolley that day. I should never have gone to a neighborhood I didn't know to meet a boy I hardly knew. I should not have been wearing such short shorts, or such a skimpy tank top. I should have been smarter. I should have been less trusting. I should have fought back.

As anyone knows who has tried to run from their demons, suppressing a horrific event only makes them bang and scream and prattle on inside your head with increasing levels of ferocity over the years. I tried to silence the din with copious amounts of drugs and men. Marijuana, cocaine, ecstasy, methamphetamine, cigarettes and, once I got my hands on a fake I.D. at age 18, booze. Men, like the boys who raped me, did not care, and it cost me two abortions, surgery and the constant threat of cervical cancer from the HPV virus. As I look back on these years, I'm surprised that I didn't kill myself, because it sure seems like I was trying to. I'm even more surprised that over the past eight years I managed to earn a GED, a cosmetology license and a college degree.

I think a lot of my ability to just sweep my rape under the rug for so long stemmed from my role in my family, and the ongoing drama within. My earliest memories are of violent fights between my parents, which ended with broken glass and the police being called. They finally divorced when I was 10. When I was 12, my father came out as gay, and moved to the city to live with his partner, while my mother dated a string of questionable men in retribution. Around the time I was 14, my mother attempted suicide and was hospitalized and was later diagnosed with Borderline Personality Disorder. At 15, I moved to Philadelphia to live with my father. The same year I was assaulted in Philly, my mother had a child by a man who turned out to be a lying, cheating, abusive bastard who had a whole other family living an hour away. My father, disturbed by my increasingly erratic behavior and its effect on his new romance, kicked me out of his apartment in Philadelphia and sent me back to live with my mother. I moved into her basement and shortly after, dropped out of high school. I spent my days high, looking after my new baby brother and looking out for his father who wasn't taking the breakup so well and had a full hunting arsenal. As I look back on these events now, I realize that I kept my rape a secret for so long because, in addition to the shame, I felt that my family simply could not handle one more ounce of drama. Both of my parents were smack dab in the middle of their personal crises, and I judged them emotionally unavailable to handle mine, too.

About two years ago, I finally cracked, and told a counselor at college and then my boyfriend at the time. I kept breaking down a sobbing when we tried to have sex. I was full of rage, and small arguments would frequently escalate to me throwing large, hard objects at his head. He wasn't quite sure how to respond to such a bombshell. His continued desire for sex and intimacy felt like a direct affront to my need to heal. He couldn't understand why I couldn't just put it behind me. I was too embarrassed to tell him what happened in any detail. Our relationship, like my counseling sessions, didn't last.

As I look at where I am today in terms of recovering from the trauma of being raped, I feel both frustrated and hopeful. Two months ago, I finally told my parents about my rape, which I feel is a major step toward recovery. Writing this essay is a step toward recovery. I am currently seeing a man who is understanding and patient with me. He is supportive and willing to listen, and he is helping me to regain my trust. I feel good that I have finally been able to identify and choose a healthy relationship over a destructive one.

Despite these steps forward, I feel I still have a long way to go. I still struggle enormously with pent-up rage, and years-old drug-abuse habits. Just recently, I grabbed a full-grown man around the neck and yanked him off his bar stool to the ground. He did nothing to provoke me. I don't remember this because I was blackout drunk. I could have killed him. I'm paranoid. When I come home from work at night, sometimes I can't shake the feeling that someone is waiting in the shadows, in the closet, or under my bed to attack me. Social situations stress me out; I'm afraid of going new places and meeting new people.

All these years later, I still live in Philly, although I am currently making plans to leave this city. When I ride the trolley to work or walk down the street, sometimes I look at the faces around me and wonder if one of them could be the face of one of my attackers. They were teenagers, just like me. It drives me crazy that I have probably walked right past one of them and neither of us ever knew. I wonder if they ever think about me. I think about the abandoned house they raped me in—my haunted house. I know it sounds crazy, but for some reason, I feel like if I could return there, walk down that same street and scream at the top of my lungs; "I WAS RAPED HERE," it would give me some peace of mind.

Elisabeth F.

Gender: Female
Age: 40
Race/ethnicity: Caucasian
Occupation: Special-events representative
Location: Atlantic City, N.J.
Age abuse occurred: 8

IN 1994, I SURVIVED a shoot-out that took place in front of my house. But if you were to ask me what was worse—being molested or surviving a shoot-out—I'd say that being molested was hands down way worse. I wouldn't wish what happened to me on anyone.

I am so tired of keeping this secret. It happened when I was 8 years old. For so long, I kept it inside and didn't tell anyone or even start to deal with it until I was 20 years old. For so long, I couldn't figure out why I didn't tell anyone what happened to me. The answer now seems so clear: I was trapped.

I was sexually abused by my babysitter's kids—her 14-year-old son and her daughter, who was my age. The abuse started when I was about 8 years old and would sleep overnight at the babysitter's house. One night, I was sleeping over, and the babysitter's daughter showed me a stack of *Playboy* and *Penthouse* magazines in her closet, and told me that her mom put them there and told her to perform the sex acts depicted in the magazines with her friends whenever they slept over. So here was this girl's mother sexually abusing her daughter, who was in turn abusing me. This is why I felt trapped: Who could I have asked for help? It scares me to think what further abuse the babysitter would have had in store for me if I had approached her for help. (I believe the daughter was just as much of a victim as I was—can you imagine having a mother who forces you to perform sexual acts on your friends?!)

What's really twisted is that my babysitter was a pillar of the community—always sitting up front at church, involved in the PTA, etc. No one in our community would have believed the things she was doing behind closed doors. I mean, it happened to me, but even I find it hard to believe.

My story gets worse.

My babysitter's 14-year-old son attacked and sexually assaulted me. I was in that fuzzy twilight state where you're happily drowsy and falling asleep when he burst into the room and came at me. I blocked and repressed the memory of him attacking me until I was 19 years old. One time, I was sexually harassed at work, and it triggered the memory of the son coming at me and attacking me. I remember writing in my diary that, *Oh my God, [he] sexually abused me when I was 8*. But I pushed the memory even further to the back of my mind because I just couldn't face it yet. But when I was 20, I started remembering and got into therapy. (I need to credit two groups with saving my life: Women Organized Against Rape and Survivors of Incest Anonymous. I received so much love, acceptance and support from the people in these groups. They literally saved and changed my life.)

As a result, I suffer from severe Post Traumatic Stress Disorder. In addition to the PTSD, I developed severe depression. When I was 28, I was diagnosed with Bipolar Disorder, which I really believe was brought on by the abuse. I know there is a genetic component to Bipolar Disorder, but I truly believe being abused caused me to develop it. And right after the abuse is when I developed a lifelong sleeping disorder. I literally cannot sleep without taking a sleeping pill. I jump at the slightest noise when I'm falling asleep.

After the worst of the abuse—after the son attacked me—I ended up in the hospital for treatment of a heart problem, which was no doubt brought on by the stress of trauma of what happened to me. I completely freaked out the hospital staff when I didn't sleep. They sent doctors in to ask me why I didn't sleep. They sent in a child psychologist. And still I repressed what happened to me and didn't tell.

But who could I have told about the abuse? My dad wasn't in the picture at that point, and my mom was exhausted and depressed from working a full-time job, going through a divorce, receiving little support from her family, all in addition to taking care of me as a single mom. To this day, my mom feels awful that she couldn't prevent the abuse. Mom, it wasn't your fault. You did the best you could with absolutely no one helping you. I love you and, again, THIS IS NOT YOUR FAULT.

I think people who haven't been affected by sexual abuse wonder why survivors never told anyone about the abuse right after it happened. The truth is, sexual abuse is so devastating that we survivors go into denial of what happened to us.

I also have major issues with forgiveness. I was raised Catholic, and they teach you about forgiveness. But how I can I forgive people who nearly destroyed my life? And as strange as it may sound, I have had the hardest time forgiving myself. For years, I kept thinking there was something I could have done to stop the abuse. But, finally, I am learning to love myself. It's not easy, but I'm getting there.

It has been a long, hard road surviving the effects of sexual abuse. There is still so much stigma attached to it that, until now, I haven't told my story to many people.

I know that for this essay I need to explain the challenges I've faced in trying to heal from the sexual abuse. But if there is one thing I've learned from this, it's that you don't heal. You learn to survive. And thankfully, I have survived. I am fortunate to have a wonderful doctor who believes and supports me, and I have been so lucky to receive unconditional love and acceptance from friends as well as from fellow survivors. There are things that help. Finally being honest with myself and with others about what happened helps. And sharing my story with other survivors through Survivors of Incest Anonymous, and listening to their stories, helps. But I believe that some wounds are so deep that they never heal. And there's a lot of sorrow that comes from being sexually abused. Sorrow for the little 8-year-old girl I was whose innocence was so brutally taken away from her. Sorrow that the abuse changed me forever.

To be honest, I'm scared. I'm afraid to come forward because I am afraid of how people will react. I have spent so much of my life hiding from the abuse, so coming forward is probably the hardest thing I will ever have to do. But if sharing my story can help someone else who's being abused, then in my mind it's worth it. And this is why I chose to use my real name for this essay—I am tired of the secrets, and I am tired of being ashamed for something that WASN'T MY FAULT. I spent so many years ashamed, depressed and traumatized. But there is one thing that cannot be taken from me, and that is my voice.

There is a silver lining to this dark cloud—I am so much more understanding and compassionate toward others now as an adult. I've learned not to judge others, because you honestly never know what they have been through. I am so grateful to *Philadelphia Weekly* for giving us survivors a voice. The only advice I could offer to others trying to heal from sexual abuse is that living well is the best revenge. Getting up each day is a victory. Learning to laugh again and enjoying life are victories. And coming forward and shining a light where there used to be only darkness is a victory.

Holly K.

Gender: Female
Age: 51
Race/ethnicity: White
Occupation: Human resources and career consultant
Location: Chicago, Ill.
Age abuse occurred: 4-14

WE LOOKED, BY ALL appearances, like the typical, well-adjusted, middle-class family. My dad was the chief financial officer of a university, my mom, a special-education teacher. We celebrated all the Jewish holidays with our big extended family. My parents had lots of friends. My sister, brother and I excelled in school.

No one would have guessed the horror, darkness and pain that were hidden behind the sunny picture window of our suburban house.

Although my dad was active in causes promoting social justice, that value vanished within the walls of our home. He had frequent, frightening, red-hot, raging tantrums, screaming at the top of his lungs and violating our physical space with his large body, thundering on and on about minor annoyances like a missing receipt or a messy room. The rage came out of nowhere, striking at all times of day for no reason. When it hit, all of us, including my mom, were ordered into the family room where he berated one or more of us for an hour at a time, screaming names at us, like, "You slob, you pig." We lived in fear whenever he was home, always on the lookout for the next explosion.

He was crude, bragging openly and often about his sexual prowess and enjoyment. Portraits of nude women lined my dad's office walls in our basement. *Playboys* and *Penthouses* were strewn around the house. The hyper-sexualized environment in our home made me feel gross inside, ashamed of my body, ashamed to be a woman. As I started to develop, I walked with rounded shoulders and wore loose, tomboy clothes, battling against and trying to deny my femininity.

But my dad saved the worst for night. For it was then that he completely pulverized my body, mind and spirit as he raped me repeatedly over a period of years I am still too pained to quantify.

My mom never tried to stop him from his rages or his rapes. Never. I struggled against that truth, confused by her polished public appearance versus her cowardly private persona. I desperately wanted to hold onto the belief that I had a good mom.

It wasn't until 10 years ago, just after she died when I was 40, that I could even allow myself to begin to see and feel, through gruesome flashbacks, the soul-searing agony of my mom's betrayal. Instead, I turned on myself. From an early age, I felt like something was wrong with me, with my spirit, my character, a belief that only intensified as I matured. What else could explain the residue of black sludge I felt inside—a bottomless hole of unimaginable shame and loneliness that I constantly fought against because outwardly, like my family, I appeared happy and successful. A nationally ranked tennis player with an MBA from Northwestern University, a fulfilling career, a loving husband and two beautiful girls, I had to fight off suicidal thoughts as I saw no other way to escape the excruciating emptiness and heartache that haunted me.

Finally, it got so bad that I sought help and started working with a wonderful therapist who I believe saved my life. She and I slowly unwound my life story, helping me understand the cause of my enormous loneliness that manifested as a deep, soul-felt longing for an older woman, a mom figure, to care for me. The longing for a mom figure heightened the shame. After all, for much of my life, I bought into the outward myth of my family. My mom was the best ever, I thought. So I falsely concluded that the loneliness and unquenchable need for love that I felt had to be a defect within me. I hated myself for it but I couldn't make the wish for a mom stop.

It took years of therapy for me to fully understand that my deep longing was a normal response to horrific circumstances. I was searching for the mom I never had—someone who would be brave enough to rescue me from my dad and stop the abuse. I needed a mom to hold me and say, "I love you and this is not your fault. I'm so sorry this happened to you."

Grasping the truth about my need for a mom was a revelation to me. I was so used to feeling defective. But the hard work was just beginning. Trauma overwhelms normal cognitive functioning, and lives in the body. For me, this long-held, dissociated body pain was the cause of intrusive, painful flashbacks and constant heaviness in my heart. It needed to be physically released.

So week after week, in the safety of my therapist's office, my body shook as I cried in anguish, sobbing. I felt the physical pain from the rapes as if they were happening in real time—one flashback after the next. My therapist sat with me while I saw the violent images unfold. As my body shook, she would gently ask me where I was, what I was seeing, but I was incapable of speaking. She comforted me, and when I asked her to, held me through the most wrenching pain. She reminded me I was safe in her office and that the worst had already happened.

I would often send my therapist an email to describe the memories because saying them out loud for the first time felt like a root canal of the heart. She gently followed up on each email, helping me process and integrate the horror I saw. She helped me understand that the overpowering shame I felt was not mine to bear. It was not my fault. Then, as each memory was released, I felt a sliver of relief, a slight lift of the heaviness in my heart, which gave me the strength to keep going, to get through one more day.

I also used every available tool to cope with the pain outside of therapy. I did extensive research about surviving sexual abuse. I joined online support forums where I connected with generous, compassionate survivors with whom I share similar difficulties including flashbacks, feelings of unworthiness, body shame and the unquenchable need for love.

Upon my therapist's recommendation, I also tried a local group for survivors, led by another therapist. Unlike the Internet forums, this support group was hurtful, not helpful, because the group leader was inconsistent and disrespectful. I had heard similar stories of poor therapeutic treatment on the Internet boards, and after going through this experience, I felt renewed gratitude for the consistent caring of my own therapist.

I wrote countless unsent letters to my parents, expressing my hurt and anger. I used a punching bag and lifted weights. I tried eye movement desensitization and reprocessing (EMDR), acupuncture, guided imagery and Reiki to release the body pain.

The healing process has required every ounce of courage, determination and strength I have been able to muster. For a few years, I had to shut down much of my life to deal with the gruesome flashbacks. I couldn't work and had no energy to see friends. All I could do was make it to the next healing step and conserve enough energy to be available for my two girls.

As I gradually faced the truth of my past and began to heal, I started to find my voice and speak about what happened in our house. First, I confronted my dad. His response was that he couldn't remember, which has since evolved into complete denial. I knew my dad well enough not to hope for an acknowledgement and apology, so I was not surprised.

Next, with my sister's support, I told our extended family about what happened, naively believing that they had seen enough of my dad's temper and sexual inappropriateness over the years to listen and extend their support. With few exceptions, they told me they did not want to take sides and continued to invite my dad and me to the same events as if nothing happened.

My family's neutrality felt like another heart-wrenching betrayal. Sadly, like many incest survivors, I severed those relationships. It was too painful to continue to pretend that all was well in our family.

My favorite aunt as well as the rabbi at my progressive synagogue told me I should forgive and move on. Their advice only added to my heartache and feeling of isolation. Of course I wanted to move on. I was already doing everything I could to heal as fast as possible. I was an achiever, used to setting and surpassing goals, including a goal to heal. But my body and the heaviness in my heart had its own time frame for healing. Trying to push it faster by simply deciding to forgive was not possible. In actuality, their advice to me felt like a directive to keep quiet so they could move on more easily, the truth too painful to absorb. Incest is a disgusting, soul-crushing crime that feeds on secrecy and silence. It's so much easier for society to look away. In my case, the truth was that I had been quiet for 40-plus years, and I needed to release anger, pain, and grief to create room for acceptance and self-compassion. Only then could I begin to feel self-love and eventually forgiveness. Forgiveness follows, not precedes, a healing process. My process is ongoing. My heart has lightened slowly and steadily, bit by bit.

Instead of telling me to forgive, I wish my aunt and the rabbi had said, "I'm so sorry for what you've endured. It's not your fault. You're not alone. I'm here to listen. Would you like to tell me more?" Those words would have softened the pain and helped me heal. I would have felt less alone.

We have made such an effort to ensure that the truth of traumatic events like the Holocaust or 9/11 is fully expressed, and that its survivors are supported. Trauma survivors, of any kind, especially incest victims who are betrayed and violated by the very people they need to trust the most, require a similar process. They need to speak the truth, grieve the loss, and receive support and compassion.

As it turned out, the rabbi's hurtful response at a time when I was very vulnerable resulted in my decision to leave the synagogue. Ironically, however, the healing process has caused me to find and feel an important, healing, spiritual connection. I was in such great pain that, for the first time, I turned to God and found comfort.

I have become a spiritual seeker. I journal and ask God for help. When I am able to quiet my mind and listen, I find peace and guidance within my heart. On occasion, I can even feel aligned inside my body, a very rare and precious feeling for someone whose body has previously only known shame.

I used to think that if I worked hard enough to heal, I could eventually vanquish the pain and only then would I feel better. Ironically, as my long healing process has evolved, I have come to realize that the pain from the abuse will always be with me, and instead of trying to conquer it, I need to give myself time and space to attend to it and feel it with compassion when it flares. It takes a lot of strength to willingly go toward pain but when I do, it eases and releases, restoring my equilibrium.

Recently, I have gained a new perspective. Throughout most of my 10-plus years of healing, I could only see one snippet of my life, one age, one flashback at time. Now, however, I can integrate the enormity of what happened to me, not just at one age, but as a life story. I see the impact and I know the full extent of the loss. I accept that there are some things I will never fully recover, like the ability to fully feel comfortable in my body and the ongoing wish for a mom, which has eased considerably but will always be there. This new understanding has opened up space for more self compassion and a sense of calm that has previously eluded me. I feel lighter inside. I am able to appreciate my own courage and strength in working through and facing down unimaginable, hellish pain during this long healing process. I feel proud of myself and quietly confident knowing that I persevered instead of running away.

In addition, I feel a sense of tremendous inner emotional depth that I believe is rare and mostly attributable to surviving through so much, and correspondingly, an ability to feel enormous compassion and sit with others when they are in pain. The relationships I have held onto have also deepened. My husband has been supportive throughout my long healing process and our marriage and family bond is stronger than ever. I am grateful for the support of my sister, who has stood firmly behind me through some very difficult times. I appreciate the encouragement of my closest friends and the support of a few family members. These are my personal and very meaningful silver linings.

Finally, my experience through this arduous process has provided me with a sense of purpose. I know the terrible loneliness that sexual abuse causes and I want other survivors to know that healing is possible and there are people who understand. I also hope that by doing my part to shatter the secrecy of sexual abuse and incest in the community, when the next survivor finds the courage to tell, instead of facing a stone wall of denial they will be believed; instead of being told to forgive and move on, they will hear you compassionately say to them, "I'm so sorry for what you've endured. I'm here to listen." And they in turn will feel the spark of hope.

Ari Benjamin Bank

Gender: Male
Age: 38
Race/ethnicity: Caucasian
Occupation: English professor, published poet, grief counselor, volunteer
Location: Philadelphia, Pa.
Age abuse occurred: 6

I NEVER WANTED to be a good swimmer, but I always was. My parents had an in-ground pool in the backyard, big enough for laps, with a diving board and a deep end, a "real" deep end, and my dad, whose parents had a pool in the backyard, too, and who was also a good swimmer, taught me every stroke he knew: the crawl, the breaststroke, side and back stroke, elementary. He got me in that pool almost before I can remember, and the water felt good and cool. I learned something new each summer: how to cup my hands and kick my legs, how to turn and breathe, turn and breathe, how to tuck my head in and dive without even making a splash. Of course, he gave me good head starts in races and let me win most times, I think. The summer after my 6th birthday, I could swim stronger and faster than any kid twice my age and twice my size. I didn't want to, but I could, and I knew, even then, watching my dad, and my mom, too, sometimes, looking back at me swim, that I was pleasing them, and that part I liked.

Still, I never wanted to be a good swimmer, but I was anyway, and in the summer, my parents sent me to a day camp that seemed so far away (though I had started going when I was just 4). The camp had tennis courts and soccer fields, arts and crafts and cookouts in the woods and, of course, swimming pools. Early in the mornings, before recreational swim time, the kids from my beginners bunk would change into their bathing suits and then follow one of our counselors, marching off to the pool for their instructional swim, their tender feet getting wet from dew still on the grass. I would go to another pool with another counselor, the pool for the more advanced swimmers—most times anyway. Sometimes that didn't happen. Sometimes we stayed back after the bunk was empty. Sometimes I started to change into my bathing suit but then he'd tell me to stop. *It's OK. I took mine off too. Look, we both have one. You can touch it. Why don't you touch it? There, that feels good. Now I'm going to touch yours, OK? Doesn't that feel good?*

We'd sit together in that quiet, dark plywood shack, the one window and door closed, and I'd think about those other kids in my bunk, learning how to dunk their heads and make bubbles, and I'd wonder why his got so long and hard when he told me to touch it that way, and I'd wonder why it hurt so much when he put it inside me, but I never cried or yelled because he said I was being good. I didn't know why I didn't have to go swim with the bigger and older kids those mornings, but I didn't feel like I belonged with them, either, and he always told me I was different, and that it was really OK, and that no one else should know because we had a special shared secret. But even that part, I didn't like.

I never wanted to be a good swimmer, but I knew I always would be. Each day, I'd come home from camp, and my mom would unpack and find two wet bathing suits scrunched up in clear plastic bags, one wet from recreational swim, and the other wet, too, though sometimes soaked from being held under a water fountain and put in my camp bag just before getting on the bus to go home. Home felt even further away somehow, and less recognizable when I walked back up the driveway. And the pool in my parents' backyard, that too felt strange now, even with my dad's voice calling to me from the backyard, inviting me to join him for a swim, just a quick dip before we barbecued hotdogs and hamburgers, asking me to maybe show him and my mom what I had learned that day.

Panic attacks began that summer. One on camp picture day, when, after me and my brother had our photograph taken together, he grabbed my hand and we ran back to join our bunks. My bunk had instructional swim. I stopped running. Fell to the ground crying and screaming. He didn't know why. Sleepless nights started to build one on top of the other, nights before I had gym class, a basketball or baseball township league game, anything athletic. My dad would watch some TV with me and tell me I'd fall asleep soon. But I wouldn't. He didn't know why. I became introverted. Shied away from the world. My mom would say that was always my nature, but there was much more to it. She didn't know why. How could anyone? I never told. Some years later, I made a choice to try to be average in every way, hoping no one would ever notice me. I aimed for C's in school. That didn't work. I started to shut down on the inside. I started getting in trouble. My parents sent me to a psychiatrist who told them I had a self-sabotaging personality, that I locked a ball and chain around my very own ankle. But someone else locked that to my leg years ago.

Sex wasn't something I wanted to have. A no-brainer. Why would I want to do something so vile with someone I liked and cared for? In my teenage years, I went on dates, had girlfriends, but we never did anything. Then, for some years, I did have sex, but only with women I didn't really know or want to know. Once, I tried to have a relationship, but I only loved her because she treated me horribly (I felt I deserved it). Best friends would begin to have healthy and long relationships, and I was left behind. I lived by myself for a decade. My only company was an amazing cat, Boo, who, in a weird way, found me. I gave all of my heart's love to that fuzzy little guy, and he loved me the same way. He was my companion and I knew that when he would die, I would have to die, too. I had a plan, but plans don't always work out the way we think.

The cat lived long enough until I would find Kirsten, my wife. Maybe he brought me to her, and her to me; Kirsten is allergic to cats but was not allergic to Boo. She called him the "magic cat." Kirsten is the most compassionate and empathetic person I know. While engaged, she stood by my side as I told my parents what had happened to me. We were at their house. It just came out. I grabbed a family photo album and showed them a camp photograph. "That one!" They knew. I didn't feel ashamed like I thought I would. I felt relieved. Still, I would never be OK.

Depression: check. Anxiety disorder, prone to sudden panic attacks: check. Post Traumatic Stress Disorder: double check. Pharmacy techs at the Rite-Aid down the street used to call me the "high-roller," the "heavy-hitter," when paying for my meds. I take much fewer meds now at least.

Found a wonderful psychiatrist. Listens. Understands. Took so much time. Finally. Just 100 milligrams of Zoloft every morning and a benzo for the times when I see a yellow bus pass by; when I catch a strong whiff of chlorine; when someone cracks a joke about fathers and choir boys in church; when a Sandusky story is on the news; when a commercial for *Toddlers & Tiaras* in which children are being told to shake their butts and chests for the judges; when a sudden scene in a movie with a kid being molested appears on the screen; when I drive by a camp (the one I went to is still open). I have a list of triggers, I guess, but the anxiety is manageable. Mostly now it's just talk therapy. I need it. Helps. My doctor tells me it won't really ever go away after I sheepishly ask her if I will ever be able to get past this. She does tell me that it does lessen, and my physical reactions and dips into depression don't have to be like a roller-coaster ride anymore. She's honest. I trust her. I feel better. Still, there are questions. How did I take the extraordinary physical pain when it happened that summer? How do I take the emotional and physical pain ever since? In his book, *The Noonday Demon*, a work about depression, Andrew Solomon writes, "The human capacity to bear pain is shockingly strong." I concur.

There is also a scene from *Rocky* that keeps me going from one day to the next. It's the scene when Rocky lies in bed with Adrian, the night before the big fight, realizing that he just can't win. More importantly, he doesn't want to win. He says he just wants to "go the distance." He knows he's not even in the champ's league, but, if he is still standing when that 15th bell rings, he'll know he made it, that he is somebody, that he counts. I like that. I like that a whole lot. Life will always throw you punches, and some punches will knock you straight to the ground, but what's important is that you can shake it off, get back up, and be ready for the next punch. If you can do that, then that's all that matters. I tell my students this when they see me in my office and notice the miniature Rocky statue on my desk. Then they open up about all sorts of things: losing a loved one to gun violence; terribly abusive relationships; sleeping in cars or living in shelters while still going to school on financial aid: There's a litany of problems that stretch for miles. I listen. I try to find them help. They are my children. I resolved, years ago, that I didn't want to be a father. I think I'd be a good dad, but, because of what happened to me, I just can't.

Then there's that camp photograph. The one with the counselor who stole my childhood. In the picture, he is standing a few feet behind me, smiling. Surprising to most, I imagine, it's actually still in one of my parents' photo albums. I think I understand why it is still there. For them to take it out, to leave a white square on a page yellowed by time, would mean that they would have to face what happened to me, with no looking away. That might be too hard to do. They are my mom and dad, I am their child, and they love me too much.

And when it comes to water, we have an unusual relationship. It feels strange just writing that I have a relationship with water, but why wouldn't I? (I'm an Aquarius after all.) It's a love/hate relationship, I suppose. Sometimes the water feels good and cool again, and other times, I think of quick little responses when someone asks me to go in, but, I just can't: "Oh, too chilly for me, but you go on ahead and I'll watch our towels and chairs." Sometimes the water in a swimming pool seems to be like an old friend who has been waiting for me for such a long time, waiting for me to jump back in without thought or care; other times, the water in a swimming pool looks like it is staring at me, reminding me: *Better be careful, you know what this led to so long ago.* I'll never know what will happen, how I'll react, if I'll go in or not. I do know that this is a part of me, and I can live with that. I can live with a lot. I survived. I healed. I have scars, but I healed. I think we all can if we want to.

Anonymous

Gender: Female
Age: 50
Race/ethnicity: White
Occupation: Physical therapist
Location: Bucks County, Pa.
Age abuse occurred: 3-18

I WAS SEXUALLY abused as a child by three generations of men: my grandfather, my father and my brother. The abuse started at a very young age, and I coped with the pain and the terror by dissociating from it. I was able to protect myself by leaving my body. It wasn't a conscious decision. It would be more accurate to say that I had been chased out of my own body. Each incident of rape caused me to vacate myself a little bit more, numbing me to the pain and memory of the trauma and leaving a little less of me behind. This split between my mind and body allowed me to lead an outwardly appearing "normal" life, but the price I paid for this was high and it eventually took its toll on me.

A diagnosis of breast cancer at the age of 36 triggered deeply held emotions of terror and rage to become unearthed, and my walls of denial began to crumble. The veil of secrecy was ripped away and the illusion of my happy and normal family, one I had clung to so desperately, was shattered as violent and terrifying flashbacks consumed me. I was left reeling. I was immersed in darkness and despair as I tried to confront the reality of what my own father had done to me, what my grandfather had started, and what my damaged brother had re-enacted with me.

I knew on a very deep level that my healing from cancer required me to heal from my past. I felt that everything that I had buried and repressed was finally coming up through my body to be healed. The beginning of my healing process was excruciating, disorienting and overwhelming. So often, I would be swept away by a raging sea of memory fragments, body sensations, images and intense emotions. For the first few months, I was practically nonfunctional. My husband took over most of the every day tasks and care of our two young children. I was barely keeping it together between my visits to my therapist. But over time, I was able to contain myself and pace myself as I worked though the difficult material that was coming up.

Healing from sexual abuse is a slow and arduous process. It takes incredible courage to face the pain and the truth about what happened, especially when the perpetrators are beloved family members. My father and grandfather had been dead for years before I remembered the abuse. My brother, as well as the rest of my family, has steadfastly denied that any abuse ever took place. They are still deeply entrenched in the denial that once held me. I miss the family that I once believed I had. I have had to redefine what family means to me and have created a family for myself of people who love and support me. I am sad that I don't have my family the way I would like, yet I am grateful that I am free and that I have been able to find and integrate the child in me who was so hurt and lost. I have reclaimed the lost parts of myself. I have painstakingly picked up the shattered pieces of my heart and mind, one by one, and have reclaimed them. I will not let sexual abuse define me and I do not call myself a sexual abuse survivor or a victim of sexual abuse because I am so much more than that.

It has been 14 years since this journey began, and as I write this now, it's hard for me to remember those desperate times. As I look back, I am in awe of how much I have healed and am grateful for the many ways in which healing has come to me.

I have found healing in my tears and have experienced how each tear washes away a little more of the pain.

I have found healing in my husband's love and support. He has been my rock of strength and stability, which has allowed me to go to the dark and scary places necessary for my healing. He has been the glue that held our family together with his constant and steady support.

I have found healing with my therapist, who is that one person on this earth who knows most intimately my pain, my grief, my terror, my rage and my shame. Together, we have created a healing space that I will carry within me forever.

I have found healing in the light and laughter of my children, whose innocence and sweetness have helped me recognize and embrace my own.

I have found healing in music, which has helped to release many deep emotions in me. The lyrics of many singer-songwriters have been my companions along the way and have made me feel less alone. Thank you, Sinead O'Connor, Patty Griffin, Sarah McLachlan, Alanis Morissette and Tori Amos.

I have found healing in my journal, a place where, through writing, my heart, mind and soul feel free and safe enough to transform the darkness into light.

I have found healing in the hands of body workers and therapists, whose compassionate and safe touch helped my body to let go of the pain of the past and return to the present.

I have found healing in the sunlight, its warmth radiating deeply into my core and illuminating the light within me.

I have found healing in nature, where perfection and beauty becomes a mirror for me.

I have found healing in the hearts and the hands of so many people who have been brought into my life: my family, teachers, doctors, therapists, nurses, friends, neighbors, colleagues, clients and strangers.

Most importantly, I have found healing by looking within myself and re-connecting with my spirit, that part of me that could never be damaged by anyone's actions, intentions or words. My spirit may have been trampled on and buried, but it has always been there, beckoning me and waiting for me to find her.

Iya Isoke

Gender: Female
Age: 45
Race/ethnicity: Black
Occupation: Office administrator; Harrisburg's poet laureate
Location: Philadelphia, Pa.
Age abuse occurred: 16

I LOOKED THROUGH the peephole with my almost 17-year-old eyes and saw it was a friend of my boyfriend's. I opened the door for him even though I did not know him very well. I remember thinking that my boyfriend seemed to know him rather well, so if he trusted him, I trusted him. "Hey!" He waved through the peephole. "Dude told me to scoop you up, he's running late."

This partial stranger entered the room smiling. He waited and told me jokes while I put on my sneakers. I went through that door and with me went the last naïve thought I ever had. It was the last time I ever blindly trusted the word of anyone. It was the end of my innocence. When we arrived at what I believed to be his house, he turned on the radio and offered me a seat. He told me to make myself comfortable, telling me, "Dude may be a while." I sat on the couch but I didn't exactly feel at ease. After all, I really didn't know this guy, and although he was being nice and friendly, I was beginning to feel uncomfortable. I asked if I could use his phone to page my boyfriend. He said, "Sure, I'll get it for you, can I get you something to drink first? I can get you some lemonade."

He came back into the room carrying an ice-cold glass of lemonade and I was thankful because it was hot and this house only had a rickety old ceiling fan, no air-conditioning. I downed that lemonade as if I had been crawling through the desert for day and I'd discovered a lagoon. Soon after draining the second glass, I began feeling light-headed, then lethargic. I saw his lips moving and heard the words, "Are you OK," but his words weren't matching the rhythm of his mouth. "Here," he said, "You'd better lay down." My eyelids felt heavy, I tried to blink but my eyes weren't opening fast enough. I tried to focus. I had the foggy image of someone undressing me. His voice sounded far away, like it was coming from inside a drum.

He drugged me, held me captive in a basement, repeatedly raped me and then threw me into an alley like trash when he was done with me. I woke up in the hospital with a urinary tract infection and damn near no memory of any of it.

I believed the fault was mine, and because of the load of shame and humiliation I carried internally, my crime went unreported. I've been asked time and again why I didn't report such a violent intrusion on my life. In my family, you just did not go around airing out the dirt accumulated in your household. When I was a child, my Nana told me that "our personal family business is our personal family business, so don't go out there airing out your dirty drawers." She was adamant about not telling people in the street about the things going on in our house. It was nobody's business how much we did or did not have, who was or wasn't working, who was drinking too much or whoring themselves out. If I came to school with a broken arm or a broken fingernail and the question of "who did it" arose, the reply had better been the same. "Nunya." None of your damn business.

And because of the Dirty Laundry Philosophy, I kept my dirty drawers to myself for years. Unfortunately, this philosophy has been so deeply ingrained in families for generations, crossing economic, educational, cultural and racial boundaries, that we've become a community of secret keepers and pall bearers of pain.

It wasn't until I began self-therapy through creative writing that I realized I need more help than the pen and paper could provide. I carried guilt because I opened the door. I got in the car. I walked into the house. I drank the lemonade. Years after my assault, I sought counseling. In some communities and cultures, therapy is a taboo word and the very idea of therapy falls under the soiled blanket of the Dirty Laundry Philosophy. We've instilled the message that admitting you need therapy is like admitting you have a weakness and as a result, the cycle of pain continues. But in fact, asking for help is about the strongest thing a human being can do.

That's why I reject the Dirty Laundry Philosophy. My life has become an open book, a 24-hour laundromat, if you will. Now, when people ask me, "Why are you putting your business in the street?" I want them to understand that there are a lot of people who are hurting in the street. They are hanging on the corners, thinking they will never survive past the pain. They need to have a glimmer of faith, a shard of strength, a moment of understanding, not shame or embarrassment.

I share my story because survivors need to see me standing, taking care of my family, being strong, not bitter, laughing, loving and enjoying life because this will give them hope that they, too, will move past the pain. And when you have hope, you can get help. It wasn't until I sought counseling that I was even able to say the word "rape." When you're at your lowest point in life, I want you to know that I have been encased in darkness somewhere before, but I am a direct result of measured steps taken to reach the light.

Break the cycle and you will find help, relief and direction from people with a story like mine or, more importantly, a story like yours.

Jane E. Johnson

Gender: Female
Age: 57
Race/ethnicity: White
Occupation: Casework Supervisor II with the Rhode Island Department of Children, Youth and Families
Location: East Greenwich, R.I.
Age assault occurred: 48

ON NOV. 8, 2003, my life changed forever. I was the victim of a horrifying rape, sexual assault and physical beating. I suffered a multitude of bruises to my body, human bites to my back and breasts, compounded by clearly visible trauma to my vaginal area. My assailant preyed upon me mercilessly for hours in my own home. He spit in my face and forced his fingers down my throat to keep me quiet. He put his hands around my throat and choked me. I thought I was going to die. He shoved his fist up my vagina and pulled clumps of hair out of my head. I fought him for as long as I could, and then as victims do, I went into survival mode in order to live. My assailant was not a stranger, but someone I knew. When I picked up the phone to call 911, little did I know how my life was about to change. My once "normal" life quickly spiraled downward. I ran away from my friends, my family, and my life. I kept my assault a secret for more than a year, because I was too ashamed and embarrassed. After all, rape happened to other people, not to me! Staying silent from my family and friends was a decision I later came to regret.

I am a casework Supervisor in the Rhode Island's State Department of Children, Youth and Families. I have spent countless hours of my professional career in court. As savvy as I thought I was navigating the legal system, I quickly learned just how naive I was. I quickly learned not to trust anyone. I was the victim, but I was often treated like the criminal.

In 2004, I gave testimony to a grand jury, and after deliberation, my perpetrator was indicted on six counts of first-degree sexual assault. In 2005, a trial was held in Kent County Superior Court in Warwick, R.I. I gave hours of testimony to a jury depicting the events of Nov. 8, 2003. I remember being shown photographs of my injuries and having to describe each one in detail. Having to identify the photos was so disturbing for me and having members of the jury looking at the naked photographs of my badly bruised and beaten body took its toll on me. Unfortunately, this jury was unable to reach a decision and subsequently returned a verdict of a mistrial. I watched my assailant walk out of court that day with a smirk on his face. Once again, I was victimized.

In 2006, I faced my assailant again at a second trial. Pictures of my injuries were flashed on television screens that were positioned in the courtroom for the jury, and anyone else who happened to be sitting in court that day to view. Although very effective from a prosecutor's perspective, it was very personally damaging for me. I felt like I was in the fight for my life and if a conviction had not come down, I honestly don't know if I would be sharing my story with you now.

The jury deliberated for one hour and found him guilty on five of the six counts of first-degree sexual assault. Finally, someone believed me. It was the first time since the assault happened that I was able to take a deep breath and feel safe. He was led out of the courtroom that day in handcuffs to begin serving his sentence. A month later, he was sentenced to 50 years in prison: 25 to serve, 25 suspended. He was ordered to register as a sex offender and was to participate in offender counseling. I was given an opportunity to read my victim impact statement to the judge at his sentencing. The news media were in court that day covering it.

Now that my assailant was in prison, it was my time to begin my healing. I didn't realize the emotional and physical toll this whole process took on me. I continued working with my therapist in an attempt to erase the horrible memories that haunted me. I was diagnosed with PTSD and depression. I experienced flashbacks when I drove down Route 95 and passed the prison, which was situated on the side of the highway. I knew he was in there. I could feel my body freeze in fear. While working, I found it difficult to even walk into the courthouse or in the parking garage, because I knew he had been there. I didn't realize at the time, but I was dissociating from all of the pain. It was my only way of escape.

It is said that time heals all wounds. The years passed and slowly but surely, under the guidance of some excellent therapists, I did get the tools I needed to help put this experience in perspective and move forward in my life.

In April 2009, I was notified by the Attorney General's Office that my assailant had hired new counsel and had filed an appeal with the state Supreme Court. Although horrified at the thought that his conviction could be overturned, I was confident that the court would never let this dangerous man out on the streets to harm another woman. I was confident the court would review the photographs of my injuries and would have no question as to his guilt. It had been such a long road, but I believed in our legal system. These well-respected justices on the highest court in our state had been entrusted to protect me. I believed they would.

Never did it cross my mind that they would set a convicted rapist free.

In October 2009, the Supreme Court overturned the lower court's conviction based on some legal technicalities, which I felt had nothing to do with me or my rape. *The Providence Journal* reported that the conviction was overturned. I am sure in their readers' minds that meant he was not guilty. Another blow for the victim. Although my assailant was released from prison after serving three years and six months, the charges still stood. This case could be tried for a third time. The attorney general came to my home and asked me if I would be willing to testify—*for the third time*. At this point, the word "if" was not in my vocabulary. I wanted to know when.

A brief period of time passed, and I was advised that his lawyers were attempting to plead the case out. He would be willing to admit his guilt but would not serve any more jail time. He would agree to a 30-year probation, with three years and six months time served, and would register as a sex offender. This was not the outcome I had fought so hard for, but the outcome that the state settled for. I understood their reasoning for accepting the plea, but as a victim, I felt like I had fought for nothing.

On April 14, 2010, I found myself in front of Justice William Clifton delivering my second victim impact statement. My assailant was present in court along with his two attorneys. All three sat at their respective table with their heads down as I delivered my statement. I told the judge about my journey as a rape victim in the state of Rhode Island and all I had to endure since 2003. I told him some of my friends called me a hero for having the guts to go through two rape trials in order to get a conviction. I told him I was certainly not a hero, but that I was a strong woman who prayed for the courage to do the right thing and felt I had a moral duty to all women to keep him off the streets. I told the judge that I wanted to find a way to take my story and message out to other victims and help them avoid the nightmares that I had endured in the halls of justice within our court system. I concluded by posing some questions to all who were involved in my assault case. I asked: If another woman asks me if they should come forward and report a similar heinous act of violence, what do you suggest I tell them? Is this the path you suggest a woman take to seek justice? Where is the rule book a woman must read prior to an act of violence to make sure that everyone reaches out to help her act and speak appropriately? Where is the instruction manual that will prevent another costly obstruction of justice?

When I sat down, Justice Clifton looked at me and thanked me for delivering my statement. He looked directly at me and said, "Ms. Johnson, there is one thing I disagree with you that you said. You are a hero." I then knew that this nightmare had come to an end and now, after countless hours of therapy and second-guessing myself, that I had made the right decision in my fight for justice. I sat and cried silently and listened to my rapist admit his guilt and then listened to the sentence imposed on him. He walked out of court that day a free man despite the fact that he is handcuffed to the probation system for 30 years and wears the "convicted sex offender" label forever.

The Providence Journal was not present to learn that he finally admitted his guilt. Unfortunately, the residents of Rhode Island were not privy to learn the name of the newest sex offender in their state. The last story that *The Providence Journal* reported on regarding this crime was that his conviction was overturned.

I share my story with you because I am so passionate about victims' rights. I now volunteer my time doing advocacy work at an organization in R.I. called Day One, which provides counseling services to survivors of sexual abuse and seeks to educate the public about sexual violence. I belong to a group there called One Voice that is made up of survivors of sexual assault or childhood sexual abuse. We are a survivor advocacy group dedicated to using advocacy and public speaking as a vehicle to end sexual violence. Members of One Voice share their personal stories to help dispel common stereotypes and misconceptions about sexual abuse, and to send a message that survivors can end up in a healthy place. I have spoken at the Rhode Island state House of Representatives with Gov. Lincoln Chafee at an event sponsored by Day One during National Sexual Assault Month. I have spoken at various conferences sponsored by Day One, and I have been interviewed on television, radio and in the newspaper. My picture has been in Day One advertisements on the sides of the public buses with this message: "It's Time to Talk About It." I have shared my experience with nurses who work on the front lines with victims in the hospitals and with volunteers who assist victims on emergency calls.

I am attempting to lead by example and encourage other victims to come forward and report their crimes. Victims need to know that there is help and healing on the other side. I am no longer ashamed or embarrassed about what happened to me. I proudly stand up and share my experience for all of the victims who have yet to find their voice.

You see, I am no longer a victim of sexual assault. I am a survivor.

Brittany Brubaker

Gender: Female
Age: 25
Race/ethnicity: White
Occupation: Lab technician
Location: West Chester, Pa.
Age abuse occurred: 13-14

TO MOST PEOPLE who know me, I am a sweet and honest person who loves to make art and enjoy life as if I'm still a kid. I'm blessed to have a close relationship with my awesome family and to have friends that I also consider family. My life isn't perfect, but I generally love living and couldn't imagine life being much better than it already is. The ones who weren't there growing up alongside me or raising me always seem so shocked when I share the dark tribulations of my childhood. My past is such a part of me now that I'm always surprised when someone is shocked at how normal I turned out. The things that happened to me are both a blessing and a curse. I flip between wishing they never happened and knowing that the great life I have now wouldn't exist without my past.

I was about 6½ when my mother no longer wanted to stay married to my father. She moved my brother, sister and I into an apartment across town. Before I turned 7, another man had entered the picture—mom's new boyfriend. He seemed very nice and I was OK with the fact that he was there. I believe he even brought me a stuffed Barney doll. It was a good way to start off our relationship because I loved stuffed animals. He even brought some gifts for my brother and sister, too. After that, we would see him every couple weekends or so. It felt as though he belonged with us. He became a second father to me. Eventually, my mom decided to move us three hours across the state of Pennsylvania so we could live with him.

After four years of being together, my mom and him married under the tree in our yard. It was a small ceremony with only close friends and family and our Amish neighbors, who stopped and watched from across the street. Unfortunately, the happy times didn't last long. That fall, my mom went back to school to become a nurse. At some point, they started arguing consistently, and on some nights mom would drag us out of bed, put us in the car and search for him at the local watering holes. He decided he liked drinking and cheating on my mom.

I took the whole situation very hard. I had already dealt with my parents' divorce and didn't want to lose my other dad, too. I would write letters telling him how much I loved him and wished that things would work out between him and my mom. I couldn't sleep at night and would crawl into my sister's bed after she fell asleep to feel comforted, even though she didn't know I was there.

They eventually split up, but did not get a divorce. We moved into one apartment, while he moved into another. Over the course of the next two years, they fixed their problems and we all moved into another home, and we all became a family again. Over the last year of those two years, my stepfather started to groom me. He started by treating me differently than my younger two siblings. I believed this occurred because I was older and reached a point where I was allowed to do more. He groomed, used and sexually abused me between the ages of 13 and 14.

We moved at the end of seventh grade. When I started eighth grade, I joined the basketball team. Coming home with sore muscles became a reason for him to step up the abuse. Inappropriate names, sexual comments and porn-sharing escalated to touching. A massage went from appropriate touching to inappropriate touching to asking me if I liked how it felt. My answer was yes even though I hated every second of it. My first major memory of being molested was followed by, "Don't tell anyone. If they find out, I could go to jail." It's obvious now that I should have ran and told someone, but I took that comment, along with the fear of disobeying him, as a reason not to tell anyone. I loved and trusted him, and I knew my family did, too. I didn't want to be the reason for destroying that. I became entrenched in a war between right and wrong, and I didn't even know which was which.

For the next several months, he continued to abuse me without anyone knowing. He made me watch him masturbate to porn. He made me dress up in my mom's "sexy" clothes, would call me sexy and then take pictures. He'd finger me, give me oral and use dildos on me to teach me how to masturbate and orgasm. He almost raped me once and I believe he would have had I not been freaking out so much. All of this lasted until the day we were having a completely normal conversation by our new standards. Mom returned from dropping off my siblings without either of us hearing her, and she freaked when she saw her naked husband talking to her daughter. They fought and he told me not tell her, but I fearfully did so anyways. From then on, it became he-said-she-said, and dealing with him lying to my family about how I made it all up. By the beginning of ninth grade, I had dealt with the women's shelter, the police, the social workers, the trial, being forced to choose which parent I wanted to live with, and moving to another school.

For the next few years of my life, I would be deeply affected by these events. They sent me into serious depression. My self-esteem and sense of self-worth not only hit rock bottom, but they crashed through it and continued to fall endlessly into a dark pit of nothingness. I was constantly upset and unable to enjoy life. Half of the time I didn't even know why I was upset, I just was. Sometimes I even felt the need to hit the closest wall near me. This obviously solved nothing, but I saw no end to the pain I was feeling. A lot of days I just cried until the lump of agony and misery in my chest went away.

My family bore the brunt of my chaotic emotions. Since I didn't talk about my problems, I would lash out at them. I don't believe they ever deserved the things I said and did. I only lashed out at them because I knew they would still be there, despite my anger. I wasn't even angry at them. I was angry at me when I should have at least been angry at my stepfather. I constantly worried and told them that they didn't love me. Seemingly harmless sentences and actions would send me into a tizzy. I wasn't the only one who was suffering. They were too.

I was no longer the slightest bit outgoing and I talked to no one at my new school. No one knew what I was going through and no one knew exactly how I was feeling. I felt as though I couldn't talk to anybody. I joined tech-crew and marching band, but still formed very little close relationships with anyone I went to school with, despite some classmates' best efforts. I kept to myself and did my best to earn straight A's. If I received a grade lower than an A, I saw it as just another failure to add to my list of perceived failures. I needed to be perfect at everything I did, no matter what.

In the beginning, I only told my mom what happened along with the social workers and police who questioned me. They heard every detail of my story because they needed to know. Afterward, I rarely talked about what happened in any great detail. I wanted desperately to confide in someone about what I felt and what had happened. I didn't want to burden or bring people down by talking about it. Terrible thoughts and images scrolled through my mind daily. Why should I subject someone else to them? Besides, it was my problem, no one else's, so I figured I should be the only one who has to worry about it. Yet, I wanted someone to hug me and tell me it wasn't my fault even after they knew it all. I didn't tell anyone what exactly took place for years, for fear they would see me how I saw me. I didn't believe anyone could love me if they truly knew, because I didn't love myself. In fact, I blamed and hated myself for "letting it happen." To this day, only a small percentage of the people I know actually know my story. And an even smaller percentage knows the story in great detail.

I've seen multiple therapists over the years. The first two weren't of much help, so my dad found another one who specialized in such cases. I was willing to at least talk to her and work on some of my issues. I saw her for a couple years until I believed I was all better. Sadly, I wasn't. It still affected me in many ways; I just didn't know it at the time. It wasn't until my first year of college when I decided to tell my cousin what happened, that I knew I still had many issues to work on. I ended up writing a few essays about it and going to the school therapist. There, I finally learned to stop blaming myself for all that had happened and realized it wasn't my fault.

Some days I still blame myself for what happened; subconsciously, I always will. It helped tremendously when I finally came to the realization that it wasn't my fault and that he deserves the blame. However, sometimes it doesn't make me feel better at all. It may not be my fault, but why did he choose me? Was I an easy target, easy to manipulate? How could I be that naïve and stupid to not at least know what he was trying to do? I've always been one to do what's asked of me and generally without any hesitation. I've always been shy and quiet. I've always loved my family and never wanted anything bad to happen to them. I wouldn't consider any of those to be bad qualities.

The complexities of the situation are at times overwhelming. The layers are stacked sky-high. The fine line between knowing what's right and wrong is obscured like visibility in a blizzard. Attempting to trust people after one of the closest people to you abuses you is practically impossible. There is a constant struggle in trying to convince yourself it wasn't your fault. Constantly attempting to jump, climb and claw your way over the next mental hurdle. I spent every day for years just trying to make it to the next one. I was waiting for that one day when I would wake up with a smile on my face, knowing everything was OK.

I woke up to that day a long time ago, but there still isn't a day that goes by where I don't think about him or what he did. Most days, I make it through without any problems and it doesn't bother me. However, it's still very hard to tell someone or write general details about what happened. In fact, I can't even tell the people closest to me details without a computer in between us, because the thought of telling them in person leaves me panic-stricken. I know there are still hurdles in the distance that I'll face and that there may never be a last one. Fortunately, I'm now able to rely on the people around me to help me through the hard times. Every day, I can wake up, appreciate what I have and find something to live for. While the events of my past make up a large part of who I am, they are not all that I am.

My past has led to many countless blessings. I took up drawing as a hobby and a way to cope. I love to draw. After high school I went to college for art. Upon graduating, I managed to land a job, not in the art field, but a job I enjoy nonetheless. I still draw to this day to help deal with the stresses of life, but mostly for fun and the occasional commissioned project. Going through such an ordeal showed me that I should appreciate all the small things in life. This allows me to find ways to have fun in any place or situation. I enjoy helping people and animals. I currently work with animal-saving nonprofits and recently went on a missions trip to Guatemala.

I believe that being shy and guarded allowed me find the best friends possible while avoiding ones that wouldn't have my best interests in mind. My whole family and I faced many obstacles after the abuse. We managed to overcome those obstacles as a family and became closer because of it. While the abuse devastated me, I know that I wouldn't be where I am today without it.

Joel and Nina

*　*　*

Joel Hoffmann

Gender: Male
Age: 30
Race/ethnicity: White
Occupation: College instructor/government employee
Location: Philadephia, Pa.
Age abuse occurred: 4-6

EYES CLENCHED, HANDS CLASPED against my forehead, I lay in bed praying, for a sign, a vision, a memory to put my mind at ease. After a year of intense psychotherapy, I was finally coming to accept what happened to me in the mid-'80s, when I was 4, 5, 6 years old, when I could barely write or read. I no longer had to ignore it, but despite all the evidence, despite all I'd heard and seen, I was suddenly stricken with doubt.

Lips quivering, tears trickling down my cheeks, I thought of my estranged mother and how she'd failed me, of my siblings and the pain that made me so distant. I wished we could be a family again, but it didn't seem possible—not with so many unresolved issues, not with so many secrets.

Before my wife could hear me, I sprang out of bed and shuffled toward the bathroom, where I quickly started to dry heave. There was no imminent threat to my safety, yet my body was bracing for attack: chest seizing, heart speeding, bowels clenched.

As I rocked over the toilet, I worried that Nina would hear me. The door was shut—as I always made sure it was in those moments when I couldn't shake off the anxiety—but I was still afraid of being caught in such a pathetic state: so vulnerable, so depleted.

Thirteen months had passed since I promised her I would tear off all the bandages and honestly assess the damage. In a few days, on April 28, 2012, I would publicly admit that my stepfather, Danny, had sexually abused me when I was too young to understand the concept. But for all of the progress I'd made, I was still confused and at times ashamed. I was still trying to reconcile the facts of my past with the gaps in my memory, and now I was besieged by the sickening feeling that I'd made it all up.

Pain surged through my body and a torrent of anger, betrayal and grief rushed to the surface. I cried so hard that my face ached, and as I sat gathering what energy I had left, a wave of relief washed over me. Reluctant as I was to let it happen, the purge always made me feel better.

The truth was, only the sickness could heal me.

BY THE TIME I met Nina in September 2008, I had come to accept my past was dead. The boy, the victim, was buried deep in the recesses of my subconscious, and he was never coming back.

At first glance, I was a self-absorbed, sarcastic prick who didn't care about anyone else. The muscles in my face were frozen in disdain, and I was quick to cut everyone off. The only joy I felt—and I'm not sure you can call it that—was the mild sense of accomplishment that academic success provided. My emotions were blunted by antidepressants and a deep, lasting numbness that shielded my fragile mind. The more I sank myself in abstraction, the easier it was to escape the pain of reality.

As I sat in an uncomfortable desk chair two columns away from Nina in a graduate-level journalism theory class, I suddenly felt less irritated. She spoke with easy confidence, and I seized the opportunity to insult her reason for returning to Philadelphia from San Francisco—to be a copy editor at the *Daily News*. I withered under her glare. This woman wouldn't take shit from me. I slumped back in my chair, conceding defeat.

A few days later, I apologized for my behavior. I scaled back the sarcasm, and she soon agreed to grab a drink with me—then another. After a few dates, it became difficult for me to keep opening up to someone so honest, so open, so normal. I had long operated under the assumption that I could only be with someone as damaged as me. This assumption failed me every time, but for the brief duration of my flimsy relationships, I felt less alone. I felt as if I could be myself: broken, self-loathing and cynical.

Nina had seen through the smokescreen, and I was terrified that she would leave me if I showed her everything. As I had so many times in the past, I ended the relationship and declared myself incapable of love.

As the semester ended and Nina's job was threatened by a looming round of layoffs, we started talking outside of class again. I had never seen her upset before, and in some sick way it made me feel closer to her. She loved the *Daily News*, and I had grown to love it, too. I hated anyone who would try to ax Nina and her colleagues. They didn't deserve to suffer for the sins of the industry, but it seemed they surely would. Satire and profanity seemed to ease Nina's pain. It made me feel better, too.

We started dating again, and I brought her home for Christmas. By New Year's Eve, I was ready to marry her. The transformation surprised everyone, especially me. My parents had divorced when I was 2, and most of the relationships in my family seemed contrived, unstable or both. Yet despite the dearth of good examples, I found myself drawn to Nina, the tide unyielding. With a clarity of mind that only champagne and cheap beer could provide, I dropped to one knee and pledged eternal commitment to her. She pledged hers in return. For once, everything was good.

Even before we got engaged in June 2009, the dynamic of our relationship had started to change. I felt safe with Nina. I finally had a reason to be happy, and I ignored the signs that I was heading for a crash.

The more we saw my family, the more she would point out how different I was around them, especially when we went to my mom's house in Delaware County, Pa., where I had lived with my stepfather. I would dismiss her concerns as a lack of understanding. Dysfunction was normal to me, and she simply wasn't used to it. Besides, I felt as out of place around her family as she felt around mind. Eventually, we would adapt— or so I thought.

On the eve of our vacation to Belize, I asked Nina to marry me. Despite my aversion to romance, I had spent days trying to find a non-clichéd way to present the ring. Finally, I realized there was only one place I could propose. I picked her up from the *Daily News*—the editor, Michael Days, had saved her job—and I drove past the airport toward a park near my mom's house.

Fourteen years earlier, my dad had taken me to that park and asked why I'd been sleeping with a steak knife under my pillow. I told him I didn't want to live anymore. He knew my mom had decided to let my stepfather back in the house. He knew I was afraid.

My dad checked me into the Philadelphia Child Guidance Clinic on May 18, 1994. I was 11 years old. In the waiting room, he handed me a yellow legal pad and asked questions about my stepfather. More than five years had passed since I first told my dad that Danny had stuck his finger and a toy jeep in my ass. My mom had dismissed the allegations as Danny "goosing" me, and because there was no evidence of penetration when I was examined by a doctor, the child-welfare investigators determined that the abuse was unfounded.

Still convinced that I had been sexually abused, my dad brought it up again. I couldn't speak, but I answered his questions in writing, growing visibly more upset until the nurse intervened. He fought back tears as he read my responses:

> *fooled around*
> *acted like complete moron because he was drunk*
> *it would seem like he was gay*
> *sort of like tickled it*
> *it was sickening*

During my stay in the hospital, child-welfare investigators revisited the case. By the time I left on June 22, 1994, I had provided "a clear, consistent and credible" account of being sexually abused by my stepfather. On July 27, 1994, Danny was arrested by Gloucester County, N.J., detectives on charges of sexual assault and endangering the welfare of a child.

Much as my dad wanted to take the case to trial, the prosecutor advised him against it. There was no physical evidence, and there was a strong possibility that I would be further traumatized by the experience. We reluctantly settled for a plea bargain. On April 21, 1995, Danny agreed to one count of endangering the welfare of a child—a sex crime under New Jersey law. He was sentenced to a year of probation.

As I sat staring at Nina, stalling to prepare myself for what I was about to say, I realized that I'd never fully healed from what Danny had done to me. The sexual abuse had only been a small part of it, as had the few instances of physical abuse. This sadistic man had steadily eroded my self-esteem until I no longer wanted to live, and I'd spent years clawing back my dignity.

I turned down the radio and reached for the ring. I told Nina she had given me a reason to live, that I had brought her to the place where I lost all hope to show her she had restored it. I handed her my pledge, forged in diamond and white gold. "You are my salvation in this world," I said.

The post-engagement bliss ended too quickly, ushering in a 20-month struggle to recognize and accept the growing rift between us. What started as a disagreement over the thinning frequency of our sex life became a bitter, sometimes hostile dispute, fueled by my implausible excuses. We're too busy, I said. Too tired. Too familiar. Things change when you get married. None of that changed the fact that Nina wasn't getting what she needed, what she reasonably should have expected from her spouse under normal circumstances.

The more she pushed for answers, the more I retreated, until finally, on Valentine's Day 2011, she threatened to leave.

I had always felt weird talking about sex. It was something that happened naturally, I reasoned, not a topic for discussion. But I was now so afraid to talk about it, so unable to say the word without feeling a deep sense of shame, that I had no choice but to admit that something was seriously wrong.

On some level, I grasped that the abuse had tainted my sexuality, but when I allowed myself to consider the depth of the problem, I was disgusted. My perception of intimacy had been warped by the abuse and chronic familial dysfunction. I felt feeble and diseased.

All of my previous relationships had become unbearable once I allowed myself to be vulnerable. Physically, I would still be present, but I wasn't there—not really. I didn't see how sex and emotional closeness could coexist for me, but that's what Nina needed, and she was willing to wait so long as I made a good faith effort to get better.

"I wouldn't blame you for leaving," I said.

But Nina stayed. She stayed as I took so much and gave so little. She stayed as my body cringed and quaked. She kept her distance to protect herself, but she would not let me break. *I believe that you can beat this*, she said, *but you'll never get better if you can't accept what happened to you.*

On April 16, 2011, Nina and her mother took me to a sexual-abuse awareness rally hosted by Women Organized Against Rape. I hid my face as we marched in the rain, afraid that someone would see me. Later, as I sat and listened to survivors speak in the Independence Visitor Center, I felt less alone. If they were brave enough to talk about their abuse, what was stopping me?

My eyes and nose burned with acid tears, but I sat quietly until a man in his 50s strode to the podium. He had only begun to accept that he had been abused in his mid-30s, and he was now finally getting the treatment he needed to heal. He had struggled twice as long as I had, but he refused to let the pain ruin the rest of his life. I was stunned by his courage, but I couldn't take any more. I shuffled to the bathroom, slid to the floor and wept until there was nothing left.

AS MUCH AS I wanted to stay in touch with my family while I was in therapy at WOAR, it was clear that I wouldn't make radical changes in my life unless I could proceed without worrying about how they felt. My mom had long believed that I would heal by compartmentalizing the past, but that wasn't possible for me. I now understood that I couldn't move on if everything remained the same.

The separation filled me with guilt and grief, but it gave me the perspective I needed to get better. I could finally see the dysfunction as abnormal and unhealthy. I could finally see that I'd been passively waiting for those who had hurt me to make things right, and I accepted that it would never happen. I loved my family, but I had to prove to myself that I could survive without them. Only then could I find peace.

At a safe distance, I began to access repressed memories, which allowed me to deconstruct the belief that I had fabricated the abuse. Young children tell tall tales, but not about molestation. If I had made it all up, why, then, would I keep drawing attention to a lie? The guilt would have faded, and I would be relieved to have gotten away with it. Wouldn't I?

It was clear that I had perpetuated my mother's denial. Sure, she believed me after I ended up in a crisis center, but her initial response had clouded my perception. I wished she had believed me sooner. I wished she had taken my side.

The anger and sadness were often overwhelming, but every time I let it flow through me, I felt so much better. I was reluctant to purge at every step, but the suffering was worth it.

THE SPEECH FLUTTERED in my hand as I stood at the podium, surveying the room for signs of danger. I had just publicly outed myself as an abuse survivor, and I was waiting for someone to call me a liar. In a room full of strangers, I was somehow safe. My voice choked with grief, I paused then continued to speak.

"I wish I could say that Danny's conviction resolved everything for me," I said. "I wish I could say that my mother fully accepted the gravity of what had happened and did everything she could to help me heal. But that didn't happen.

"She had convinced herself that everything would get better if we all just moved on. And when I would crash and burn after weeks, months, years of ignoring it, she would beg for forgiveness she hadn't earned, then let my dad intervene so she could go back to pretending everything was fine.

"She still doesn't get it, and I'm not sure that she ever will.

"There's the incident, and there's the aftermath. Pure logic would have it that the event itself is far more painful than the recovery, but we all know that's not true. Rest and medication won't do much for an infection of the soul. It takes years to flush out the poison, not weeks, and that's assuming that the survivor is trying to get better.

"I've learned that you can't move on by sitting still. I've learned that you can't let it go until you let it in.

"I've spent the past year assessing the damage. I've unraveled much of the shoddy logic that has prevented me from enjoying my life. I've begun to access memories long buried, but I am not whole. I don't know that I'll ever feel whole, but I can accept the abuse as a proportionate part of my life. I feel well enough to move forward, to start letting go. I am more hopeful than I've ever been. I am far less cynical.

"I am not the first survivor of child sexual abuse, and I know I won't be the last. My voice, my story is one among many. I will continue to speak out along with countless other survivors and advocates."

I thanked the audience for listening and sat down next to Nina, squeezing her hand for comfort. I had never done anything so courageous, and it was difficult to comprehend. I looked at my father, at Nina's parents, and

I knew they understood me. But it was more than that. Only a day had passed since Nina told me she was pregnant, and I realized the baby had given me the strength to keep going.

Something had clicked. Something was different. My past didn't matter as much the future I wanted for my child, and I couldn't let anyone or anything get in the way of it.

A few weeks later, I felt obligated to call my mom and tell her about the baby. Our last conversation hadn't ended well, and I was afraid that she would still be upset with me for cutting her off around the holidays. I didn't hate her, but I couldn't trust or love her until she could accept how deeply the abuse had affected my life. In order to accept the gravity of the abuse, she had to accept her role in it, and I didn't think she was ready for that.

There was no resentment in her voice. She was genuinely happy to hear from me. She wanted to know how I was, how Nina was feeling, and I humored her with more details than I'd expected to give up. But when she said how excited she was to be a grandmother, I had to redirect the conversation. She listened quietly as I explained what it would take to resolve the issues that prevented us from having the relationship I wanted. She agreed to read about the effects of sex abuse and said she would attend counseling with me.

Still, I was skeptical. She had pledged so many times to help me move on without ever moving forward herself. She still had my stepfather's last name and continued to live in the house they had bought together. I wondered how much progress she could make.

Finally, she started following through. It had been 18 years since we attended a therapy session together, but she had read the research and she was ready to listen. I held nothing back, explaining in painstaking detail how the abuse had tainted everything good in my life. She lamented her failures and said she wanted to be the mother she should have been. I told her it was too late. What I needed now was for her to recognize that the abuse would always be a part of me. I couldn't pretend anymore. She said she understood.

When we talked on the phone several days later, I was stunned by the conversation. She hadn't completely transformed, but she finally understood that her betrayal had lasted for years after the abuse. She acknowledged the depths of our family dysfunction and recognized it was time to choose a new direction. She talked about selling the house someday, about helping my sister come to terms with the truth about her father.

"I never realized how much the abuse traumatized us all," she said. "I'll do whatever it takes to help us be a family."

Letting her in was risky, but I gave her another chance because she didn't expect or demand it. I was willing to suffer for her in the way Nina had suffered for me so long as she was willing to be honest with herself, so long as she was willing to tear off the bandages and air her wounds. She had been abused—physically and emotionally—by both of her husbands, and it was time for her to purge, to grieve. I sensed her reluctance, but something was different. Something had clicked. She saw the damage for what it was now, and the truth was, only the sickness could heal her.

*　*　*

Nina Marie Hoffmann

Gender: Female
Age: 30
Race/ethnicity: Mixed-race
Occupation: Senior editor at *Philadelphia Weekly*
Location: Philadelphia, Pa.
Relationship to survivor: Wife

WHEN I MARRIED Joel on Oct. 2, 2010, I didn't know how to be a wife, let alone the wife of a survivor of child sexual abuse. I thought all guys basically wanted the same stuff: home-cooked meals, sex, love, support, the emotional and physical space to do manly things. Despite all the affection and kindness I showed him, it wasn't enough to make him happy. I thought for a long time that it was because of something I did or said, or perhaps because Joel realized I wasn't the right woman for him. His silence, his lack of affirmation, his inability to communicate to me that, no, it wasn't any of those things, fueled my feelings of inadequacy and loneliness.

Joel was a deeply troubled, unsettled man. He had yet to accept that his stepfather had abused him physically and emotionally. He had yet to fully comprehend that his well-being was neglected after the fact, and that that in itself was a form of abuse.

Neither of us realized how much pain he was in until after we got married.

When we started therapy in the late spring of 2011, our counselor told us that, sometimes, it takes a huge life event for a survivor to face his past. In Joel's case, that's exactly what happened. We were stuck in marital purgatory: not able to move forward, not able to take it back—at least, not wanting to go through with a divorce. Looking back on Joel's emotional breakdown, the near disintegration of our marriage, and then, finally, our reconciliation, I can say that I did not understand what love was until I was forced to fight for it.

That's why, more than anything, my story is a love story.

IN 2008, I STARTED over. I left California and moved back to Philly, started a new job at the *Daily News* and, in the fall, began the graduate journalism program at Temple University. I met Joel on the first day of school. The first thing I noticed about him was his green eyes. They were the kindest, gentlest eyes I had ever seen. I had always been drawn to green eyes.

For the next couple weeks, we talked in class, texted, messaged each other on social media. On our first date, Joel kissed me. He took my breath away. We dated for about a month until one day, when I told him I really liked him, he backed off.

I like you too, but I don't think I'm interested in a relationship.

The next class we had together, he spoke enigmatically about various issues he had with relationships, love, family, you name it. It seemed as though he was trying to tell me something. I didn't know what. I was hurt.

We stopped talking for a while. Class was tense and awkward. One day, I was riding the subway to work, daydreaming about Joel. I missed my stop. Walking the extra few blocks back to my office, I thought: what the hell is wrong with me?

I barely know you, but I know I love you.

I couldn't explain to anyone, least of all myself, why I loved this man, despite how clear it was to me that he had a lot of unresolved emotional problems. And even weirder was that I had a nagging feeling that he loved me too.

To my surprise, on the last day of class, Joel said he wanted to get back together. The answer seemed like a no-brainer—so we did. That weekend, he told me he had been sexually abused as a child. He showed me the newspaper clippings, the court transcripts, the notes that his doctors took while he was living in a mental hospital at age 11. It was all-very disturbing to me. I sobbed, and he just sat there looking at me. Like he was waiting, *expecting* me to walk away and never look back. *This doesn't change the way I feel about you*, I said. The very next day, he told me he loved me. I said it back. I knew I would marry this man.

We were engaged six months later. We moved in together. That's when I started to notice changes in the relationship that concerned me. Joel seemed more and more uninterested in sex. Every time I brought it up, he would say, very affectionately, "Look, we're both busy. You're in school, and you work nights. Things will calm down soon." I brushed it off time and time again because we were happy, and he clearly loved me. Yet the feeling nagged at me. In that time, I switched jobs—mostly because I wanted to work during the day so that we could have a normal life together. I thought that would fix the "problem." It didn't. The frequency of our intimate moments kept declining. I thought maybe for a time it was my fault because I had been living with undiagnosed thyroid disease, which does a number on a person's emotional state. I'm sure that didn't help things, but I knew there was something else.

Something was happening to Joel. I started to notice some periods of moodiness and depression. I thought of every reason in the world to justify what I was seeing: *He's stressed at work. He's stressed about the wedding planning. His allergies are really bad. He's hung over.* It felt to me like my husband was disappearing, slowly being replaced by a man I didn't know—and, frankly, didn't like. And his insistence that everything was OK made me feel more and more disconnected from him.

Up until this point, sexual abuse had not come up a whole lot in our conversations. I knew his story, how he didn't get much family support, but nothing about the effects, what it does to people years later, how it can wreak havoc on relationships. A couple months before the wedding, we talked about intimacy again. And again he tried to convince me that we were doing all right.

Things will get better after the wedding.

They didn't.

On our honeymoon, Joel simply did not want to have sex. When I initiated, he recoiled. He offered no explanation, only an apology.

I'm sorry. I'm just so tired. I didn't realize you wanted to do it now.

I was trapped in a hotel room in Mexico with my husband and my rage. I wanted so badly to leave—to just get back on a plane and go home and leave him there.

The next couple months, I grieved in silence. A powerful wave of anger crept into my heart, my soul. It crushed my spirit, left me feeling ... numb. Cold. I did not recognize the person I was starting to become.

Is this what depression feels like?

I started to resent Joel. *Did I make a mistake? Does he still love me? What happened to the man with the kind, green eyes?* We went through the motions of life. Work, dinner, bills, school, TV. Sex was completely emotionless. I usually absconded to the bathroom to cry immediately afterward. Or I'd simply roll over and choke back tears. At that point, our pain was so out in the open, it didn't feel necessary to keep hiding my sadness. We argued all the time. He said I confronted him too much, wasn't understanding enough, wasn't patient enough. I'm not a religious person, but I prayed for an answer to this hell.

On Feb. 14, 2011, I exploded. I came home to find Joel burning a Valentine's dinner he tried to make for us. I laughed it off, but he seemed irrationally upset by it. I suggested we go out, and he agreed. I gave him his card, but instead of opening it, he set it down on the counter and walked away, as if to say, "Thanks, I'll get to it later." Every perceived slight since the honeymoon fueled my pain and my anger. But this one set me off. I threatened to leave him if he didn't start owning up to what I saw as a complete emotional breakdown. On the one hand, I finally realized that he had not come close to healing from the abuse and its aftermath. On the other, I hated him for it. The gravity of the situation knocked the wind out of me.

Why is this happening to me?

With few options on the table, Joel called Women Organized Against Rape to set up abuse counseling. We waited five months. In that time, we fought almost every day. He was a ghost, walking around completely numb. I threatened to leave him time and time again. He even agreed it might be the best course of action. The sex stopped completely because we decided that, at that point, any physical interactions would further traumatize him. He resented me, too, for bringing the issues to light. For wanting him to communicate with me. For wanting *more* from him. He said I was asking for too much. It drove me deeper into depression.

I cried every day for months.

Looking back, there were periods of time when Joel and I felt the *exact same emotions*. But I couldn't see past my pain to really understand his. I felt like the victim. *He's doing this to me. He's making me feel this way. I didn't deserve this. I didn't ask for this. Why can't he just move on?*

"If it were possible to get over the effects of sexual abuse by pretending it didn't happen or by forgetting it, most survivors would gladly sign up for a class in memory loss. Healing is . . . agonizing."

In my first individual counseling session at Women Organized Against Rape, I received some photocopies of sections from a book titled *Allies in Healing: When the Person You Love Was Sexually Abused as a Child*. My first assignment was to learn exactly what it meant to be a survivor of sexual abuse. Joel and I agreed that I needed to be in therapy; plus, I needed to know what I was dealing with so I could accurately gauge if I thought I was strong enough to handle the drastic changes that were about to happen in our household.

For months after Joel started therapy, he barely acknowledged my existence. He was completely immersed in his own thoughts and feelings. Each counseling session would render him uncommunicative or in tears for hours on end. It was exactly what I wanted him to do. To really heal this time. And yet being so completely alone drove me to a new level of sadness. That's how powerful pain can be, even if it's motivated by a good intention, which, in this case, was recovery.

All I really wanted was for my husband to pay attention to me. I just wanted to be held. At that point, though, Joel was simply incapable. There were times when he would avert his eyes when I was undressing. I felt ugly and disgusting. I would waver from feeling asexual to completely obsessed with having sex. I started fantasizing about other men. Ex-boyfriends, complete strangers—it didn't matter. *I could sleep with this person and Joel would never know.*

One weekend, I went to my parents' house in Allentown, alone. I sat on my bed and bawled for hours. I just sat there, my head in my hands, repeating over and over. *Please, God, bring him back to me. I can't do this.* I contemplated really leaving Joel.

That night, I laid in bed with *Allies in Healing*, reading a chapter titled, "My Needs and Feelings."

"Not everyone wants to be in an intimate relationship with someone struggling to heal from child sexual abuse. Give yourself permission to leave ... That way, if you stay, your commitment to will resonate with the power of free choice. (See page 87 for more on the decision to stay or go.)"

I kept turning to that page but finding no clear answers. *Don't fake a commitment that isn't there. Do we have a mutual dream? A sense of where we're going, what we want, a commitment to something bigger than our individual struggles?*

In the middle of the night, I decided, once and for all: Yes, my love for Joel was greater than my struggle. I would not leave my husband. I would be the person he needed. I would sacrifice more to give him the love that no one else did. Joel simply needed to heal, and I needed to help. It wasn't his fault. It wasn't my fault. *But here we are.*

It wasn't easy. Feelings have a way of asserting themselves even as you try to manage them on your own. But assuring Joel that I would stay renewed his mission to heal—which made things better for both of us.

I continued my counseling. I came to understand that abuse survivors suffer from post-traumatic stress disorder just as cripplingly as soldiers returning from the battlefield do. The more I learned about PTSD—the more I grew able to identify and decipher the meaning of Joel's reactions to certain situations—the more I learned to anticipate his needs. I learned, albeit slowly, how to restrain my temper. I learned how to walk away if I thought he was using me as a crutch. I learned that it was OK to tell him, "No, I can't listen to you today, I'm sorry." It established boundaries. Joel couldn't use me as an emotional well, and I didn't have to pretend I cared *all the time.* It kept me sane, and forced him to deal on his own.

In the meantime, I was trying to rebuild my shattered self. My therapy assignments required me to get out of the house and be with other people. I met my mom at the King of Prussia Mall a lot. Sometimes I was happy. Other times I wasn't. Sometimes I faked it because I couldn't bear to tell her how sad I was. I'm sure she knew.

Other assignments required me to write down a list of my needs, to talk with Joel about which ones he could meet immediately and which ones he would need more time with. I did. We talked. It was the first time we compromised on anything in more than a year. One of my needs was physical interaction. Hugs. I knew even this would be difficult for him because at that point in his healing, any sort of touch or prospect of touch would elicit a very visceral reaction. So the compromise was that, if I needed a hug, I would *ask*. It sounds silly, having to negotiate innocent touch with your partner. But it gave Joel the power to decide for himself— the power he didn't have when he was abused. Usually, he wanted to—I just needed to ask.

Another need was that I wanted him to ask me how I was doing. At that point, I had done 99 percent of the listening. Part of Joel's therapy now was that he *had* to fulfill certain husband duties, no matter how small. So he would put reminders in his phone. Every day at 6 p.m., his alarm would go off and he would come find me. He'd tell me how he was feeling, and he'd ask me how I was. If I felt like talking, I would ask if he felt like listening.

Life turned into a series of negotiations. But they filled me with more and more hope.

We started couples counseling so we could talk through our issues with the same person at the same time. Learning how to compromise through effective communication was our primary goal. On Tuesday nights and Sundays, Joel required alone time to do therapy work. We agreed that Saturdays would be our "fun" days, and were not to be used to discuss anything therapy or abuse-related. They weren't *that* much fun, since we inevitably both ended up crying. There were never any specific triggers, but we were both grieving in our own ways, really exhausted emotionally, and needed to feel that release. Some days, I would just sit and cry because of how I felt, and then he would start crying because he saw how unhappy I was. He would apologize and promise it would get better. Other days, I would see him suddenly break down, those green eyes so wounded and full of sadness, and it would bring me to tears. I could not bear to watch him live in so much pain. I encouraged him to keep moving forward in spite of the pain, that it would get better. Eventually, we'd clean ourselves up and go out for ice cream, and those small, weekly moments of happiness seemed to be enough to keep us going. We were united by grief.

Meanwhile, every Wednesday, we each got to talk for 10 minutes, uninterrupted, about our own feelings. It was a time for us to say things without the other person trying to rebut, deny or justify. This part of the routine was mostly created for my benefit, so I could release some anger without scaring Joel, or making him feel guilty for not fulfilling my needs. He would always listen.

On our one-year anniversary, we suffered a setback that left me reeling. We had been given intimacy assignments so that we could rebuild our sex life. We got a room in the same hotel we were married in. It proved too much for Joel; he felt too pressured. I was quietly disappointed and angry, but I didn't lash out. I refused to argue, and, more importantly, I decided I would not acknowledge his anxiety. It wasn't my problem. The next day, he said, "You went to sleep and I had to deal with that by myself. Thank you. I'm so sorry. I'm not giving up."

We kept trying. Some nights, we would just lay in bed listening to music. Sometimes it would lead to kissing. Sometimes, it led to fighting. Sometimes, we just *were*. Months went by, and Joel was still not feeling confident in the bedroom. He would prefer that we didn't speak of it, let alone do it. Yet every weekend he tried to connect with me. I was happy as long as he tried. Our success rate improved.

One Sunday night, we made love. Five weeks later, I found out I was pregnant. Joel's reaction was surprising, but what I'd hoped for. He was legitimately happy and excited to move on, together, as a family. I told Joel that our baby was created as a result of healthy, consensual, loving sex— something he never thought he'd have. "That will always remind you of where we were, and where we are," I said.

We still marvel at how hard we fought to save ourselves so that we could stay together. To me, that is what it really means to love someone.

I don't know what life will be like once our daughter arrives. But I have my husband back, and I finally feel like I have a partner, a best friend, a lover. No doubt there will be arguments to resolve, physical and emotional needs to negotiate, navigate. None of it will be worse than what sexual abuse did to the man I love.

Darlene C.

Gender: Female
Age: 51
Race/ethnicity: White
Occupation: Paralegal/student/advocate
Location: Rhode Island
Age abuse occurred: 10-12; 20-30; 46-47

IT IS HARD to believe that the person I am now is the same person who first endured sexual abuse at the age of 10. My journey to becoming the strong, outspoken woman I am today has been a battle that has left many scars, both physically and emotionally. However, I wear those scars proudly as badges of honor in the war against the abusers in the world. I have discovered that when people in my life learned of the indescribable experiences I had endured, many were in denial and many decided I should have been stronger and shut me out of their lives. Throughout my journey, I have lost my home of 16 years, attempted to commit suicide because I could no longer deal with the pain of the abuse, and lived in a shelter for a while.

When I was 10, my family had taken in a patient from the local VA hospital as a boarder. The sexual abuse began slowly, and eventually, my abuser was forcing me to perform oral sex on a daily basis. My abuse continued until the age of 12, when my abuser was sent back to the VA hospital. By the time the abuse ended, it had escalated to total vaginal penetration. My abuser continuously threatened my life as well as my family. My parents were not aware of this abuse until I was in my late teens. My abuser had brainwashed me into believing no one would believe me and that it was my fault.

The consequence of being sexually abused at such a young age has had multiple effects on my life. I have had difficulty trusting people, as well as establishing and maintaining relationships. I became promiscuous in my teenage years. Looking back, I believe it was a way to have some type of control over my life. For as long as I can remember, until recently, I have kept people at a distance. The fear of being so intimately betrayed remained for decades. I always ended up in some type of abusive relationship, whether it was physical, verbal, emotional, or a combination of all three.

The abuse worsened again when I married for the first time at 19. My now ex-husband was a very insecure person and attempted to lower everyone else's self-esteem and self-confidence to his level. He physically and verbally abused me. I was forced on multiple occasions to have sexual intercourse with him in order to protect my children from his abuse. Once my husband began to take his anger and frustrations with me out on my children, I gathered all my inner strength and kicked him out. I was married to this monster for more than 20 years. He did not give up easy and constantly stalked me. On numerous occasions, he broke into my home to leave threatening notes. The threats and fear became so severe and frequent that I ended up having the local police keep a constant watch on my house. Eventually, my ex-husband realized how serious I was and moved to another state. Unfortunately, his threats and abuse have continued through a second marriage. The last I heard, my ex-husband is in a psychiatric hospital. He has repeatedly and proudly stated to his psychiatrist that he will kill my children and me if he ever gets out. I have been reassured he will never be freed.

The largest pothole in the road to my recovery began in 2007, and came to a head in 2008. While I was living in a shelter, I met a man who I entered a relationship with, which from the beginning should not have happened. He was more than a decade younger than me and had a completely different upbringing and outlook on life. After a brief period of time, I moved into an apartment with this person. At first, this person seemed too good to be true, but within a few months his true self appeared. On a daily basis, I was abused verbally, physically and sexually. My mental state at the time of this relationship was not as strong as it needed to be to fight back. I was not allowed to have contact with friends and family and was completely isolated from the world.

The final straw was when my abuser knocked me down and attempted to strangle me. He told me I would never see my family again. Somehow, once again, I found my inner strength and got up and ran out of the apartment. I went to a police station nearby and my abuser was arrested after an intense police search. I obtained a restraining order but the order appeared to be more of a temptation than determent to my abuser. He would continually break the order and be re-arrested and another court hearing would be scheduled. Whenever the newspaper would publish an article about the incidents, including the charges of stalking and assault and battery, my abuser would attempt to contact me, saying that was just the beginning. In October 2008, I returned to my apartment after grocery shopping. As I was putting away groceries, I heard a noise in my bedroom closet. Before I realize what was happening, my abuser jumped from the closet and pushed me to the floor. He repeatedly punched me in the face and eventually broke my cheekbone. Every time I attempted to get up, he would literally pick me up and throw me against a wall and kick me in the legs. He smashed glasses and ripped down curtains. At one point, he had thrown me to the floor and was laying on top of me, strangling me with one hand and with the other attempting to undo his pants. I saw my life flash before me. After what felt like hours, my abuser finished raping me and beating me. As he hit me one last time, he said now it's your family's turn. The inner mother bear monster came to life inside me and somehow I pushed my abuser off me and knocked him down. He attempted to grab my ankle to knock me down again. I said, "You do not threaten my family." I am not certain how, but somehow I made it to my phone as he attempted to grab it away from me. I hit my abuser over the head with it and dialed the police. At that point, my abuser sat down and began crying. He ran out of the apartment before the police arrived, but they eventually found him.

After multiple court appearances, my abuser was going to be let free yet again. At that point, I told my court advocate I wanted to address the court. I told the judge that a restraining order is nothing more than a temptation to my abuser and I wanted it on record that when my abuser ended up in succeeding in killing me, the court could explain to my family that I was dead because the court allowed my abuser to be set free again, believing he was not a true threat to my life. The judge deliberated for a while and then sentenced my abuser to one and half years in jail, with 18 months of parole after release and three years' probation.

I always wondered how I would react if I came face to face with my abuser again. On Christmas Eve 2010, I had my answer. I was in CVS and came face to face with my abuser and did not run or turn away. I looked him right in the eye as he attempted to engage in conversation. Later that day, I received a Facebook message from my abuser stating it was great to see me and we would have to do it again soon. I sent him a brief reply explaining I wish him luck in the future getting the help he needs and if he ever contacts me again I will contact the police. That was the last time my abuser has attempted to contact me.

Today, I know I am truly a survivor and not a victim. My life is finally on the smooth road it should have been on for a long time. I have a fantastic, supportive husband, a full-time job and I am attending college full-time to obtain my master's in social work to help other victims become survivors. I also volunteer on weekends for Day One, a statewide agency that assists victims of sexual assault, domestic violence and hate crimes. In addition, I have recently joined a subsidiary of Day One called One Voice. This is a group made up of sexual-abuse survivors who speak out in different public venues attempting to educate the public on the lasting effects of sexual abuse. One Voice is also attempting to change the laws that at times protect the abusers more than the victims. When I first started working as an advocate, I was not certain how I would be able to handle seeing people in the same situation I had been in multiple times. I must say after my first trip to a hospital, I knew deep in my soul that I had found my life's mission and true calling. I know everything happens for a reason and I know the reason for my enduring the abuse for so many years was to shape me into the strong woman I am today. I am not saying there aren't days when I recall some of the situations I have been through and want to crawl into a big ball and stay in bed. However, I remember all that I have overcome and that remaining the victim gives the abuser continued power. I have in my own way forgiven all my abusers so that I can move on in my life in a positive direction. I will never forget what they did to me, but I refuse to let them control my life any longer.

Every person, male or female, who has endured any form of violence or abuse has their own road to travel. It may be difficult to talk about at first and to get past the self-blame and loathing stage. I think one of the most important things for any victim of abuse can remember is you are not alone and there is a world of people who are willing to help.

It has been a long journey, but I know I had to experience the rocky roads to become stronger and appreciate the smooth sailing even more.

Kathy H.

Gender: Female
Age: 52
Race/ethnicity: White
Occupation: Owner of house-cleaning business; in school for social work; full-time caregiver of mother
Location: Philadelphia, Pa.
Age abuse occurred: 5-25

ALL THE EMOTIONS that I am running from are here. I wonder why I am working so hard, over-doing everything. I cannot say no. I try to fix everything. I never have an idle moment. I am distracting myself from feeling. I feel like I am a robot, getting things done, trying very hard to be good enough, and the "good enough" feelings never last. It's never enough, so I try again like a hamster going around a wheel searching and searching. I have difficulty trusting people, have difficulty getting close to people. I crave love that I never had as a child, yet I push it away. I have so many emotions going on inside of me, yet I am scared to let this stuff out. I hear thoughts of "Don't be a baby," conflicted with "It's OK to be honest." Then shame takes over and the voices say, "What are the people going to think of you," or "Nobody is going to believe you." Secrets keep you sick, and I know I must erase all the "don't tell" messages. These are old tapes inside my head. The voices inside my head never stop.

I feel so much shame inside, and scared to allow anybody to see who I really am. Nobody can see the darkness inside, because I appear to be functional on the outside. No one can see my pain. I want a miracle. I want to be healed miraculously. God, where are you? Why am I drowning? I have done years of therapy, why am I not healed? I look fine but my heart feels like a crane that has come in and ripped out a part of my chest.

I am a victim of sexual abuse, physical abuse and emotional abuse. I grew up the youngest of four children, living with a father who drank, two brothers and an emotionally unavailable mother. My parents fought all the time.

The brother closest in age to me, he and I were scared little children when our parents fought, and we only had each other. There was constant fighting and bickering back and forth and there was no adult around to care about me. He was three years older than me. He sexually abused me, at first taking photos of me when I was just about 6 years old. He threatened that if I ever told, he would die, and nobody would believe me because, after all, I was posing for these photos. Then he started touching other places of my body, and using me to give him pleasure. Sometimes, he even touched me under the dining room table, while we were supposed to be having a family dinner, but the parents were fighting so nobody noticed. This brother was violent, and he hurt me, and he got turned on by hurting me. This went on for about 20 years.

My older brother, who was eight years older than me, also sexually abused me, and told me never ever to tell my other brother or anybody else. I never told. He was the gentler person, always taking care of me sexually, teaching me sex positions, and other things. I was very young, and never told anybody. He gave me lots of attention, and I liked this brother for that. He was the only one who was nice to me. He took me places with him, and always played with me.

My older brother sexually abused me for about 20 years, and it became a secret to the other brother. One day, my brothers came to me laughing because they had been comparing notes all along about which one was having better sex with me.

Then, after my two brothers abused me, my drunk father would have me sit on his lap, and get aroused. I was so needy for attention that I liked sitting on his lap. He also got inappropriate with me in bed whenever he could. He thought I was enjoying touching him. I loved my father because he gave me attention. Then, after my father sexually abused me, my emotionally unavailable mother would touch my genitals when I had menstrual cramps. She wanted to relieve me of my cramps, so she masturbated me. I was never close to my mother, and always hated her.

After I had been sexually abused by my family members, my father used me for his friends. His drinking partner started touching me, and then in church I was touched sexually. I thought something was wrong with me. I just never knew the word "no," and thought my purpose was for pleasing people sexually. I thought that I had to do whatever anybody wanted me to do and just shut up and "take it."

Growing up, I felt alone, isolated, and never trusted anybody. I was always trying to befriend teachers, and they called me a "pest" because I never wanted to leave school.

At 24, I married a man who was emotionally unavailable. He also had Asperger syndrome. Sex became a chore, and a challenge, and every time I would have sex, I would emotionally freeze. I hated touch, was paralyzed to go to a dentist, or a doctor, paralyzed to go places, and became depressed. I find it impossible to see a gynecologist because of my sexual abuse, and impossible to get any kind of tests done on me. I also find it impossible to be put to sleep because of my deep trust issues.

I joined a 12-step group called Survivors of Incest Anonymous (SIA) 10 years ago, and became very involved in the program. I learned to deal with feelings, and discovered that I was no longer alone in this journey. That others felt the way that I did. I learned how to cope, and gave back what I learned in the program. SIA and my wonderful therapist of 18 years have saved my life. It took me about 10 years to trust my therapist with my deepest secrets. I also see a homeopathic psychiatrist, and fought to stay off medication, only using alternative medicine.

I have tried to take my life two times, and was admitted to a hospital for depression. A psychiatrist told me if I did not take medicine for the rest of my life, I would live the rest of my life in and out of a mental institution. To this day, I am a functional adult, living my life on homeopathy and no traditional medicine.

My incest experience has affected my only daughter, who is a grown woman today. (The reason I have only one child is because of dealing with incest.) Eight years ago, my father moved in with my husband and I because of his failing health. I chose to care for him in my home until he passed away on hospice of cancer to the bladder. I was his sole caretaker. I currently take care of my mother, who is ailing from late stages of Alzheimer's, and she lives in my home. She is currently an invalid and needs 24/7 care. I have learned to forgive her. It has been challenging to take in both of my parents, but I have learned to change my heart through the years.

I still yearn to have a mother love me. I still yearn to be protected by a loving mother, and yearn to have a mother who would just listen to me. I still search for those needs in others.

I know my journey is not over. Sometimes I am not sure where I am heading, but I do not want to go back to the starting point. Sometimes there are flat tires on this journey, and I must stop and fix it. Sometimes there are detours, or I go the wrong way, but I always find myself back on this road. Sometimes it is uphill, and sometimes it is down hill. I tell myself over and over again I can do it.

It has been helpful to mentor somebody just coming into the SIA program, because I understand where they are in the healing process—I have been there.

I also mentor needy children, and give them the love that I never received in my life. I volunteer to run workshops and retreats, as well as speak at various events on recovery. I have gone through several programs, learned many things along the way, and pass them on whenever I can.

I know life is always going to be a challenge, but I would not be alive if I kept this a secret. Even though I still have work to do in my life, to look at these deep feelings—which is challenging for me—I know that I am going to survive. I had always been a fighter in life, always trying to be better, and give to others what I never received in life.

If you are an incest survivor, know that if I survived, you can too. You are not alone, and many people out there understand why you may feel like you do. I ask you to please don't hurt yourself. You have already been hurt. Know that I care, and have much passion in my heart for survivors of childhood sexual abuse and incest.

Anonymous

Gender: Female
Age: 27
Race/ethnicity: South Asian-American
Occupation: Law student, copywriter
Location: Philadelphia, Pa.

ALMOST TWO YEARS AGO, I opened my email to find a Facebook friend request from the person who had sexually molested me as a child for almost two years. Not uncurious, I looked at our friends in common. Three. An elementary school classmate and my two first cousins, siblings, who still resided in the small town in South Jersey where we'd all grown up. The one and only time I had attempted to tell the cousins about what he had done, they had reacted with a curious mixture of disbelief and anger. I had never spoken about it with them again. I scrolled through the photos of the man who had single-handedly managed to make my childhood a time of guilt and confusion, fear and trauma. He had two photo albums dedicated to John Deere farming equipment and a lone photo of himself and his wife, a mutual friend of ours, cheek-to-cheek, smiling.

More than 30 years ago, my father first brought his Pakistani bride to America and soon thereafter, the two went on a tour of the Pennsylvania Dutchlands and emerged converted. To raise their family in the New World, shielding all the evils of secular American culture, my uber-Christian parents chose Mennonites, the car-driving, electricity-embracing cousins of the Amish. We never actually became Mennonites; my mother remained in her traditional salwar kamezes, and neither parent was baptized in the church. But myself and my three siblings grew up knowing only Mennonite friends and neighbors and attending only Mennonite schools and churches.

My mother, a college graduate who chose education as her major and taught elementary school before marriage, never had a problem talking with her children about the evils in the world. As a child, I distinctly recall her telling us, "If anybody ever tries to touch you, no matter who it is, if you feel uncomfortable you have to tell me." But I did not tell her. I did not tell her the first time my best friend's older brother, who I adored, tried to put his hand up our skirts to show us this new "game" he'd invented. And I didn't tell her the second time. Or the third time.

And he knew I wouldn't. Ever. Everyone in the community knew that my parents were going through a difficult custody battle and that a caseworker had been called to determine whether our mother adequately provided for our needs and treated us well. I knew, even at 6, that if my litigation-happy father and his attorney found out that the pastor's son had been touching me, my mother would lose custody of us faster than you could say "unfit parent."

Looking back on it and having now read the literature on sexual abuse, I know that what he was doing was called grooming and that he had done it not only to his sister and myself, but to half a dozen girls in the community. Not coincidentally, all of those girls happened to be in a certain state of vulnerability. One was mentally retarded. Another had just been adopted by an older couple. All of them were prone to attention from a certain charming, handsome young boy who said all the right things to parents. A boy who followed me and his sister around his parents' many-acred farm until we took to staying in the house, playing only under the ignorant eye of his mother.

When I finally started talking as an adult, I never stopped. I told everyone in my life. Sunday school teachers. My siblings. My mother. My friends. My boyfriends. And with each new acceptance, I grew more at peace with that part of my childhood.

The last time I saw him in person was on his sister's wedding day, days before the Facebook friend request. Despite my reservations, I had gone.

Bold, as always, he came up to me at the reception. "How are you doing?" he asked, smiling widely, his teeth as white and straight as ever, his eyes twinkly. "You're all grown up now."

I looked at him. "I am actually doing quite well, thank you," I wanted to say. "Through years of hard work and therapy, I have managed to overcome my feelings of worthlessness. I am not afraid of all men anymore. I am not afraid to trust handsome, charming men, who smile at me with straight, white teeth. I am not afraid. I don't hide my body under layers and layers of clothing. I don't eat to forget. I don't think what happened was my fault anymore. And every time I tell someone about what you did, and I do, I get back some of the confidence you stole from me."

I didn't say any of that. I wish I had. Instead, I just walked away.

Michelle S. Cahill

Gender: Female
Age: 30
Race/ethnicity: White
Occupation: Student/advocate
Location: Chicago, Ill.
Age abuse occurred: 21

MY STORY MIGHT be considered somewhat typical. I was 21 and totally enamored with the wrong guy. I had recently ended my first long-term relationship. A three-year relationship, three rather uneventful years, and now it was time to move on. I met Mr. Wrong at the local Irish bar on karaoke night. He had stopped in after work, belted out a Shania Twain song, and was on his way out the door when I shocked myself by stopping him to compliment his choice in music. I was hooked, and it was already obvious that I liked him a lot more than he ever liked me.

Shortly after we met, we traipsed along with a mutual friend to a party that had a slight whiff of a Fourth of July theme. The theme being that the host was a police officer, and he had recently confiscated some fireworks while executing the finer points of his job. We were going to shoot off said fireworks by his apartment and have a few drinks. The party had a selective guest list: myself, my date and three other guys—our mutual friend, the host and another of our casual acquaintances. I'm sure this scenario would set a lot of fingers wagging, but it never occurred to me that something bad could ever happen to me. It was simply a thought that had never crossed my mind, although violence against women was not a foreign concept to me. One of my close friends had been raped at a party, and my grandmother had been the victim of severe and brutal domestic violence. My mother made sure that I was totally aware of the risks one runs simply having been born a female. My dad always warned me not to be the girl that the guys talk about in the locker room the next day. I knew about the tricks and the lies, but I felt totally comfortable with the choice I was making. My naiveté was showing.

The fireworks had been masterfully discharged, everyone was drinking cheap beer, and we were going through the host's record collection. It wasn't exactly a wild house party at a frat. At one point in the evening, as the group sat down to watch television, I started to feel sick. I asked the host if I could lie down, as I was feeling dizzy and nauseous. He showed me to his room, which was right off of the living room where everyone was sitting. A few minutes later, one of the guests, one of the mutual friends, came into the room. He stripped off his pants and tried to get me to fondle him. As I lie there terrified, facing the wall, I tried to summon some sense of what I should do. My mother had told me what bad men do, and I knew the "stomp on his foot, gouge his eyes, kick him in the balls" tricks when cornered in a situation like this. Yet, I couldn't come up with a plan. I just lied there, feigning sleep, praying he would go away, or that someone would come and help me.

My prayers were answered, but by the wrong kind of angel. The host came in and turned the light on. I shot up, terrified, and lit out of the room. I ran pell-mell searching for my future ex-boyfriend. I stopped him and begged him not to leave me, telling him that something was wrong and that I would explain in the car. I was afraid. I was afraid of starting a fight, I was afraid of getting yelled at, I was afraid someone was going to be angry with me. I wouldn't tell him what had happened, I just wanted to put it behind me. I just wanted to get away.

I didn't get away that night. I was raped. Not by the man who had assaulted me the first time, but by the host. I was searching for my purse and I could not find it. I found it, finally, in the kitchen and the host was holding onto it for me. He cornered me in the kitchen and began telling me how great he was and how I didn't need to leave, and that he would take care of me. I especially didn't need to leave with that guy; that guy was no good for me. He wasn't good enough for me. But my rapist, he was the one.

My mother had always made it clear to me that a woman needed to protect herself. I knew that bad men did bad things and that sometimes, even good men did bad things. I learned that the second part of that statement was true when my friend, who later became my boyfriend, had explained why he had left the night I was raped. He had walked into the kitchen where the assault was in progress and, seeing what was happening, turned around and left. He said it had something to do with his own sense of self-worth. At the time I accepted that, coming from my own unhealthy sense of self-esteem. Now, if someone said something like that to me I would scream and yell, demanding to know how a man could walk away from a woman so desperately in need. Now, I know that it happens every day.

I called my mother a couple days later, looking at the bruises on my thighs in the bathtub. I had to tell her. She took me to the hospital, wanting me to be checked and get prophylactics for STIs. It was too late for a kit, but four police officers showed up anyway. They yelled my name and swore at me when I refused to turn around and look at them. I was shaking when my mother went toe to toe with the biggest of the blue-shirted bullies and told him off for treating me so disrespectfully. The nurse acted like I was wasting her time, especially after I declined Plan B. Apparently, good Irish Catholic girls don't get raped.

Support comes in many forms after something like this happens to a person. The blaming starts. People blame you, blame the perpetrator, blame the system. Everyone asks you the questions you are asking yourself: Why you didn't do this, say that, call this person, hail that cab, scream, yell, fight back. What were you wearing? Why didn't you bring a friend? Why did you go in the first place? Why don't you fit the image of a rape victim? Why don't you have a black eye? Where are your bruises?

These questions don't help, and they don't bring clarity. They just encourage the survivor to feel guilty. Guilty that she doesn't wear chainmail under her chastity belt, leaves the house at night without a chaperone, looks a man in the eyes.

The soul-shattering effects of rape take a long time to go away, especially when the most unhealthy people in one's life are where one focuses most of their attention. I pushed the feelings of violation and rage, confusion and hurt deep down until it began to fester like an infection. Occasionally I would confront my demons head on. I tried therapy, only to have my therapist tell me that she didn't "handle things so heavy," she really just dealt with things like divorce. I tried validating myself with sex. Then I felt more disgusting and angry. I knew I was being judged by the harshest of critics—myself. I had lost the sense that my body belonged to me, that it wasn't garbage, something to be used and tossed aside.

I was floundering alone. My mom and I didn't have a solid relationship, and I had alienated myself from the rest of my family. I really had no one and nothing. Yet, I wanted to help people like me. I wanted to be for someone else what hadn't been available to me. This was before I knew that something like medical advocacy existed. I knew for certain though that I wanted to be able to hold someone's hand when they were being judged and invaded all over again.

After some time in Al-Anon, a support group for friends and families of alcoholics, the guilt, rage, violation and desperation came bursting out. I came home from a meeting and lied down on my living room floor. I curled up and sobbed, my nose ran, I was spitting and drooling, heaving sobs, until I retched up all those feelings. All that poison that had been inside of me came pouring out all over my carpet. It occurred to me that it WASN'T my fault, that I could be angry that someone had done this to me. It didn't matter that someone might not agree or might be angry with me for speaking my truth. I didn't want friends who would doubt or judge me. "With friends like that" and all that jazz. It took almost five years.

I tell my story a lot, and I won't lie. I'm always afraid that someone will challenge me, or demand proof or say that I asked for it. And those fears are well-founded, because there are people that do such terrible things. I have been volunteering for the last three years as a medical advocate. I found that nameless thing that I so desperately needed and wanted when I was in my darkest hour. It is the purest, most real thing that I have ever done. I meet survivors who remind me every day that we are a community of people who deserve to be respected and cared for.

Unfortunately, my story doesn't end there.

I've taken classes, I've learned about date rape drugs. I am certain that my rape involved drugs. I don't generally find myself overcome by dizziness like an 18th-century heroine in a novella. I've learned as an advocate that the most popular date-rape drug is alcohol; it's cheap, easy and legal. The theory is if you give someone enough of it, you can control them. I know how easy it is to hurt someone, so I try to keep my guard up.

I went to a house party with a friend a few weeks ago, and I was careful to monitor my drinking in order to stay in control. My friend had brought a bottle of wine; a sweet, white wine. We finished it over the course of an hour or two. As I was chatting with a couple of the female guests, someone handed us a few beers. I put mine on the floor and went back to my conversation. A while later, I was talking to someone else, standing instead of sitting. I was talking to a guy (maybe) instead of a girl. I was handed another beer. I remember looking down and thinking that it was strange that someone would hand me an opened beer. It was foamy on top. I thought that it was strange enough that I wouldn't drink it. I went back to my conversation.

I must have sipped that beer a couple times, and within a few minutes I started to feel very dizzy. I sat down, realizing that something was wrong. As soon as I realized what was happening to me, I knew that I needed to get out of the situation. I stumbled through the apartment twice, once to find my friend that I had arrived with (I never found her) and the second to find my purse so that I could call my roommate and leave. I spent the rest of the night in the hospital, having blood drawn and talking to the police—there was nothing they could do, but they did commend me on "doing the right thing" and getting away, but made sure to make me feel a little guilty about leaving my friend behind. This time, I asked for an advocate from the agency I volunteer for. I knew the emotional risks of seeking help. It had gone so smashingly the last time. However, my nurse was amazing, the doctor warm and my friends and family supportive and understanding. My dad called to tell me he loved me and that he was glad that I was safe.

It was unfortunate that a similar experience had to occur, but it taught me the importance of having people around you that care and advocate for you. I felt like I got the opportunity to feel what I didn't have before: a community of people who love and care and want me to be OK, but even more importantly, the knowledge that risk of being hurt, of someone doing something to you, wanting to harm you doesn't change, no matter the depth and breadth of knowledge and experience a person might have. There are people out there who want to do terrible things, which is why we need to keep fighting this fight. We won't stop until they do, and until we can leave our chainmail at home.

David

Gender: Male
Age: Late 20s
Race/ethnicity: Caucasian
Occupation: Cook/freelance writer
Location: Philadelphia, Pa.
Age abuse occurred: 16

IT TOOK ME a long time to pin the right word to it, to call it what it was.

It happened over Christmas break, in high school. In a small town in the Midwest, teenagers were breaking into a liquor cabinet. Me, getting too drunk, taking too many shots. Me, trusting the bed of the classmate I had been fooling around with off and on. Him, coming into the room where I was too drunk to move, closing the door behind him. Him, putting his dick in my mouth. Me trying to tell him no. Him continuing. Me trying to push away with all my facilities. It took me biting down to get him to stop.

It would run through my head as the time I got too drunk—as if alcohol had excused what had happened. Maybe he just didn't know what he was doing? Maybe it was my fault for being too drunk and somehow us fooling around earlier that day was an invitation to what happened. Maybe this was just being queer in a small town.

The Monday after break at school, he came into homeroom, taunting me with the words "weiner biter," waving his finger as if admonishing a petty insult. I felt myself sink. I felt so low. The only thing I could feel was to blame myself, and I let our not-relationship continue on.

And I still never put the words to what happened that time, or the reluctant consent I felt every time there was a day off from school, and the inevitability of having to fool around again. It wasn't always reluctant, but when it was, I never felt lower. Again, I still felt like I was at fault, somehow. That this was some sort of price for wanting to be sexual or for wanting to not be completely straight or for having been the initiator of the whole situation some months before. Both it and the queerness stuck to me like my deepest secret for the remainder of high school, somewhat into college. Sometimes, the two weird guilts are intertwined, even though I know in my heart that being queer isn't a problem. It's still a side I feel like I can't trust, I can't explore, as if every man will be like this man, as if I will always be hurt. Even in "straight" sex, I can still feel the damage, as if any part of my body is some minefield of shame and hurt.

But still, it took me a long time to put the important word to it.

It took me that long to call it rape. It was around five or six years after the fact, when another friend had come forward. And for the first time ever, at the age of 22, I not only told what had happened for the first time, but called it that for the first time. It seemed weird. Though I know better now, so much of talk surrounding sexual assault and rape seemed aimed at women. But this is the same culture that told them the same feelings that I had running through my head: That it was my fault, that I somehow invited it, that something I did deserved it happening to me.

It hurts and it will always hurt. I still feel like the wound isn't healed, like my own outward trust has never been repaired, that despite my desires to the contrary, my inability to let people in will damn me to being alone. I sometimes still have nightmares where he's there. I avoided all talk of a potential class reunion this year. Sometimes, he still butts into my life, and it's as if he somehow either doesn't know or doesn't care that what he did hurt and was wrong. Thousands of miles away, I still dread the off-chance that I'll see him on a trip home. I had known him for years, and I had considered him a friend. Even when I confronted him at one point, the fact that I initiated the non-relationship was blown back in my face, that there again it was my fault for feeling queer.

I know that it wasn't my fault, that the only responsible party was the rapist, that nothing I did was an invitation to rape. I know these things. But I also know, at the end of the day, how hard that is to let yourself be closer to freeing that lingering guilt and shame and anxiety and dread. I hope I can at least believe that I can just move on and not have it hang over me anymore.

Jennifer Clare Burke

Gender: Female
Age: 38
Race/ethnicity: White
Occupation: Independent contractor
Location: Philadelphia suburbs
Age abuse occurred: Early 20s

1. Observational Techniques of the Damned

It's a strange thing to do, to stand there in outward silence, consciously trying to look indifferent, but actually sizing up another woman's victim potential, deciding if her eyes are wide-enough security cameras, if her energy tenses pit-bull ready, if she got enough calcium so that her wrists won't break in a struggle.

It's the Rape Olympics, dontcha know. They have never stopped playing in my head since the switch flipped with my own rape. They exist outside of time, as if I never knew a different way to frame my own or anyone's being-in-the-world-ness, something called *dasein*. I encounter a different awareness of my body as an object in space, of my psyche as an elastic thing, something plastic and thus malleable through an exercise of will— mine or someone else's. The *dasein* after the rape. What if it happens again, and where, and how to recover? What is the shape of my soul thereafter?

I measure every person and every location by how "rape-y" s/he/it registers in my now-Olympian brain.

There's the woman in her 80s, her hunch pronounced as she rummages in her purse with one hand, the other hand holding her phone as she bitches about the delay at the mechanic's shop where we sit. Her inspection is dawdling along, and my new tires are still unattached. I have nothing to do now but play the Rape Olympics in my head and observe frailties in everyone, seeing the ones that in some way parallel my own. The skin over her knuckles and along her jaw is so thin that I want to walk in front of her, my body protecting her.

"Sitting this long is unhealthy," she admonishes the room and no one, rising from her chair to make the point. "I'm taking a walk," her regal frown sinks deeper to emphasize the tardy sins of the mechanic. "Twenty-five minutes," she tosses at the guy at the admin desk. Her feet hit the floor with uncertainty, as if she's not sure of her balance, not sure of her body being there for her.

I wonder what she'll find on that walk, if her thigh bone can take the pressure of a nonconsensual hit, if her pelvis would shatter, if she would.

I create the world in bones and fractures. The world is a fragile place.

The Rape Olympics channel is on. It's always on inside my head, and she's one more player. Her age doesn't disqualify her. She gets to be a victim as much as any other person, including the youngest, most nubile chickie wearing a short skirt in *that* neighborhood at *that* time of night while hanging around with *those* people. You know who I mean, *that girl*, the one who was asking for it.

2. This Probably Isn't a Great Campfire Story

You can do stuff to avoid being a victim.

Project don't-fuck-with-me body language, sign up for self-defense courses, use the buddy system. But what if that doesn't work?

What if sexual assault becomes part of your life's narrative? See a therapist to heal, find the right doctors to repair your naughty bits after the fact, proactively ponder the way disgust, attractiveness, violence and degradation conflate with your body.

I think your marshmallows are burning. Or is that you catching on fire?

3. A Reason To Shank the Well-Intentioned

"I think the world of you, you know, for being honest about this stuff." [1]

What stuff?

"The way rape can impact you, the way you choose to reveal your experience."

I'm not choosing, not really. I'm not consenting to the way my body insists on shouting its history so that medical intervention is mandatory. Whether I consent or not, my body is screaming as it needs to scream. I hear it in my bones. I didn't want to go for treatment or to be touched by medical people whom I didn't want in my life or in my twat in the first place. But I had to. I'll write *The Handbook to an Involuntary Universe* and teach you.

"Still so brave to be so open and so honest. I think the world of you, really."

What world is that?

4. The Misbegotten Arena

In 2000, I discovered I had the pedestrian plague of those who were sexually active: cervical dysplasia caused by exposure to the HPV virus, which was detected on a routine pap. I could have contracted it from assault or from partners. From there, the odyssey of colposcopies began.

Before the dysplasia, my OB-GYN and I were already in troublesome matches against my vag. Getting on the examination table with my ass positioned on the edge was a rodeo of lassoing my knees that were already shutting, whether I wanted them to or not. The smallest speculum was an instrument of blunt-force torture that left me squirming and grunting over the table as I tried to focus on a mobile of butterflies suspended from the ceiling, fluttering above the stirrups.

These problems were then gently broached in the nonclinical room reserved for talking after the re-trauma-ing medicalization. It crystallized for me then, those stories I had heard of the subsequent reality for many who had endured sexual trauma: the healing, saving intervention can often resemble the original act of destruction in unsettling, quietly horrifying

---

1. I have had more than one person make such comments to me.

ways. I immediately thought of a story I heard years before: A person refused to eat after being forced to perform fellatio, and she then needed a feeding tube forced down her throat to survive.

Once my abnormal pap results were identified, my OB-GYN explained the need for examinations and biopsies to prevent cervical cancer. All of this discussion meant one thing: The already unbearable pelvic exams would become more intense and more prolonged. What's more, they would require a greater opening by the speculum, the very stretching I couldn't give.

We had to find a way to make it possible, which was difficult, because I—or rather, my vagina—was becoming more difficult. The rare acceptance of a tampon became rarer as pelvic spasms ruled my lower half. I could sometimes ride a stationary bike in the gym, sometimes not. Pain came just from sitting in snug jeans. Sex was a constant negotiation with partners who grew confused and with genitals that asserted their will independent of my wishes.

"One way to address this difficulty is with therapy in the traditional sense, with talk therapy, and there's also physical therapy for this kind of vaginal pain, which has been successful," my OB-GYN said.

"Physical therapy, like touching me and exercises?"

"Yes. It has a great success rate. I can give you information on it. Do you want to try it?"

"I want to learn about it, maybe think about it. I don't know yet if I could handle that."

He handed over pamphlets and a directory of practitioners.

"With the colposcopies, you'll need to be emotionally and physically able to get through them as comfortably as possible."

He was right.

I'll go to the space between hyperextended joints and be silent. I'll hide in the pores of broken bones, anywhere with a bit of nothingness.

Where will I be in my body during those times, I wondered. Where will I be in my head? If I'm on a table with a speculum in the locked position and a sharp tool against my cervix, what to do with myself if I want to make sure my cells stay safe?

Insertion and the resulting pain will dissolve like dreams of a

mirage. They'll be images on overexposed film, drifting pollen in the sunset, mute ghosts haunting a forgotten birdcage.

Sometimes you can't talk a maladroit vag into dancing. I thought all the right things. They didn't help. I decided to try the physical therapy.

My intellect and verbalizations couldn't have been farther from twat realities. Battle zones were drawn on my body, an en-fleshed conflict. Oddly, my body's topography lent itself well to this purpose. My collarbones have always been more pronounced than the flashiest jewelry. Even my mother has commented on their stark straightness, with their length on unusually broad shoulders for a petite woman. They became the granite wall between well-reasoned affirmations above ("I need medical care to which I am fully consenting to take care of myself") and a shockingly articulate combat zone below ("Stop launching another attack on me, or I'll fight back").

I made an appointment for pelvic floor retraining with the specific purpose of getting vaginal compliance ("thou shalt obey my will") and less pain in my life as the threat of cervical cancer—and the needed colposcopy—loomed.

The invasion is coming, and the resistance has claimed me. I'll bury myself beneath scapula. I'll find kingdoms in a yawn, way stations in tear ducts.

The physical therapist's name was X. This type of work was all she did. No knee strengthening, no stroke rehab, no back injuries. Just this. I wanted to see what X could offer. When I met her, I looked through her skin and tried to assess her bone density. She seemed strong.

I was first brought to a nonthreatening, nondescript room that looked like every other institutional room where people are Supposed To Talk. I recall that the walls were a soft color and the lighting was neither bright nor glaring, something different from the vibe of an interrogation room. This room existed for questioning nonetheless—my history, my symptoms, my demographics, my insurance card, please. Each of these things blended into the others until my symptoms became my basic info, and medicalization became my narrative of self over time. It wasn't only that rape altered vaginal functionality. It was that it altered who I told myself I was right down to the bone.

5. Reimagining Circuitry

I see a pain-management doctor, Z, who shares her research finds with me. I delight in new knowledge as much as she does. These pieces are better than toys; they're tools to unhinge and hammer cooperation from my body.

She loops the red leads of a specific-frequency microcurrent machine around my thigh.

"There's research that we're actually hard-wired for negativity. Think about it: when we were primitive, if we saw a black form on the ground in the dark, we should think it's a snake and be prepared to avoid a venomous bite."

She loops the black leads around my calf. Now there is a circuit with my knee as the target. The chronic swelling and pain in this joint responds well to this type of treatment.

"It's called a negativity bias, and it was about survival. If the black thing on the ground turns out to be a stick, well, fine, but if it were a snake, we would need to fight or flee. The problem comes especially for traumatized people and people in pain: They're already dealing with hypervigilance and are already experiencing the worst. They're amplifying the parts of the brain that are already there telling us the world is bad and dangerous. The adrenal fatigue alone is rough, let alone the emotional experience."

She adjusts the machine's intensity. Already I can tell the program is working. A deep, unexpected peace arrives, a zen in the mind that isn't willed but achieved.

"But with meditating 30 minutes a day for three months, you can change structures in the brain to modulate that fear response. This is documented in research and in images of the brain. You can change the brain."

The frequency on the knee is exactly right. Specific-frequency microcurrent is strange in that I know my knee is getting the right treatment—not from my knee's sensations, but from the calm throughout my body.

Change your brain, change your vagina?

6. We Are Our Own Poltergeists

X brings me to the clinical room.

What I would prefer is to hide indefinitely in the waiting room, as if it weren't my turn, and to stare at other patients, wondering what broke them so that they needed help, wondering about their vitamin D levels, wondering if other people wonder about other people's skeletons in an attack.

"You can leave your shoes and socks on, unless you don't want to, but everything from the waist down comes off. We'll use this sheet so you're covered. I'll knock to see if you're ready." With her long legs, she's in the hall in three quick steps.

The room is colder than I would like. Once my boots and jeans are in a heap under the gurney, I miss them promptly. The sheet is thin, but I'm covered as I lie down, eyeballing the room. Opposite my bed sits a computer monitor. My eyes land on it easily as the monitor is directly in my field of vision. Near it, a series of leads and wires snake in different directions that don't make sense to me.

I wait, pantless, for a therapy I've never had before with a stranger who seems nice enough. I feel things now that I don't anticipate, including a hollowing alone-ness, a walling-off of connection to others, a sentencing, a clinical chill that every bit of pain and raw immediacy can be reduced to an emotionally removed, slow-paced excavation toward functionality.

Monet once left his completed canvas in the rain for an entire night. When he returned the following morning, he saw morphing shapes and lifted colors bleeding into the mud. "From this," he said, "I will build my new earth." I'll cull the mangled parts, the shifted mind. I'll make wreckage into art, art into a place I can live. I'll find the words I once lost in my body.

In the well-lit medical calm of "pelvic floor retraining," who I am doesn't matter. My insurance will be billed like so many other patients' insurance companies. The sheet covering me will be laundered, just like every other sheet on every other body. The rape itself doesn't matter. Everyone here has been hurt or is hurting, and everyone wants it to end. All that matters is my right-here, right-now comfort and focus so that the real patient, a wayward twat, can be brought into compliance, into better form.

I want to live.

X returns and explains with placid neutrality how this kind of PT works.

"I'll attach electrodes to you, and they'll indicate the level of muscular contraction on the screen."

The wires and leads that didn't make sense to me earlier are all too clear. Now they loomed as invading octopus tentacles, poking into everything, consuming knowledge of me they shouldn't have.

"Electrodes where? Inside?"

"Yes. Both inside and out."

"I can't handle anything inside. The OB-GYN is bad enough. Can I see first what the outside ones do?"

"Sure."

And like that, lightly, I set parameters in invasive medical settings as quickly and assuredly as I do in accepting or rejecting jobs, parking places, social outings and places to live. I ascertain the threat level and decide what I'm willing to live with in the aftermath. If things go badly, I'll know that at least the onus was on me from start to finish and that I was willfully present and consenting. There's some comfort in knowing that you, only you, are behind your own pain.

From my right side, X leans over my bed and lifts the sheet near my feet. I barely feel her hands connecting electrodes near the vagina, rectum, inner thigh and hips. I think about the prospect of swimming again while I have my period because I can manage a tampon. I see a tsunami of activity and color on the screen with no white space anywhere.

"That's indicating your total contraction level, and it's the highest level."

"I'm not doing anything. I'm not lying here squeezing. I'd feel it if I were."

"You actually are doing something. And you're feeling the pain of constantly being in this state. Watch the screen to see what happens when you consciously interact with the muscles under the sensors."

She stands a few feet away from me, watching the screen and my expressions, letting me acclimate to a new way of decoding my body's logic for protecting itself. There's a reason why a speculum, a tampon, a body part can't enter: I've decided nothing will because my body learned the resulting agony, and the body's intelligence is cruel, effective.

That's not gonna fucking happen again.

I notice some of the on-screen patterns flatten at certain points in my breathing, allowing me to see a little of the white space at the top of the graph.

"The goal is to have the colored part as low as possible, which indicates relaxed muscle—where it should be in a resting state."

At the end of an exhaled breath, my pelvis naturally tilts, and my body loses its grip for a second. Here the colored wave abates.

"If you can learn how to un-contract the muscle a little, that's a start. That can get you through the exam with less pain or almost no pain. Just see what

you can learn with the sensors about controlling your muscles."

I learn how to make the color go away, breath by breath. I learn that my entire pelvic region can listen again to my will instead of only my fear. Having control there feels unnatural. I see her each week, where I learn more.

One activity involves her gloved hands. The feel and smell of latex and lube already has me inwardly disgusted. Color captures the entire screen.

"Do what you've learned to relax."

"What exactly are you going to be doing?"

"Stretching just the outer muscle of the vagina, nothing deep. We'll think of a clock. You'll feel pressure upward toward your pubic bone at noon, pressure out toward your left leg at 3, toward your right at 9, and downward toward your rear at 6. OK?"

"We'll see."

"If it's too much, you tell me. Here we go."

Her touch isn't the deeply penetrative probe of the OB-GYN searching for pathology in the uterus and ovaries. It stays confined to the outermost muscle. I relax. The screen confirms my action, until the six o'clock mark.

"Why is that burning? That spot."

"It's where it's the tightest on you, and the release can feel like a burn."

"That's so strange."

"Look at the screen," a phrase that became code for *"remember your intent if you want to manifest it."*

And the word was made flesh…

While we worked literally around the clock again, I watched the jerky balance of color and white.

7. My Geolocator Is in My Vag, and It's Really High-Strung

My twat is my compass. This is my prayer.

I know exactly where I would like to be, or not to be. I am in Mama Bear overdrive. I want to know the emotions of every person in the room before they know I walked in. I know the lighting plans of parking lots and the exit routes and fire escapes of public buildings. I gauge the attitudes of waitresses, decide on the threat levels of clerks, assess the eye contact of people walking in the opposite direction, and look closely at who ventures too close to me when they need to walk by my space.

"You're staring," my friend says.

"I know."

"You're giving people your judging face."

"That's my favorite one." [2]

I turn down invitations into the thickness of the city when I realize that I will have to walk a distance, however short, from where I parked in territory that is not mine. I stay home when I know that I might have to navigate public transportation when a Nice, Reasonable Girl shouldn't be out on her own.

What was she doing out at that hour anyhow? Didn't she know what could happen?

Paranoia rewards me constantly: be paranoid, get a good result, thank the paranoia, rinse and repeat, take your calcium.

I already think in terms of triage nurses, rape kits assemblers, and tut-tut's from the Peanut Gallery who say things like, "I know I shouldn't 'blame the victim,' you know, and I'm really not blaming her exactly, but did you notice about her that...." They will want to know the length of skirt, the tightness of the jeans, the height of the heel and how much makeup. If there are quantifiable things that a victim did wrong to earn her come-uppance, then perhaps they can avoid such wrongs, which means the world will be safe and neat again for vaginas everywhere because rape isn't flow-ing in the veins of the culture, no, not that; rape is just in that one wrong committed against one dummy.

See? Everything is still fine.

My body is more than the sum of square inches of skin. My body is the air surrounding me and how far away the nearest person is. My body is the desperation level of the people on that block beneath my feet or car: How badly hurting and needing is the nearest person, and will that person try to alter the dimensions of the body I've reconstituted? If attack can happen once, it can happen again. My body is the blindness level of a street, or the darkness surrounding a building that used to be a home but

---

2. My boss for one of my jobs is also very much a wonderful friend. He has pointed out to me more than once that I'm staring, which is a rude habit. I know. Some-times I don't realize I'm doing it. The first two lines are uttered often in my world. The second two lines involved a specific incident—my friend remarking upon my reaction to someone and my response.

is now boarded up, thereby obscuring my vision, or the angle of a car parked just around the corner so that I can't see who's in it.

Her: It's always so crowded at 6 at this gym with the after-work people. We'll have to find a space all the way in the back.

Me: The part adjoining the park that no one uses and the empty train station parking lot?

Her: Well, yeah, unless a space opens up.

Me: But the lighting is shitty back there. I don't see any foot traffic there.

Her: So? This is the gym lot. It's not like we're parking a few blocks over.

Me: I get that, but you're a few rapes— maybe three good, solid ones—from the front door.

Anyone could be waiting, or maybe not waiting, but see an opportunity and fucking go for it. Do you know how small we look to someone who can bench even just 100 pounds? Do you know your feelings might not matter?

Her: What are you talking about?

Me: We're driving to the bookstore, and hanging out, and trying the gym at 7:30. And we're parking out front, near the door, where I can see every fucking move, every corner, every distance, every person in every car. I want everyone in the gym to be able to hear my scream, or at least one other person to hear. Way out back, no one will know. Out front, I might stand a chance. This time. [3]

My body is the proximity of a stranger who's bigger and stronger than I am in the elevator. My body is the sense of how consequently screwed—literally—I might be in the next 10 minutes. My body is the distance between me and the nearest cat call I experience because I am a female walking outside. My body is how I feel when I'm in a neighborhood with bars on every ground-level window, no matter how much it costs to live

---

3. The above exchange in italics is half-fantasy and half-reality—I was not this verbally organized in real life. The reality occurred with a woman who went to my old gym in Willow Grove, which has since closed. That gym attracted a core of regulars but also had so many people whom I would see once or twice and never again. This woman came a few times, and while we weren't that friendly, I liked her enough to pick her up when I saw her headed there in gym clothes. As you might imagine, she and I did not become more familiar with each other after this moment, and I wound up not seeing her again because she never came to my former gym again, as far as I know. The fantasy element of the above includes the detail, clarity and smoothness with which I responded.

there, no matter how nice the nearest restaurant. My body is adrenaline when I have to walk from my car to my destination and the unknown breathes heavily beneath every parked car I pass, inside every doorway I can't see, and on the other side of a building wall. My body is the nearby neighbor who sees a chance and is willing to bet that I won't approach the authorities about it. My body is the nearness of someone who has nothing to lose and a shit ton of grudges with no otherwise available target.

The Rape Olympics continue so loudly in my head. Each assessment of my potential victim status is a fracture. The world breaks over and over.

8. Another Reason to Shank the Well-Intentioned

"Why didn't you go to the police? To court?" a friend asks.

"Because I was already badly hurt and didn't want any further encouragement to kill myself. It was already too tempting."

"But you could have hired a lawyer, gotten some justice."

"Because I was sick of the torture of feeling ashamed and fearing blame, so going to the police and going to court were luxuries I just couldn't afford. Because back then, I was made of huge gaping holes, right down to the bone, one raw gash all over, one used tissue in walking form. Because the legal path was one thing I could say no to, and that was fucking sweet to have some control over what would happen next. Because the judge, the prosecutor and the defense team can put any spin on me they want and then take every shred of truth I have just to turn it against me. You think I wanna get fucked twice against my will?"

"But the justice system wants to help victims, it does, really."

"You're so cute when your worldview is threatened."

"…"

"I would like to have faith. I'll try, OK? But you'll never get me to say that I should have done differently with my decision about pursuing a case. I'm still okay with what I did, or rather, didn't do. I have total empathy for that person who just didn't have the strength to go forward over a decade ago. And I have total respect for who I was then, someone who just wanted to survive and get through another day. I won't apologize for my legal decisions any more than I'll apologize for the rape itself."

"OK."

"Let's make our own brand of lipsticks. We'll call the brightest, deepest red 'You Deserved It, Whore' and the medium pink one 'Shameful Hussy.' At least we can critique the double-edged sword of accentuating attractiveness while making a buck. We should give it a go."

"Are you seeing a therapist by any chance?" [4]

9. Dasein Revisited

I don't follow scripts well.

I'm a vagina-bearing person who was married in a black suit with men's tailoring and an eminently sensible button-down shirt underneath. I couldn't imagine being excessively female-ized in a bridal dress, the white institutional fabric blaring a message about my sexuality that simply wasn't true, both by choice and by force. I also didn't spend my sexually active life, starting around age 13, thinking much about the sex and/or gender identity of my partners. For all these complicated years since then, I've decided how to fit my gendered body into the world so that neither crushes me.

I didn't go to the cops or to court as I was ideally supposed to. I didn't "bounce back" physically as I was supposed to. I also didn't turn away from sex or sexuality, which surprised enough people both in and out of bed. On all three counts, I was a bad conventional victim.

My sexual functioning was altered in what I could actually do in bed (e.g., penetrative activities), but my sense of myself as sexual —and as sexually powerful and joyful in that aspect of self—was never changed. I don't know why specifically; I have been asked that question more than

---

4. This is a combination—like the section above—of both reality and fantasy presented in one exchange to achieve the most impact for this essay and to show how the total effect of these interactions sits in my consciousness today. The reality is that I ranted and made these points with people whom I considered friends. The fantasy aspect, like the section above, is how well I responded above versus how I tripped over my tongue in conversations in real life over these issues. My thoughts in reality were communicated as sputters and rants, not as the self-assured statements you read here. I can think of three people with whom I've had these conversations—one of them I trusted with my sense of humor (though I recall that I suggested far worse names, so some editing occurred for this essay).

once by people hoping to access that key. From the time I was a child, I had a deep, intuitive sense of my sexuality as exquisitely my own, as something akin to any thought in my head: No one could get in there and take that from me, no matter what happened. As it turned out—for me, at least—that was the case, though I know it is far from the truth for other survivors, whose losses and grief I don't want to downplay.

I could accept a range of physical changes, even sexual ones. When I was diagnosed in 1998 with an incurable, painful disease (systemic lupus, followed by Sjögren's syndrome and fibromyalgia) that sometimes put me on a walker, I still managed to do much of what I wanted to do, including finding sexual partners (even at my most unattractive because of illness and treatment) and finding ways to achieve in the world (e.g., a graduate degree, a doctoral-level degree, publications, paying off private student loans, to name one area of my life). On some level, altered sexual mechanics did not strike me as any different than having to navigate the world with a limp at times, something to which I also did not consent.

My sexual functioning made me emotionally uncomfortable at times. It annoyed and frustrated me, but I took partners with this in mind and entered environments that allowed me to focus on the point of the connecting-and-getting-off deal: pleasure, whether or not I achieved orgasm. I thought in terms of moment-by-moment enjoyment rather than working toward a goal. The trajectory of what constitutes "normal" sexual coupling was yet another script I refused to internalize, especially since I noticed that even the "normal" people weren't able to conform to it, including orgasming consistently through intercourse.

"Know what I like and can do tonight?"
"Show me."

I would never idealize my limitations, though I can obviously find my assets easily in the bedroom and in a post-rape survivor mentality. If you asked me if I would trade vaginas with a woman who could fuck with abandon by her own will, of course I would want a vag that behaves in a way that corresponds to desire and context. But that's not what's on my plate, so I've constructed my subjectivity from what looks like mud and bits of life gone awry. As such, I'm not dismayed over cultivating an inventive, wider-ranging sensuality and opening partners' eyes to other ways of seeing what "getting off" can mean.

"Wanna see something?"

"OK." [5]

Apart from the technical difficulties of tampons, pelvic exams and sex (oh my!), the biggest loss I have suffered is the impact upon my being-in-the-world-ness. I don't roam as freely or easily as I once did. I'm not as comfortable walking the earth when I know the ground beneath my feet can become a rape altar.

I think about, and then investigate, the minutiae of transportation details, the risk of a medical incident from lupus during the transportation, how rape-able I am during such an incident while commuting during the length of my route, whether or how my destination is itself a rape trap and where exactly, and who my allies might be from start to finish. Before I venture out, I think about how I feel, given the intensity of my lupus symptoms that particular day. I decide whether I could put up a good fight or run well.

"How do you know?"

"I listen to my bones."

I still do what I must, like accepting a decent-paying job (i.e., one that gives a decent wage after taxes for an independent contractor) in the city, a place I find overwhelming, instead of sticking to the suburbs, where I feel I usually have more space, fewer people, and more control over my environments. That was a concession born of needing adequate money to live, to medicate, to pay student debt, to handle family needs.

But I refused to accept a job for which I would park in a garage or a lot or along a street that made me thoroughly feel like unprotected bait, and ditto on any needs for public transportation that would similarly leave me feeling like a waiting target. Before my involuntary dasein shift, I would have simply accepted that parking conditions and train stations are not ideal for plenty of people, especially women, and that life is a risky, terminal ordeal for everyone.

But now in my bones, I hear a roaring, articulated response to such conditions and to anyone who would expect me to negate my feelings because that's how the world is for adults: "Why don't you go fuck yourself,

---

5. The two bolded lines here as well as the two above are presented as tropes in this essay, but I've used these lines often. In this case, what is presented as trope/fantasy is reality.

since I'm not letting that become my fate again." I have accepted jobs, and even not-great living conditions at home, because they nonetheless have met my dasein criteria. My twat is my compass. My vag doesn't need any person's or institution's subjective (and usually arbitrary or ill-informed, at best) proclamations on what reality should be for me, on which options I have available—for anything. My twat is my compass. There have been no laws, no precedents, no reasons, that would compel me to accept other than my dasein criteria for myself, as long as I can find a way to get by in this world.

And I do.

I wish I had learned to be that kind of Mama Bear for myself before a torn vag taught me how.

Pre-dasein shift, I didn't think about routes, risks and other people's desperate moments, ravaged histories and rationalized predatory needs. I simply went. For example, I once drove from the Philadelphia Museum of Art one long night into Detroit in a straight shot with no map in my lap. Instead, I put my trust in two male travel companions—people I had recently met through acquaintances, no less— who seemed able to navigate, a talent that still challenges my limited spatial abilities. The chick on those star-lit, post-midnight roads with two new friends didn't know yet that her body could be turned against her, against her will, not like this. I'm happy that I had those experiences, but I'm also happy that my survival instincts are honed into something less reckless.

"Less reckless" has entailed mapping out routes as step one, but then how to handle anxiety-causing new places and new roads? My solution wasn't to force myself into solo action. I wasn't going to make myself panic-stricken and then frustrated through going by myself: Who can drive well while panicking, and who isn't frustrated when unable to find a destination? As a terrible map reader and a worse intuitive navigator, I enlisted the help of friends and family in "rehearsals": We mapped a route together on paper, then with a verbal accounting of road names and landmarks, and then we picked a time to hit the road with me behind the wheel so that I could practice taking on new territory with a buddy. This is not the chickie who decided to flounce off to Detroit at dusk, roads unseen, navigators unknown.

For my current job in Philadelphia, I needed a friend to drive with me roughly six times to my new work place from my home. I needed each run before I felt confident enough about neighborhoods, turns, mergers and timing. I have remained terrified of getting lost and looking vulnerable, becoming an easy pounce.

10. Willfully Naked on the Job

Once, an accident on a highway overpass along my appointed route to my Philly job left me stranded in the same spot for over an hour. From the sea of idling cars' nauseating exhaust fumes, I made an apologetic call to work, where they were following the news and understood I was telling the truth (*"Well, we know where to find you, heh, heh"*).

When I arrived at work another hour later, my supervisor said to me, "Why didn't you just use the earlier exit instead of fighting through to your usual one?"

The answer to me was as unremarkable as bone and completely obvious: That route had not been practiced. Duh. The roads off that exit had never been vetted with people I trusted so that I could learn to trust myself on them and to find the possibility of safety in a world where too many rape kits clutter too many shelves in too many cities.

I decided to risk a bit of honesty on this point.

"I can't bring myself to take on roads where I don't know the lay of the land. That's asking myself to panic or to get into a situation that makes me nuts. And I'd want to know the crime stats for that area—whether they're bad or angelic, I just need to know what they are."

I said everything I needed to convey.

"I get that. There are a few other women here who are the same way." [6]

I heard generosity and acuity in the response.

---

6. The supervisor who uttered this sentence made other supportive remarks. She showed me her GPS because she's a bad navigator at times, too. She showed me how she has everything set up on the GPS for all the places she normally goes in case she gets stuck with a detour, or if she needs to find a different location. I'm positive that she has no idea of how helpful to me she actually was.

Anonymous

Gender: Female
Age: 33
Race/ethnicity: African-American
Occupation: Biomedical researcher
Location: Philadelphia, Pa.
Age abuse occurred: 4-7

WHEN I SAW the announcement for *The Survivors Project*, I thought it was an opportunity to share my story. I was conflicted as to whether to submit my story as an anonymous entry or boldly (and proudly) include my name for publication. After much thought, and anxiety about missing an opportunity to include my story, I have decided against being so forward.

Many people who know me would be very surprised if they learned I am a survivor of childhood sexual abuse. People attribute my drive and success to a foundation of supportive people in my life from early childhood until the present. It would shock them to know that I was molested by my brother from the time I was 4 until I was around 7. And I suppose it would be even more shocking to them if they were to realize, as I later did, that my mother was aware of it, but complacent.

The abuse was sporadic over those years, but I can still remember every incident. The complication of the abuse was that I trusted my brother more than I trusted my mother, though neither one of them actually did the right thing—whatever that would have been in the situation.

I was about to turn 30 when I found the mental push to start talking about the abuse. I didn't go to the source, but went to a support group for survivors of child sexual abuse. The day I walked into that room was actually the hardest thing I have ever done. It was easy for me to pretend that I had a wonderful supportive family instead of one that was horribly fragmented. Going into that room made me have to strip off the shell of competence that I was hiding behind for years. But going into that room was also the bravest thing I ever did.

Joining the support group made me realize that was I not alone in my feelings, that there were other people out in the world that had a shockingly similar, sad story. Although I sometimes feel sad that I have met some wonderful people because they were also sexually abused as children, I also feel comforted that these same people understand me more than people I have known my entire life.

I have not mentioned what became of my relationship with my mother and brother after I admitted to myself that I was a child sexual abuse survivor. My relationship with both of them was fragmented for years. My mother acknowledged that she had known that my brother was probably my perpetrator, but she then quickly added that this was a matter that didn't involve her, it was between him and me. That one statement pretty much summed up my entire relationship with my immediate family. I decided after that conversation that I would be better off knowing a different set of people.

I never believed that I would be able to have a trusting, loving relationship, but I have one with my wonderfully supportive boyfriend. I have also experienced true loving relationships with a large circle of friends that I consider my family. I want people to know that they are not alone, and they are not forced to continue the cycle of complacency that thrives in families such as ours.

Alice*

Gender: Female
Age: 44
Race/ethnicity: White
Occupation: City employee
Location: Philadelphia, Pa.
Relationship to survivor: Daughter

NOTHING IS LONELIER than taking a taxi home from the hospital—especially if it's a psychiatric hospital. It was early December, during the blizzard of 2009, and Philadelphia was already blanketed with the first of three feet of snow. The cab driver picked me up at the Belmont Center on City Line Avenue, eyeing me suspiciously. "You work here, right?"

"Yep, I'm a surgeon," I replied, hoping he'd not noticed my hospital-grade paper booties.

I was about 40 years old that day. In a span of four months, I'd gone from earning a six-figure income in the pharmaceutical industry and living in a stylish Society Hill apartment to being unemployed and emotionally dependent on a man who had "borrowed" $40,000 from me and promptly vanished, just as the SEC was closing in on him.

I look like the typical over-educated white woman living in Philadelphia. I live in a cute house with a pretty garden. I have friends, I wear good clothes and I have a decent job and nice teeth. But under the veneer is a woman with a sketchy history. Two suicide attempts, anorexia, bulimia, four psychiatric hospitalizations, a divorce, a stalled career, years and thousands of dollars seeing a therapist, less-than stellar grades, broken friendships and an addiction to unavailable or abusive men that spans 20 years. I have been on 30 different psychiatric medications and have conducted desperate visits to shamans, psychics, acupuncturists, herbalists, psychiatrists and healers of all flavors. I've spent more than $12,000 on a doctor who uses a magnetic device to electrically jump-start my brain out of depression. My friends and family are baffled and angry, and I am hopeless. Why do I keep screwing up my life, I ask myself, when I have so much to be grateful for?

My theory is that I am a second-hand victim of sexual abuse.

Our family made regular trips from the suburbs into the city to see my extended family. My parents maintain that it was "car sickness" that made me throw up at each visit, but I never got sick in the car any other time. Looking back, it must have been a by-product of the anxiety these excursions caused.

You see, my mother could not bear to be around her family.

They'd all be there. My aunt, who'd reinvented herself from a poor Northeast Philly kid to a Main Line socialite. There'd be my two uncles and my grandmom. And the bottles. Everywhere, empty beer bottles crowded the table and most of the floor. The cigarette smoke hung in the air and yellowed the insides of the windows. It was hard to take a breath. At the center of the alcohol, cigarettes and bawdy talk was one of my uncles. He was a stocky man, maybe 5-foot-7, with a blustery manner and flushed face. In my memory, his wife and kids aren't even present, but they must have been. In my memory, his porkish figure eclipses all else.

This uncle, he stole my childhood.

This uncle raped my mother. Not once, not twice, but over and over again for several years, well into her teens—a period of time stretching between the end of World War II to the Korean War. Not only did he violate her while she pretended to sleep, as she compulsively recited the Hail Mary to distract herself until he was done, but he and a chum would regularly take her to an isolated baseball field dugout and molest her. The horrified neighborhood mothers of other little girls would come to my mother's childhood home, screaming at the front door. It seems my uncle did not limit his predatory ways to family. And somehow my grandmother was able to ignore this.

The result of the constant and savage incest and trauma my mother endured was an adult woman with a laundry list of psychiatric problems. Close to 80 now, she suffered more than any kid or adult deserves to. Anorexia while pregnant with me; agoraphobia so severe she couldn't leave the house when my sister was a toddler; locking us kids out of the house so she could privately scrub her arms with bleach until they bled. Suicide attempts, hospitalization, depressions, flashbacks, nightmares, insomnia, trust issues, bonding problems with her kids and explosive anger. Her fear of dirt is so great that after a day of playing outside, the three of us kids were routinely forced to strip down to nudity each night in the foyer of our split-level home and be carried to the tub for a group scrub. Her self-consciousness about sexuality was so deep that she'd put tape over her breasts underneath her clothes to hide her nipples from view. Her despair was so frustrating that my father often resorted to either hitting us with his belt or retreating to the basement to "pay bills." She tried to be a good mother to us, but it's hard to be a mom when your own childhood was the most dangerous place on earth.

Nobody stopped my mother's abuse. Not one adult, sibling, parent or teacher stood up for her when it had to have been obvious that in that tiny Bustleton Avenue house, something was terribly wrong. The abuse only stopped when, as a teenager, she stopped it herself. Home alone one day, her brother turned up back from a stint in the Army. Wanting to pick up where he'd left off, he grabbed her. But she'd grown up a bit while he was at war, and she had a kitchen knife when he went after her. She stabbed him so badly he ended up not only in the hospital, but in a psychiatric unit for months. Now, my uncle is in a nursing home, his brain pulp.

Unfortunately, I'm the other result of the constant and savage incest my mother endured—another adult woman with a laundry list of psychiatric problems.

These days, I spend a lot of time in church basements, with other addicts, and we talk about "working the program" and "a higher power," nervously twitching in folding chairs and eyeing each other, wondering what monster lies beneath the 12-Step jargon. I feel like a ghost of myself. Someone who fits in nowhere. Maybe at some point I will feel a commonality with these folks. I hope so, since these meetings are my last-ditch effort at becoming a somewhat normal person, at having a calm and loving relationship with a man, at not wanting to die the moment I open my eyes every morning.

My mother, who has long since retired, does not talk about her childhood; she seems to have healed somewhat with age. But me, my healing is just getting started.

Nicolas McMahon

Gender: Male
Age: 29
Race/ethnicity: White
Occupation: Adjunct professor
Location: Tavernier, Fla.
Age abuse occurred: 4-6; 18

ORAL, THROAT AND SINUS cancer, freak accidents, amputations and burn injuries are the worst diseases and circumstances that can disfigure the face and body. Missing jaws, trach tubes and deep scars are often irreversible. Scars can occasionally act like text, giving the viewer the ability to read what has injured a person in their lifetime. The face is a mirror into a person's soul. This mirror can be changed in an instant.

Instead of fearing the possibility of a personal injury permanently changing our appearance, what if it were possible to look as we actually felt—our secrets and mental illnesses available for everyone to see? What if our depression and personal issues became that permanent reality, like an irreversible scar that cannot be removed?

Currently, I carry two life sentences. I was molested as a child by the husband of a babysitter over a period of two years. Later in life, at the age of 18, I was raped two months after arriving in Philadelphia for college. Simple sounds, touches and smells can bring me back in an instant. My outward appearance developed into how I felt. My life in Philadelphia continued on a strange autopilot while I battled addictions and eating disorders, which led to my eventual weight of nearly 400 pounds.

It was painful to walk as my legs constantly rubbed together, which created a weekly line of new boils and chafing. A normal-sized bottle of stain remover lasted me a mere two weeks to combat the blood and pus stains from my pants at the laundry. My checklists for leaving the house were my keys, cigarettes, shoe laces and menstrual pads. The keys and cigarettes were for obvious reasons. The shoe laces for keeping my pants up by making a knot at the belt loops when the button or buckle would inevitably break from simple tasks such as bending down to tie my shoes. Finally, the menstrual pads for being more absorbent than Band-Aids and preventing the blood stains from showing on the inside of my pants from my legs rubbing together. On one occasion, while wearing shorts, a bloody pad fell out and landed next to my shoe to the horror and curiosity of the passengers on a crowded bus.

In 2009, I received my M.F.A. from Penn's School of Design under a beautiful canopy. Instead of being excited for my future, I was more worried about the chair breaking underneath me. Despite attending Penn for two years, I knew almost nothing about campus due to the difficulty of my walking anywhere, let alone the uphill slope of Locust Walk. I had a highly detailed knowledge of the entire SEPTA system to avoid walking a mere seven blocks.

Approaching 30, and after losing nearly 200 pounds over three years, I am lucky. My years of extreme obesity, pills and cigarettes never showed on my face. I got a second chance to create some kind of normal.

To combat the damage of sexual abuse, one must yearn for a normal life despite our sentences and their machinations. The way we create this varies from person to person. One must learn to laugh and reach out to people. Despite the dysfunction of my life due to my sexual abuse, I will forever laugh at the memory of the crowded bus and my bloody pad falling on the floor. I can only imagine what my fellow passengers were thinking.

Recovery can be a tedious process, with many instances of gained and lost ground. At my sickest, when my weight crept past 400 pounds, I knew at the age of 25 that I was dying. I realized that when my end came, I would regret everything and wish to live my life over again.

After my graduation, I withdrew and moved to be with family in the

Florida Keys on a small island town with one red light. I have not left since. Instead of planning a career full of creativity and gallery shows in New York like many of my classmates, I am merely learning how to continue with a life full of missed opportunities and waste. After losing all of my weight, I look much younger than my age; I am often confused for a 19 or 20 year old. I am not ashamed to say that I usually do not correct people when, in fact, I am nearly 30 with a master's degree and an entire past that I prayed I could relive. Sometimes I feel like an imposter.

Despite the fact that I got a second chance, I have to deal with the inevitable fact of aging despite all the years I have lost. The thought panics me as I feel as though I have too few years to fill with new memories. My newfound future is full of the excitement of discovering the joys of simple things that I was never able to enjoy due to my crushing weight. Despite the fact that it is sometimes easier to fall back into what I have known, looking forward to a new experience has kept me on my path.

The emotional aspects have been devastating. The substances that kept me numbed still call and it is still nearly impossible for me to eat in front of anyone. The simple act of a deli counterperson at the grocery store offering me the extra slice of cheese taken from the scale evokes panic attacks. My abusers have continued their lives without any repercussions while I suffered immensely. I am beginning to cast away my anger, as it will only hold me back. At times, I feel damaged, but with the continuation of my life and my example, I have not let them win. I look forward to the day it is emotionally possible to leave this island and return to Philadelphia to pick up where I left off at 18. Until then, I do the best that I can with each day and challenge. It is the best that I can do.

Tish R.

Gender: Female
Age: 32
Race/ethnicity: White
Occupation: Speaker with the Rape, Abuse and Incest National Network (RAINN)
Location: Poconos, Pa.
Age abuse occurred: 3-9

LIFE ISN'T AT ALL what I actually lived. There's a deep secret that they made me hide. I hid it from everyone, including myself. I have to face reality: My grandfather sexually abused me for more than six years.

Born to teenage parents, life began rough for me. On the run from her parents, Mom was 14 when I was born. Daddy was 16 and had the financial support of his father. Living in hotel rooms, my parents set the stage for a life of instability; as I grew up, I would be in constant search of comfort. By the time Mom was 19, she had four children from two different men. She was single, and alone with us, but she did the best she could. By the time I was 6, Mom's parents were her only source of support, and even then life was still rocky. In January 1987, I returned from a long day of first grade to find that Mama had "friends" over. She instructed me to place my favorite toys in a red milk crate because my siblings and I were leaving with these nice adults. We stayed in a foster home for five days, and then arrived at our maternal grandparents' home. Mom's brother-in-law came over from Georgia and took my sister and brother to live with them. I stayed with Nana and Pop while the baby of 18 months went back to live with Mama. Over the next few years, the three of us kids would go back and forth between family members until Mom eventually ended up with the boys, and Daddy got us girls. Giving us away would prove to have disastrous consequences for us all. The family dynamic was changed forever.

I lived with my daddy until I graduated high school and left home. Years of living with an alcoholic father, who was verbally, emotionally and physically abusive, made me even more empty inside. I left that small town and headed north two hours to the only people who had always been good to me—Mama's parents, Nana and Pop. I found great comfort in them because I could see them every day. Nana was more of a mother to me than a grandmother. By the time I reached 30, she was my best friend. Our phone calls were so important to me and I loved all the advice she gave me on parenting, home making, family and even spiritual guidance. I loved my conversations with Pop about politics, news, family drama and yes, football. They truly were important figures in my life. So important that my husband called them for permission to ask for my hand in marriage, and Pop even walked me down the aisle to my handsome groom. They both helped me try to understand my childhood.

In 2011, our family moved to the Poconos. A year before that, I had begun to have extreme physical pain while living in New York, where I was diagnosed with fibromyalgia. Nana, a retired RN, helped me understand my medical condition. When I moved to the Poconos, I had to find new doctors, including a therapist. This is around the time when the reality of what happened to me started to set in. Huge black holes in my childhood memories began to come into focus.

I'm 6 years old, living in the apartments with Nana and Pop. My aunt and I share a room. I am sleeping on the bottom bunk, with my back to the wall. The hall light comes on, and soon I see Pop sitting at the edge of my feet. He moves the blankets and slides his hand up my leg. Soon he has his hand over my panties as he is rubbing my vagina. I'm starring off at my tall dollhouse, yet I pretend to be asleep. Maybe he will stop. He doesn't. I want to cry but tears won't stop him, nothing ever does. Finally, he is done with his extracurricular activity, and I have survived one more night.

As I recall this memory, I am a 30-year-old wife and mother of two—but inside I feel like that scared 6 year old. I try to function in every day life, but I can't. I feel like a child having to make adult decisions. Only in therapy am I allowed the freedom to express my emotions of hurt, anger, confusion and disgust. At home, I have to function like a normal wife. I can't go on. I sleep all hours of the day, pretending to be OK for our children, hoping my husband would understand that my world is shattered. But he doesn't understand. Nobody understands. I can't stand to look at myself. How did I get here? I hate who I am, I hate my body, I hate this pain inside me, and I just wish I could die. It's like the abuse is happening for the first time. I hate that I hid this from myself. I was better off when I didn't know—or was I?

More memories come. I'm trying to comprehend it all yet remain in a relationship with Nana and Pop. I have told only Nana about my repressed memories of being sexually abused. She is extremely adamant that repressed memories don't exist, that there's "no way this could have gone unnoticed for 24 years." I'm so confused, yet I know that these memories are true. I know that I have to confront Pop. I have to tell him that I know the truth. I'm scared of what this would mean. What if Nana leaves him? He is 72 years old, he can't be alone, and he needs her. My heart aches for him. However, I can't live with this secret. I reach out to the only person who would understand, my aunt. My mom's oldest sister was sexually abused by Pop. I have always known that. Pop and Nana told me many times that he did it, but that it only happened once. During our phone call, she tells me that it happened to her for three years. I am shocked. The truth is clear; I must tell him.

The very next day I sit in my truck and place the hardest phone call of my life. It's a sunny Tuesday in June as I dial his number. Pop answers and I begin: "Pop, I love you very much, and never want to hurt you, but I have to tell you something very important. I know that you touched me sexually when I was a child." I describe the memory and he responds, "No, you are a liar. You need to see another therapist. I only touched your aunt." I close the conversation with, "I'll always love you but I know the truth." On the phone, I was cool as a cucumber, my voice steady and quiet, but when I hang up I come undone. I collapse under the strain of fear, shock and disbelief. What have I done? I return home and email Mama and Nana. I have to tell them now! It's all out!

I've finally shared my secret. Yet no one helps me.

Mama was just diagnosed with lung cancer. Nana says we can't focus on this, we must focus on Mama and Mama alone. For the first time in 11 years, my birthday comes and there is no phone call from Nana. It's official—I'm all alone! Mama doesn't call, text or contact me either. For two weeks I'm all alone with my memories. How could I do this? I should have kept silent. At least then I would still have them.

Mama got worse so I finally went down to Georgia. The cancer was in her lungs, lymphnoids, adrenal gland, breast, liver and in her brain by the time it was detected. She was given months to live. I rushed down to be with her but I was nervous because I would have to see Nana and Pop. For two long weeks I stayed with Mom, trying to put the past in the past so I could have my family back. But it made me even more miserable. When I finally returned home, more memories had flooded the gates. And I couldn't shake them.

I'm 8 years old riding in the car with Nana. I am in the front seat; we are following Pop and the other kids in the truck. It is raining so hard we can barely see the vehicle in font of us. Nana is talking to me. "He does it because he loves you." Her voice is shaky. "You two have a special relationship. You must not tell the other kids, or they will get jealous." The sound of the windshield wipers going back and forth ring louder and louder as I hear, "You can't tell anyone" and "No one will understand" and "The other kids would be jealous." At 31, my heart is broken and I'm sick to my stomach. I can't believe it: SHE HAS ALWAYS KNOWN.

I'm in therapy when I realize that I need to find my voice. I need to speak up. I rush home and call RAINN (the Rape, Abuse And Incest National Network). I have been searching for a place to "belong" since I realized the truth. RAINN had the word "incest" in its title and I knew they would understand. I phone them asking for help. Desperate to find answers, they refer me to the rape center in the Alabama town where all this took place. I tell them my story and then find myself on the phone with the local police department. The dective listening on the other end is very kind and compassionate. He takes my story down and all the information that I can give him. Two hours later, my aunt calls me frantically, and says, "I can't believe how selfish you are." She says that Pop is down at the police station. At that moment, another call comes in and it is the detective. He tells me that Pop confessed to sexually abusing my aunt and I. To this day

I remember the words "He confessed." As I prop myself up by the nearest tree outside, I listen as the detective tells me what happened. As the call ends, I fall to my knees, screaming through tears, "I'm not crazy, I'm not crazy." I called Mama and she was angry. *How dare you do this?* She said that she wasn't going down this path with me. I said, "I love you, Mama, but I have to do this." I really couldn't blame her; she was fighting for her life and finally had the one thing she longed for her entire life—love from her mother and father. She couldn't give that up to be with her daughter. It would be the last real conversation I would have with her. On Sept. 23, I called to tell her I loved her, but she was already near the end. On Sept. 29, she died. I couldn't go to the funeral. My husband and our children and I had a small ceremony for her at a local lake, where we released red roses and balloons.

After six months of trying to determine how to handle this, I flew down to Alabama and signed the official warrant to have Pop arrested. In August 2012, just a year after the phone call and the confession, I went and testified in front of a grand jury. Twenty-four strangers. A week later, he was indicted and charged with child sexual abuse.

TODAY AS I type this, the DA called and offered me his plea: guilty, 10 years (with time served), registered sex offender for life, and a paternity test to be conducted to determine if he is my birth father. I have accepted the terms.

It's been a long year and half since the memories of what happened to me came alive. I've come so far in my healing, yet I have so far to go. I have no contact with Nana and Pop. Many days, I still miss them but what I miss is a fantasy of a loving relationship that never really existed. A healthy, happy, true relationship we did not have. I no longer worry about Pop being alone. I pray for him to be alone with his thoughts, memories of his actions and his shame. He needs to heal from his sins.

I have come to accept the manipulation, the lies and the truth. Pop started touching me when I was 3 years old and continued until I was 10. The memoires are so vivid and clear; how I wish I could make them go away. Some have been dealt with but there are many more to go through. I just have to find the strength.

I joined a support group, where I learned that I was and I am worth fighting for. What happened to me was not my fault. It was his decision to act, but it's my decision to speak the truth and fight for my healing, which makes me stronger and stronger each day.

I am a speaker with RAINN, have counseled a child that was abused by a peer in his class at school, and continue to see my therapist (probably always will). When this all started, I was depressed and full of anxiety, fear and uncertainty. Now I know I know I needed to go through that so I could free my inner child. She was trapped, living in the constant storm. But I have helped her heal. I know I still have a long journey, and I accept that. I have learned through all of this that is it under extreme pressure that diamonds are created. When I am finished with this journey, I hope I am one giant carat!

Anonymous

Gender: Female
Age: 35
Race/ethnicity: White
Occupation: Nonprofit
Location: Philadelphia, Pa.
Relationship to survivor: Daughter

IT'S A HORRIBLE FEELING to know that your mom is broken, her family was the culprit, and you are powerless to help her in her suffering. I first had this realization when I was just 12 years old.

Perhaps it was intuition, or just an accurate reading of nonverbal cues, but when we had our first discussion about her abuse I somehow already knew, although I couldn't put it into words. Her emotional mood swings, heavy drinking and victim mentality were already very apparent to me; I didn't know the back story but knew it must have been awful.

At 35, it's still difficult to write about. I've been looking over old journal entries and this one from 1996, for a college class called Sexual Assault in American Culture captures how this has affected me and my family.

11/26/1996: "My mother is an incest survivor. She was raped on a regular basis from about age 8-12 by two of her brothers. In some ways, I kind of feel like a secondary survivor of rape. This has obviously affected her entire life and how she has led it. She has taught me to not trust men whatsoever. In fact, she once told me not to trust my own father. She'll go through periods when she's mad at everyone for no reason, or will take out her frustration on family members who had nothing to do with making her mad. What really frustrates me about all of this is that she won't stay in counseling. She'll start, and soon after quit. It makes me mad that all of her anger and fear are directed towards everyone else except her attackers. She needs to deal with her inner demons, and she won't. The most frustrating thing for me and my family is that there seems to be no way of convincing her to help herself, and any way we try to help her directly doesn't work. I know first hand that rape affects more people than just the survivor involved, and it doesn't go away. Even 30 years after the fact, even after all the time that has passed, it is still a major wound for my mother and my family."

Being the child of an incest survivor puts me in the position of wanting to be there for my mother and support her on the one hand, and on the other hand makes me want to scream, "You're fucking driving me crazy with the shit you're dumping on me!" I want my mom to be well, but as a child and teenager there was no way that I could help in any meaningful or practical way. Yet her mood swings, anger and irrational behavior continue to haunt me. I've struggled with these roles in my own therapy sessions as an adult.

If she were independently wealthy and the day-to-day demands of a lower-middle class life were of no concern, perhaps things would have been better. But she was married with five children. She stayed home until the youngest went off to kindergarten. My dad was a high school teacher. The seven of us lived in a two-bedroom house and got by with the help of subsidized school lunches and thrift-store clothes. This meant that despite her extreme dislike for my father, which mostly had to do with her intimacy issues stemming from the abuse, for better or worse she had no other economic options for securely raising five kids.

I know all about my parent's failed marriage because I was their de facto therapist. Whenever one was mad at the other, I was the one who heard all about it. Particularly on long car rides, I was the confidant who listened as they rambled on about the other's failings. According to my mother, everything was my father's fault. I tried to suggest pragmatic solutions to their conflicts. I'd ask things like, "Well, does Dad know that? Have you told him that upsets you? Have you asked him to do stop doing that?" She almost always said no, because in her mind it wouldn't matter. She assumed he would never change and there was nothing she could do about it. This is a common victim mentality for incest survivors, being unable to navigate conflict and therefore not knowing how to advocate for themselves. This made me the emotional garbage dump, all her anger and frustration heaped upon my young ears.

She was so emotional. And yet her emotions were often incongruent with actual experience. You could get yelled at for something petty and small, so it made it difficult to take it seriously when we actually did something bad. I once bought some hand lotion with my own money, an early expression of my teenage financial independence. When she borrowed it without asking, I asked her not to do that. She yelled at me and said maybe she shouldn't have paid for me to go abroad my sophomore year of high school and bought a bunch of lotion instead. But when I staggered home drunk on the weekends, rarely did I get the third degree.

Perhaps this is the normal, motherly guilt trip that many experience as they grow up. But it was always everyone else's fault. She was never at fault, even if it meant bringing up how you wronged her many years ago; it was all your fault. And nothing would change, so why try—just get drunk and bitch about it.

That was the worst, when her grumblings were infused with booze. Sometimes, because of the actual things she said, but more often her actions. I remember many instances as a child while in the car with her and she was obviously too drunk to drive, the worst being when three of her children were in the car with her and she started to go the wrong way to get on the highway. This was after I had literally tried to wrestle the keys out of her hands but could not.

And what was my father's response? He's more logical, and would try to use logic and problem-solving skills to help my mother. No matter how irrational she was being, he would go into teacher mode to advise her about what she needed to do. I understand why this drove them both crazy; she just wanted to vent, and he wanted to fix her. I have the same inclinations. I'm more like my dad in that sense, but they both would have been happier if they could have found a middle ground. They didn't, and a year after I moved out to go to school, they got divorced.

A year after graduating from college, I moved to Philadelphia. My mom was not happy about her baby moving 500 miles away. When I first mentioned the fact that I was looking into jobs outside of my hometown, she immediately said something like, "You don't have to. I had to move away from my family." My inner dialogue screamed, "Yes I do!" but I said nothing. My decision wasn't singular and all her fault. There were many other reasons for wanting to move to a new city, but this was definitely a consideration. Although much less extreme than what she dealt with, I needed to get away from it all for a while. After I left, the second oldest, my sister, took over my role as therapist and peacemaker. She even said something like, "Whoa. I didn't realize how much of their shit you put up with now that it falls to me."

Some of my mother's extended family knows about her ordeal, but many, including her sisters, don't believe her. Those who do, or are also sexual-abuse survivors of her brothers (unfortunately my mother was just one of many), want to talk to my mom about it, but my mom will not. She moved away from her small Ohio town more than 45 years ago and has left them all behind. These two brothers have never been brought to justice, and for all I know could still be predators. It really sticks in my craw, so much so that I view it as karmic retribution that one of them recently suffered the loss of a 14-month-old granddaughter who died in a freak drowning accident. I realize how awful that sounds, and I feel horrible for thinking this way, yet the pain of knowing what he did to my mother without a single repercussion inclines me to believe this. Ideally, they both should be rotting away in a prison for life. I'm an atheist; otherwise, I could take some comfort in knowing they'd burn in hell for all eternity.

As I said earlier, this is difficult to write, but even more difficult is: Why? What's the point of sharing my story? It's not to make my mom seem like a monster. We have our issues, but she is a good person and a good mother. She has many friends and people who think she's great, including her young grandchildren from my siblings. I guess the point is to let survivors know that there are people who love and care for you, and want you to do the best you can. Please get the help you need.

Sarah B.

Gender: Female
Age: 34
Race/ethnicity: Caucasian
Occupation: Nonprofit executive
Location: Boston, Mass.
Age abuse occurred: 1-4; 11; 17

WHEN I WAS 11, my parents, brother and I went to visit my grandparents in Oregon. Like most kids, I loved visiting my grandparents. My grandmother was full of energy and creativity. We would wake up early and go pick blackberries by the ocean, talking about life and sharing stories. My grandfather was somewhat of a mystery to me, but I had great affection for him, especially because he was sick with Parkinson's disease.

On that trip however, in the summer of 1988, my grandparents molested me. My grandfather felt my breasts while my parents and brother were out for a walk. And my grandmother took a bath with me where she touched me inappropriately.

Now, this wasn't the first time I was sexually assaulted, nor would it be the last, but it was the first time I told anyone. That night, I told my mom what had happened and I remember that all the color drained from her face. I thought she was mad at me, and I felt scared about what was going to happen. She left the room, and I heard lots of talking and whispering. The next day, my dad sat my grandfather down for a talk. I heard muffled, intense voices. And then we stayed the rest of our visit. When we went home, we tried to move forward. Except I couldn't. Over the course of the next six years, I just felt worse and worse. I tried to cope with my feelings the best way I could, but I was just a kid. My parents didn't have any support either, and were told by a trusted therapist that what happened to me wasn't that big of a deal and that I'd come to them if I wanted to talk about it. Nothing could be further from the truth.

Throughout high school, I cried out for help in many different ways. I wrote about my experiences in English class. I talked to guidance counselors, teachers, friends and other adults. But because I did so well in school, no one thought I was in an actual crisis. Everyone thought someone else was handling it, handling me. So I just drifted further and further.

Then, right before my high school graduation, I was raped by a friend. It was my first time having sex as a young adult, and I wanted to stop. He said no, and he just continued until he was done. This experience made my head spin. He thought it was "great," and I felt completely violated and scared to have sex again with anyone. It made me want to just leave my body completely.

When I got to college, everything hit rock bottom. While I had always been able to keep it together on the outside, my self-harming behaviors peaked and I felt things starting to spiral out of control. Since I arrived on campus, I was on a downward spiral of starving, purging, over-exercising, drinking and cutting. The cycle started Monday morning when I woke up, promising to be good for the week by sticking to my "diet" of 750 calories per day and working out at least once a day if not twice. I'd usually make it until Wednesday, maybe Thursday, when I'd fall off the wagon with a bowl of pasta or slice of pizza on a study night. Angry at myself, the slip would turn into a night of drinking, resulting in more feelings of self-hatred, shame and despair. And then I'd wake up and start the cycle all over again. I was drinking 12 cups of coffee a day to keep myself going, and had a full class load and busy college schedule.

I knew that controlling my body and what went into it was about being sexually assaulted. I knew that cutting myself was a distorted way of feeling something real. But talking about it didn't seem to help. I just wanted to die. I didn't think there was a reason to go on but I was too afraid to take my own life. I was stuck. I needed help, and there was a part of me unwilling to give up. So I found a therapist and she helped me navigate my way back to health. I was also fortunate to find two different intensive-healing programs that really worked for me: the Opening the Heart Workshop and the Sierra Tuscon eating-disorder program. It took a lot of time and energy, and I was fortunate that my parents were willing to pay for the treatment and therapy I needed. My therapist was really creative in the way she helped me find my way; she believed that I could survive, heal and thrive. She created a space that allowed me to explore all the parts of myself, examine the places I was broken, and piece myself together again.

Healing from sexual assault is like healing from any physical or psychological trauma. I will never forget what happened to me. If I close my eyes, it's all still crystal clear. But I'm not afraid of it anymore, and it doesn't impact my life in a negative way. Like any scar, it's a part of who I am, but it's not all of me. Today, I have a healed relationship with my parents. I am happily married with a little boy of my own. One day, I will talk to him about sexual assault and it's aftermath so that he can be a compassionate ear to others. I share my experiences openly because I can. I am one of the lucky ones who found a way back. I write about my experiences on a personal blog—theenlivenproject.com—because I want to give hope to other survivors, and more importantly, open the door for friends, families, boyfriends and girlfriends to talk about these kinds of traumas without fear or shame. I speak publicly because it allows me to break the silence again and again, and not be ashamed of what happened to me.

When speaking, I am often asked: Wasn't there something good that came out of this experience? This question is interesting, because it usually starts out as a compliment. "But you seem fine now. Amazing, in fact. Isn't your amazing-ness a result of this experience? Don't you think that it was your past that made you this way?"

Well, no, not exactly.

While there are certain innate characteristics that make me who I am in the world, I can't dole out credit for them any more than I can dole out credit for my five senses. And I was also born with the capacity to learn, grow and evolve as a human being. Whether I had been born into a life in which I faced cancer or sudden death of a parent or ran around in meadows full of flowers, my journey in life would have been to understand who I am in the world and develop my capacity to live, love and be present. This answer is tough, however, because the question itself creates a causal relationship that doesn't need to exist. Do I think I turned out OK? Yes. Did I learn a lot about myself healing from sexual trauma? Yes. Did this experience require me to grow? Yes. That doesn't necessarily mean that a painful path is the only way to a positive destination or an evolved self. A painful path simply provides more frequent chances to exercise humanity and heart and to demonstrate courage than those whose path was a little more paved.

Sexual abuse impacted every single area of my life. It impacted my relationship to food and to my own body—a relationship I am just now starting to enjoy again. It impacted my experience giving birth, which was surprisingly traumatic and triggering. It impacted my ability to date as a 20-something. Every time I met someone new, I had to decide when and how to tell them about what had happened to me—and worry whether it would scare them off. It impacted my relationships with my immediate and extended family members. I feel lucky that my parents and I healed our relationship, but sad that I won't be able to do the same with some of my extended family members. My husband and I have negotiated and explored the different parts of me that are still wounded by these experiences, and I am incredibly grateful that I found someone with whom I could share myself fully and who was willing to be a partner to me in my healing and journey in life.

My story is just one of millions of stories around the world, stories of things that happen in the shadows. The antidote to shame is light, and I hope that my story can light the way for others to share theirs and to find community and healing.

Pasco Troia

Gender: Male
Age: 50s
Race/ethnicity: White
Occupation: Charity consultant/graphic and web designer
Location: Cranston, R.I.
Age abuse occurred: 10-11

FOR DECADES, I WAS full of anger, full of rage, full of hate. I felt mentally full 24 hours a day, seven days a week, but never realized why. I believed everyone in the world must feel the same way. Then, at the age of 32, a newspaper article changed my life forever.

One day back in 1990, I returned to my family home to visit my mother for Christmas. I came in from Chicago, where I lived at the time. My dad had passed away, so it was my mother, my oldest brother and I, sitting around discussing the news of the day. My mom had always been an avid reader, and the *Providence Journal* was near the top of her list. She handed me the *Journal*, showing me an article on the bottom of the front page. It pertained to a lawsuit filed by an Iowa resident and involved our local church. I had no urgent feeling to read it right away, but I decided to take a glance at it right there in the kitchen and to read it thoroughly later on. The article was about a man suing St. Mary's Church over his alleged sexual abuse by one of its priests. Then, all of a sudden, the words I read almost caused my brain to explode. They almost caused my heart to come to a screeching halt. These words were a torment for me to read: Father Robert Marcantonio, sexual abuse of a boy, St Mary's. I had never put those thoughts together before.

Father Marcantonio had been a priest at St. Mary's Church many years ago. As I read the words again, I started to yell. I started to rant that this same repulsive priest had molested me. I could not believe the upheaval this caused. I could not believe the hurt I was feeling. Years after he had sexually abused me, he did it to someone else. I could not continue reading because my eyes were so full of tears.

The story tapped instantly into memories of self-destruction I had hidden for decades. I did not know what to say or do next. I was an alien in my own body. I was hearing and seeing thoughts from my youth that I had never acknowledged. My emotions were in charge. I did not try to control them. I was losing my mind, as well as control over my physical reactions. I was becoming a little 10-year-old boy again. In my mind's eye, I saw him physically attacking me. I saw this big man overpowering me. I saw him standing over me. I watched him rape and molest me repeatedly.

The abuse had been unbearable and tough. For a year, he controlled me. He made me engage in oral and anal sex, in acts that would destroy any child to his core. I was a sexual pig for this priest. He interjected devilish tools of destruction into my mind as he planted his sperm into my body. Sometimes, when he abused me, he would be partially dressed, wearing a half-opened black shirt and his religious white collar. Other times, with his pants down around his ankles, he would drive his penis deep into my rectum, ripping tissue. I was forced to perform sexual acts everywhere: in his upstairs bedroom, in the rectory, in the back of the church, in the school located down the street, even in his car. I yelled for him to stop. He never did. It was continuous. I did not know how to handle it. I was young and scared. He instructed me to keep it all quiet. He even conned me to believe he would never hurt me. These vicious acts occurred in the house of the Lord.

I wonder at times how I was strong enough to survive. During times of self-hatred, suicide always had a cunning way of disguising itself as the ultimate form of relief. I thank God that I never followed through on those thoughts. Drinking, drugs and self-abusive behaviors were the ways in which I dealt with my inner hatred. I "saved" myself by putting this abuse completely out of my mind. This was the only way I knew.

I returned to Chicago from my mother's home with a head full of fresh demons. After reading the entire article, I learned of an additional lawsuit occurring in another state, as well as one that was about to begin in Rhode Island against Marcantonio and five other priests.

God places people in our lives and only he knows why. I was lucky to be dating a great girl who lived in northern Illinois. Within a short time, we grew to love each other and before long moved in together. I told her about the priest and all the emotions I was experiencing. Without blinking an eye, she opened up and told me how her adoptive stepfather had raped her for years in her youth. She explained her devastation as best she could and told me therapy was what saved her. She wanted to help and encouraged me to seek therapy. She contacted her therapist from years past and set up my first appointment. If it were not for her, I would never have pursued therapy, believing therapists were for the crazies of this world. But I knew I was coming apart at the seams. I needed something to help me, and for all I knew, maybe it would be in the form of therapy.

My goal was to gain back my soul. Since my abuser represented the Almighty on earth, he polluted any relationship I had with God by deceitfully distorting his trust and love for me. Nothing states it better than Jesus' enlightening words: "Beware of false prophets, which come to you in sheep's clothing, but inwardly they are ravening wolves."

When I entered the therapist's office for the first time, I sat in the chair closest the door. Upon closing the door, he took his seat on the opposite side of the room. Something about him was calming. He made me feel relaxed without even speaking. We first touched base about my work life, he asked how my girlfriend was doing; the overall atmosphere had a warm feeling to it. Then he asked the most important question: "How can I help you, Pasco?" Without hesitation, I just started to speak. I told him I did not believe in therapists, but I could not comprehend on my own what I had uncovered from my youth. I was releasing my thoughts in a rush, and was extremely nervous, venting intensely. The therapist sat and listened while he took notes. Eventually, my words started to slow down. I heard my own verbal confusion. I became silent while he continued to write. He then looked up and told me, "Congratulations, Pasco, you seem to have no problem talking, which will help us immensely during future sessions." He praised my forthrightness. He was wise and knew I needed to hear encouragement, and he supplied it for me. He knew I was hurting inside and let me know he was there for me. He showed me compassion, which was exactly what I needed at that time.

As our sessions continued, our dialogue touched on every subject imaginable, even subjects I had felt were taboo. With time, I learned to respect his profession. After a couple years of therapy with him, I started to get my life back on track. I married my girlfriend and adopted her son.

I then decided to join in the lawsuit against St. Mary's Church and Father Marcantonio, which was a lot tougher than I could ever imagine. The church attorneys were relentless. They kept sending packages of paperwork requiring detailed information about every encounter of abuse. One month, it would be a package of 100 questions to answer or be disqualified from going any further in the lawsuit. Then the next month, it would be 150 questions, the previous questions reworded to screw with my mind. The church attorneys were trying to discourage me and the remaining 35 victims from continuing with the lawsuit. They would try every angle to buy time and kill any momentum that started on our side. This continued for more than a decade.

By responding to all this endless, traumatizing paperwork and reliving all these devastating thoughts about my youth, I became extremely angry and very hard to live with. Within time, it destroyed my marriage, from the inside out.

Eventually, I signed a settlement agreement with the Church, letting them get away with stealing my childhood, as well as numerous adult years, for what it would cost to buy a new Ferrari. Considering the lifelong insecurity and mental anguish I had to deal with, along with more than a decade of being in litigation, the payout was such a joke. But I thanked the entire group of attorneys who gave their heart and soul to help win the case against the Providence Diocese for me and other victims.

Within a short time, I proceeded to write *Behind the Altar*, my book about the abuse, to help myself and other victims to become survivors. I am currently finalizing a website with the same name. By writing my book, I grew closer to God than I have ever been in my entire life. I read the Bible every morning.

A couple years ago, I moved back to Rhode Island to take care of my mother, who has Alzheimer's. Soon after I returned, I started volunteering at a local abuse and rape-crisis center called Day One. In April 2012, I went with some other survivors to our state capital and spoke about my abuse. This is what I said:

"My name is Pasco Troia and I am a proud survivor of childhood sexual abuse. For one full year, a Roman Catholic priest sexually abused me and this became my ultimate life changer. He fastened my youth to a shameful childhood, destroying any opportunity of having a normal existence. Unknowing, I hid all these memories of internal hurt, mental anguish and physical destruction from my 10-year-old mind in order to survive. Not until I was 32 years old did those memories of despair reveal themselves ever so intently. My aftermath took over 20 years to sift through, including a 12-year lawsuit I had to endure. Yet, I came through it, more in love with God than I have been in my entire life.

"Reading or listening to other sexually abused victims tell their stories always astounds me. Our individual stories of sexual abuse, either as a child or an adult, are so enormously different. Yet in the handling of the after effects, we are all shockingly similar. Many of us truly feel responsible. Many of us lug around truckloads of guilt. Many of us overindulge in the negative things in life. And many of us contemplate thoughts of suicide. I honestly believe most of us come out feeling worthless. Until the day you finally work through your abusive past, these demons of destruction silently devour you.

"To all abuse victims who have not yet worked through your personal pain, talk with a survivor and learn. Realize as a victim you are not by far the only one who emotionally suffers. You are not by far the only one who engages in risky behaviors. And you are not by far the only one who has numerous thoughts for killing yourself. Remember to talk with survivors, family members and close friends, who you can ultimately trust.

"To everyone who has a child in their life, please sit with them and ask those tough important questions, in order to save them. Do not sit back and wait for them to come and talk with you. Literally go and talk with your child. The solution to childhood sexual abuse is to remove the silence. Please talk with your child today."

Kelly Johnson

Gender: Female
Age: 26
Race/ethnicity: White
Occupation: Program analyst
Location: Washington, D.C.
Age abuse occurred: 23

"EVERYTHING'S GOING TO BE OK."

Who doesn't hear this at least once in their lives? The situations it's being applied to may differ drastically, but the sentiment is the same.

It's a nice thought, but it's a lie.

Not a horrible one, of course. Said with the best intentions, it's something that people voice because they wish it were true. It's certainly something I've said—both to myself and others.

But it's a lie all the same.

Everything's not going to be OK. There are going to be things in everybody's lives that are so decidedly un-OK that they not only slap the idea of *everything* in the face, but they also have you doubting the OK-ness of *anything*.

I was raped. Nothing in this world or any other will ever make that OK.

On March 25, 2010, my alarm went off at 3:15 a.m. A commuter, I left my apartment each morning at 3:45 to make it to the van pool at 4:15 to make it to work by 6. It certainly wasn't ideal, but I figured I could do it until I heard back on one of the other jobs I'd applied for. I got dressed, never thinking that the ensemble would be forever burned into my memory. Purple bra, red underwear, knee highs, black tank top, gold blouse with copper polka dots, yellow sweater, black wide leg pants, my favorite black Payless heels, an amber necklace and a dark beige military-style jacket. At 3:45, this was just an outfit that I would try to remember to ensure that I didn't wear it twice that week. A minute later, it was the clothing I'd never forget.

At 3:45, keys and cell phone in hand, I opened my front door. And immediately took a step back. The man crouched outside the threshold stood up, said, "Hey," and walked over to the apartment across from the elevators, quickly entering. I told myself that he must have dropped something and his being outside my door was just awkward timing. I didn't really know too many of my neighbors. It was entirely possible that he lived in that apartment. I waited for the elevator, making the subconscious choice to stand closer to my door than his. At the same moment it arrived, he exited the apartment. Moving to the elevator he held the door open and said, "Going down?"

I always thought that I had fairly good instincts, but I didn't really know what instincts were until that moment. I remember two thoughts very clearly. *Get out of this hallway. Do not get into that cage with him.* I looked down at my phone—3:46—and said, "Crap, I forgot something in my apartment." I had to turn my back to him to unlock my door. My mind continued to tell me to get inside, while another voice said I'd feel silly later. But even trying to convince myself I was overreacting, I knew that I wasn't going in to work on time that day.

Even as I write this years later, my heart pounds and I feel a case of the shakes coming on.

Get out of the hallway.

I was back in my dark apartment and closing the door when he charged. He slammed into the door, knocking me back. Given the bruise on my right temple, the door must have hit me, but it's hazy. I immediately started screaming. I've never screamed like that before. He didn't approve of the noise and began punching me in the head. When the first blow landed everything went bright white, and I finally understood what "seeing stars" meant. The beating was unrelenting as he wrestled me to the floor. He whispered continuously for me to "shut the fuck up." I wouldn't. People later told me I was so brave to have kept screaming. I can tell you that it wasn't a conscious choice. When he burst through that door, my mind shattered. It's the only way to explain it. So, as I was beaten, one piece thought, *What's happening? Is this real?* Another piece knew without doubt. He was going to rape me. He got me to the floor, placed his hand over my mouth, and jamming a finger into my eye—by accident or design, I don't know—tried to smother the sound. I wouldn't be silenced. "If you don't stop screaming, I'm going to make you stop breathing." He wrapped his fingers around my neck and squeezed. I stopped screaming, but he didn't immediately let go. At this point, my fractured mind came together for one cohesive thought. *You have to breathe.* I didn't realize this until later, but I think I blacked out for a second because, I still can't remember how he dragged me into my bedroom.

My next memory is lying on the floor at the foot of my bed while he searched for the light switch. I guess he wanted to see what he was doing. At this point, my face was swelling and everything looked distorted. He told me to take off my clothes. I barely had the strength to move. He began to remove them. I was crying, begging him to leave me alone. I told him to take anything he wanted, just please leave me alone. He told me to shut up and ordered me to take off my shirts. With a great deal of effort, I managed this. He removed my bra and then my pants, pulling them right over my shoes. Then he left for a moment and I heard him dead-bolting the front door. For less than a second I thought of running, but there was nowhere to go, and I knew he'd hit me again. He returned to my doorway and I saw the condom in his hand. He removed my underwear and then he raped me. As I lost my virginity in the way nightmares are made of, my rapist asked me a question.

"Who loves you?"

"I don't know."

"Say I do."

In my dazed stated, I repeated that back to him. "I do."

Though it wasn't what he meant, he didn't comment. It didn't really matter to him. But in that moment, it mattered a lot to me. One part of my mind was furious. He wanted me to say that he *loved* me? The rage that this inspired cannot be overstated. Another piece clung to the truth of the statement. "I do." In that moment, though my sobbing continued, a tiny corner of my mind was calm. *Yeah. I love me.* Nothing he was doing, or would do, could change that. No torture still to come would alter that fact. He couldn't take it away from me.

Then the police were outside my door. Hearing their shouts, my only thought was, *What?*

After checking to see if there was another way out, he surrendered to them. There were suddenly so many voices. A police officer appeared in my doorway and asked me what happened. I said, "He raped me." It was the first time I said any variation of the sentence I would be saying countless times over the following months. The screaming I'd done hadn't been a conscious choice, but this was. I remember thinking, *Just say it. If you don't say it now, you never will.* So I did. And I've been able to talk about it since. As the police got my rapist out of the apartment, a female officer sat on the floor next to me. She cursed steadily under her breath. There was a great deal of comfort in that. That someone else would be so angry about what was done to me. I asked how they knew to come. She said that someone had heard my screams and called 9-1-1. I don't believe I'd have lived through that morning if the police hadn't arrived. It wasn't until later that I realized it was my roommate who called them. My best friend saved my life. Just the first example of why, despite living through horror I can't adequately describe, I'm extremely lucky.

My rapist was never again out of custody. He pleaded guilty to the crime, and seven months later was sentenced to 24 years in prison. I spoke at his sentencing and wore the gold shirt from the morning of the rape. Now, when I look at it I don't see the shirt I was raped in, but the shirt that I was wearing when I put my rapist behind bars. Once, it was just a nice shirt—now, it's a statement.

On that horrible morning, I encountered the worst evil I've known. In the days following, I dealt with nothing but good. The responding officers were wonderful. The detectives made themselves available at all hours throughout the legal process. The assistant U.S. attorney assigned to the case is one of the best women I've had the privilege to know, and someone with whom I still keep in touch. Friends and family came in droves.

But I know this is somewhat unique.

On the day I met her, the attorney commented that she rarely dealt with survivors who had such a strong support system. I've heard many similar statements from people who are so happy for me because I have support. While I truly appreciate their concern for me, every time I hear this, my heart hurts. That we live in a world where people are so frequently surprised that a rape survivor has support is devastating because it shows how many survivors don't.

I couldn't have gotten through what was done to me without my loved ones. Within an hour of my arriving, the hospital waiting room was populated. My parents made the drive from New York to D.C. in record time. My brother and cousins followed suit. My sister got on a plane in Jordan and was with me within 36 hours. No one told me that she was coming, but when she showed up in our hotel room, I wasn't surprised. It never occurred to me that any of them wouldn't be there for me immediately.

Still, even I've had small experiences with "victim blaming." One came during my grand jury testimony. One juror asked, "If you knew your roommate was in the apartment, why didn't you scream to get her attention?" I'd already very clearly detailed my screaming, which the attorney pointed out to this gentleman. But for a moment, let's say that not only had I not made that clear to him, but that I never screamed. His question implies that if this was the case, then I bear some responsibility for the crime. If I didn't scream, then I didn't try hard enough to stop my attacker. If I didn't scream, then in some way I was consenting to being beaten, strangled and raped. In that moment, I understood why the counselor who handed me the stress ball before I went in had said, "Just try not to wing it at anyone during questions."

Only a few days ago, I read a story about a judge admonishing a woman by saying that she should have known better than to be in the club where she was sexually assaulted. I hear so many comments like this, people finding ways to blame the victim. Why? Because no one wants to believe that it can happen to them. If the victim did something wrong, then everyone else can reassure themselves that they're smarter than that, and therefore safe. As someone who still hasn't regained her sense of security, I greatly understand the need to feel safe. But I'm not. No one is, no matter what precautions are taken. In the months following the attack, I wanted to lock my family in my new apartment with me, so that I could watch them at all times and make sure nothing ever happened to any of us. Then, one night, as I sat in bed, dreading the dark, I wondered what would happen if I locked everyone in and then someone set the apartment on fire. We could all still die. *Nothing* I could do would ever erase that possibility.

So, to all who look to bolster their sense of security by blaming rape victims: Stop it. By ignoring the reality of the situation, you're not only unsuccessful in ensuring your own safety, but you guarantee a society in which rape continues to flourish unreported.

It's been two and a half years and I still think about it on a regular basis. I avoid going out at night and never wear skirts if I do. Neither of these actions has any relation to my rape, but they make me feel more vulnerable. I'm no longer as scared of elevators as I was immediately following my rapist's attempts to get me in one, but I continue to be extremely aware of anyone traveling with me. I barricade my front door every night, and my bedroom door on the nights I'm alone in the apartment. I haven't conquered my immediate distrust of strangers, particularly of the male variety. I doubt I'll ever get to a point where it's simply a bad memory. However, because of the happier moments of the past two and a half years, this is something I tolerate. Since being raped, I have started and completed graduate school. I've been a bridesmaid in four weddings. I've held down a job. I've traveled. And most importantly, I have not allowed the trauma I went through to taint my interactions with the people I love.

I was raped. In those moments of victimization, the rest of the world disappeared. All that existed were the seconds, and each second that I was still alive was a victory. Afterward, it was almost shocking that the world still spun. But life continued on, and I continued on with it, even when the preventive HIV medications I had to take afterward made my body ache and caused me to vomit everything up. Even when the voice in the back of my head told me to just lie down and not get up. Everything will not be OK, and even though that hurts, I can accept it. Most days, at least. I'm still a work in progress. But I can accept the things that aren't OK, because I know *I* will be. Not every moment of every day, but overall. I'll be OK. I actually plan to be much more than that. I plan to be happy.

So, instead of clinging to the fallacy of "everything's going to be OK," I'm turning to an idea that I have more belief in. If you have the courage to put in the work and effort, everything can be dealt with. It's not a fast process and it's certainly not an easy one, but it's possible. And that's the closest thing to a guarantee that any of us will ever get.

Coach*

Gender: Male
Age: 49
Race/ethnicity: White
Occupation: Unemployed
Location: San Francisco Bay Area
Age abuse occurred: 3-15

IN THE 1970S, I often was entrusted to an extended family member with whom I took road trips and had weekend stays in Philadelphia. On one particular day while on a drive, in my early elementary years, I exposed that I had a secret. From the back seat of the car, I innocently exclaimed, "I have a secret!" The wife of the driver said, "What secret?" At which point, the driver turned from his seat and violently screamed, "It's none of your business!" This response immediately silenced his wife. At that moment, fear and shame paralyzed my speech. It would be another 15-plus years before I was capable of facing the secret of sexual abuse beginning in my early childhood and extending into adolescence.

After this experience, it took some personal losses to finally bring me to the place of admitting to a trusted friend that I had been sexually abused as a child. This friend stood by me, encouraged me to seek counsel, and remains a friend today. The next individual I decided to tell was my college coach. I felt his awkwardness and that perpetuated the shame and judgment within me. Following this, I shared my abuse with other college friends and professors. Some were capable of being compassionate and others were not.

As a result of these friends, I decided to tell family back home in Pennsylvania during the winter break of my senior year. The first person I went to was my high school coach. He never asked me any questions or communicated any concern for my history. Instead, he said, "Don't tell your family, forget about it and move on." After considering his response, I saw it was lacking and decided to do the opposite by informing some of my family members. I went to my father's closest brother because he was decisive, exhibited care and that made me feel safe. He was the first one to express anger toward my perpetrator's actions. He offered to help me tell my father. Within a few days, the meeting happened. My father, who was a highly decorated combat veteran from World War II, sat there looking at me with the 2,000-yard stare and didn't say a word. At the close of our meeting, he said, "I don't think this is a good time to tell your mother."

After college, I decided to relocate to California. It was there that I met my future wife. She was an open person, and when I revealed my history, it didn't frighten her. She had great faith in human potential and noticed mine. As we got to know each other better, she encouraged me to tell my mother. When I told my mother, she expressed shock and disbelief. I remember her saying, "When did that happen? Where did that occur?" Then I told her. One thing about my mother is that she was educated, and took an active role in learning about what happened to me so that she could help me. I was glad I told her.

The turning point for me occurred at a family member's funeral. It was at the grave site that I confronted my perpetrator. I said, "Those years of abuse hurt me." He would not, nor could not, take any responsibility for his actions. Then I said, "I know of one organization that specifically works with perpetrators, are you willing to receive help?" He replied, "I don't need any help." At that point, I ended the conversation and walked away. Within a few weeks, my brother informed me that this extended family member had been arrested and was awaiting trial for sex crimes against children. His history of sex crimes dates back to the 1950s. Presently, he is serving his third prison sentence in Pennsylvania for sex crimes.

Facing my perpetrator gave me greater confidence in continuing my healing journey. Over the course of 21 years, not one man admitted to me any childhood sexual abuse or mentioned someone that had. Yet, the statistics state that 1 in 6 men experience it. I was on a relentless quest to be whole, and the Internet ended up leading me to an answer through MaleSurvivor.org. Within the next year, I attended a men's weekend retreat and there I discovered I was not alone. Shortly thereafter, I became involved in starting up a peer support group in the San Francisco Bay Area. My friends from this group informed me of another retreat for men, with the Monterey County Rape Crisis Center. The center is one of the first of its kind to address the needs of male survivors. After participating in several of their weekend retreats, one of the facilitators directed an email to me about an opportunity to appear on *The Oprah Winfrey Show* with other male survivors. I inquired and was chosen to be one of the 200. This was a historical and monumental event. Never had this many male survivors come together to expose the problem of childhood sexual abuse. Yet all 200 of us came forward to speak the truth and further release the shame.

Following the show, both my wife and I were invited to contribute to Dr. Howard Fradkin's book *Joining Forces: Empowering Male Survivors To Thrive*. Being involved in this project gave both of us an opportunity to work collaboratively to help survivors, family and their friends. It is this outward focus that has lifted the past pain and present shame. It keeps me inspired on my journey forward.

Over the years, I gained a voice—first by talking about what happened, then by finding help, and then by confronting my abuser. The power of those in the community to love unconditionally has given me more of a voice. Being heard validates our hearts and our experiences. When we confront our fears and shame, we then are able to move past the pain.

If you have never shared with anyone the sexual abuse you experienced, I encourage you to talk to a trusted friend today. You don't have to live with your dark secret anymore. There are people who will listen, understand and help you process your emotions and help you get freed from the bitterness, pain and shame. I am hopeful that despite all the odds, freedom will reign once again in Philadelphia, but this time for survivors of sexual abuse.

"He who learns must suffer. Even in our sleep, pain which cannot forget falls drop by drop upon the heart until, in our own despair, and against our will, comes wisdom by the awful grace of God." —*Aeschylus*

Jennifer Patterson

Gender: Cisgender woman[1]
Age: 31
Race/ethnicity: White
Occupation: Writer/editor/designer
Location: Brooklyn, N.Y.
Age abuse occurred: 19
Note: *This piece is from a forthcoming anthology to be titled* Queering Sexual Violence: Radical Voices from Within the Anti-Sexual Violence Movement, *edited by Jennifer Patterson. She is still seeking a publisher.*

IN ORDER TO WRITE this piece, I have to embrace all the deepest, most rotten parts of myself. I pull from a core I have formed over the years of cast-off feelings and resentments. First, this mass formed from rejected pieces of who I was. Then, that loosened; fragments fell and collected, re-formed around a new core. I am present to the secret shells of lifetimes-past fermenting in my belly. I am struggling with my memory and how it intersects with trauma. I am struggling with how linear this piece feels

---

1. I define cisgender as an identity in which self-perception and the way one presents oneself aligns with what is considered normative for one's gender.

and how memory is not linear and sometimes not even true. It all feels a little too clear but I often don't feel clear at all. But I will give you linearity and clarity. I will give you this core. I'm ready to give it up as an offering, in hopes you will listen.

The violence inflicted upon my body knows no gender, no sexuality, no binaries to which you can pin me at the end of or between. The only consistent thread was my ability to bounce back and at times, disconnect. I have worn many faces. I have existed as a survivor who perpetrates violence on another. I have failed people who have loved me. I have the potential to still do it. I have had to learn about boundaries after mine were repeatedly violated. But I also have been the stable shoulder for another survivor. I have brought comfort. I make healthier choices with more knowledge every day.

I learned lessons about violence and vulnerability as a child. I learned lessons as I tried to escape verbal abuse, shaming and humiliation. Many times, I was left to fight adult battles as my child voice elevated to match the rage of my father's. I felt like a protector. I felt like I needed to keep my family safe. I felt wise, terrified, but ready to leave the mess I couldn't clean up from a young age. The abusive lessons after childhood became frequent and continuous. I was raped, as a virgin, at 19 years old. In my early 20s, a cisgender man that I was newly seeing physically assaulted me on a date, leaving me with fractured ribs, which I discovered because of increased pain from coughing, while sick and working as a server at a fine-dining restaurant. After online, phone and in-person stalking, I pursued and received a restraining order. My first queer relationship resulted in my partner slapping me across the face as we were breaking up. Years later, a cisgender lesbian friend, nearly 20 years my senior, punched me in the face during a verbal disagreement.

I can line these reminders of violence up precariously like dominoes. Violence left me hollow. It left me enraged. It left me desperately needing to leave a body I couldn't trust. But most frustrating of all, violence left me too wounded to claim the space I needed in order to find fulfillment in the arms, heart and body of a queer relationship. In so many ways, my queerness was always there but I was too shell-shocked and splintered by violence to see it. When I finally did? It saved me. Queerness saved me.

I struggle with what feel like rigid definitions of sexual identity, gender identity and survivorhood, most especially when it is for other peoples' consumption. I actively spend my life working against nearly everything that intends to shape me because much of what I have previously encountered has worked to dismantle me. I should take a moment to define "queer," as it is frequently misunderstood and multi-layered. While queer is historically defined as odd or unconventional and has been used as a slur, I connect with queer in what I see as a more expansive and progressive way. For me, queer defines me both politically and sexually. I find it to be a radical position within the larger mainstream LGBT community; a commitment to exposing the systems that don't serve us and a space to dream of new systems that do. It is a rejection of mainstream ideas around sexuality and gender. It is the home to critical thought organized through radical love and compassion (among so much more). Once I began to identify as queer, I began to require this dreaming and commitment to change from my partners. And because I believe in self-determination, I certainly believe that some people who are perceived to be heterosexual are queer, should they choose. I am more concerned with defining myself than others. I define myself to claim myself, to foster a curated community of support. I am a queer cisgender woman who is a survivor of multiple forms of violence. Most of my intimate relationships have been with self-identified queer women[2] and people who are gender-nonconforming. However, those who wish to render me deviant search for sources of my "illness," a root for my queerness. They quickly find it when they learn I am a survivor.

Because a queer survivorhood is my lived reality, I often forget that other people see these two things about me as intrinsically linked, bound by dysfunction. They are confirmation of my perversion. The conscious and unconscious ways people pervert sexual and gender identity through the lens of abuse has been something I have noticed and experienced consistently since I began identifying as queer and a survivor. The need to pervert my sexual identity did not exist when I was in relationships with cisgender men and a vocal survivor. I spent years judging and shaming my-

2. When I talk about women throughout this piece, I mean trans and cis women. I include all women who self-identify as women. And when I talk about whom I am attracted to, I mean women, people who are gender-non-conforming and genderqueer. I have learned that I don't happen to fall in love or have fulfilling relationships with men, trans or cis.

self for being a survivor and still find myself falling prey to my own internalized oppressive ideas around victimization.

My coming out as someone who is queer and a survivor requires a relearning of how to be both, as well as navigating my own expectations of societal response to my personal experience.

As I write from this weight in my gut, I am conscious of the physical manifestations of trauma. I can feel the ways trauma is living in my body, the way it carries out its own life within my skin. With each secret revealed, I feel a rumble. This core has become a detectable block and it stands in the way of my healing. A claiming of my truths, a rejection of the shame will break it down. I have been deemed an unrepentant sinner. I have swallowed the lies fed to me, eaten them raw. I have been told I am a broken woman in more ways that I can count. I have told myself I am a broken woman in more ways than I want to remember. Even though there is release, I am reminded of all of the ways people have told me I am sick; the ways in which my mental and emotional health have been intruded upon while I was trying to connect back to myself. I wear all of this on my body, sometimes callous like steel armor, sometimes a soft shell.

I have never been a person who wanted to keep secrets. As a child, I was a tattletale. With a strong moral fiber running through my tiny child body, I stood boldly next to every underdog, whether they wanted me there or not, all the while, I was living through my own trauma. But my trauma started well before I was raped. I was also the underdog and often felt undefended against the world. At home, my father shouted words that seared my skin and left emotional bruises (which I still battle every day) while my mother loved me deeply and consistently. At times, my father did too. It was complicated. I was told daily that I was nothing, that I was a loser, didn't try hard enough, that I was troubled, too angry, had a bad attitude, spoke up too loudly and too often, that I could be sent "away" for it all. A report card in elementary school stated that I didn't work well with others, was an independent learner. I was an insomniac at 8 years old and had kidney stones at 17. I, too, believed I didn't deserve any good that came my way because I was broken. I grew up so convinced of my brokenness and so ready to leave that I kept an escape bag in my closet. That bag contained a razor that I would press firmly against my skin, daring myself to draw blood. I imagined how many bones I would break jumping out of my second-story window. Was it worth the risk? I daydreamed about killing off my body because deep inside, I was convinced I was never going to be able to survive my home. Part of me didn't want to.

I used to simply say that I was a rape survivor. This was before I connected the trauma back to my home and experienced more after the rape. The rape I survived was enacted upon me by a friend of three years. He went to my high school. It wasn't the first time he had pressured me, and I couldn't say I hadn't been warned by people. It is a very familiar story to many of us. And knowing all of this, I know it isn't my fault. Though I had been sexually active, I had considered myself a virgin, which at that time meant I hadn't experienced heterosexual, penetrative sex. I was raised Catholic. Virginity was cherished—if not expected. I was in a "True Love Waits" club. I signed a contract to stay "pure." I sang in the church youth choir. I went to youth group with my best friend (now gay, too). And then I began college. After the rape, I remember one of my strongest feelings was loss. I was silenced by a cultural and personal scream of shame mixed with disbelief, so there was a period where I said nothing. Or the story I shared didn't seem like it was mine. It was years before I told my mother because I didn't want her to know I was no longer a virgin though she has since told me that she would only be worried about the violence I experienced. But in the months after, though I couldn't get out of bed, could barely make it to my classes, and was seeing a therapist on campus, I was unable to connect this to the violence I had experienced.

When I did speak, it was fragmented. I left parts out. I didn't want people to know portions of the story because I feared for my credibility. I didn't want to tell some people that I was drinking, that my rapist was drunk and had done coke. The night after I was raped, I slept in his bed again, pinned to the wall, because I didn't want to put out friends I was traveling with. I didn't want to be an inconvenience. We had all traveled to Penn State together with both of my friends visiting their boyfriends. I could count on one hand the number of people who know that detail. When I did share some of these parts of my narrative, I was told I was lying about the rape. My father considered the possibility that I was drunk and didn't remember clearly. Friends would give me a glazed look or respond with disbelief. Increasingly, my need to expunge the violence from my body began manifesting itself in nonverbal ways. At times, my survival was only audible after downing too much whiskey, yelling too violently at the wrong people, crying too long in unsafe spaces or nearly falling asleep crying on New Year's Eve in a stranger's closet.

Queer survivors have to wade through multiple layers of oppression including, but not limited to, homophobia, transphobia, biphobia and heteronormativity, and this survivorhood is further complicated by racism, classism, dis/ablism, immigration status and sex worker status (among many others). As a white cisgender woman, I have seen myself and women who look like me centralized in conversations, organizations and movements. I have not seen the same kind of mobilization around my fellow racialized and gendered survivors. I have had my experiences marginalized because of my sexuality and mental health status. The status of my mental heath has been both magnified and erased when viewed through the lens of violence. There have been so many manifestations of "crazy" hurled my way, and while I have experienced some of them in a very real way, others seem to trickle off the end of a therapy session after I divulge too much trauma or too much rage. In no particular order, I have experienced, have been told I have or have been given medication for: major depression, obsessive compulsive disorder, bipolar disorder, trichtillomania (the compulsive desire to pull out one's own hair), bulimia, anxiety disorder, insomnia, adult ADD, suicidal thoughts, borderline personality disorder, self-harm, anti-social behaviors, and alcohol abuse. While I have only been formally diagnosed with PTSD and depression, I can feel the weight of a world of labels on my shoulders. They pile up; collect at my edges. I am forever searching for a root; a "which came first."

To believe that people "become" queer by way of violent exposure also informs a false idea of safety within our queer communities. When people imagine that I "became" queer because of the violence I experienced, they are saying to me: Queer people don't experience or perpetuate violence. You will be safe there. This is not even close to being true. All genders have the ability to experience and perpetuate violence. Many people have also inaccurately assumed that the weight of the abuse I experienced was "too much," left me "too raw," forced me to turn to relationships with women because it "made sense." This is always strange to me because my relationships are still about navigating much that I imagine people in heterosexual relationships do. I haven't escaped personal growth, accountability, developing trust or reliability. I still have to emotionally, spiritually and physically connect with another person. For me, it is true that trauma leaves permanent scars, and my scars have demanded that I map out my interactions with all genders. When I was in heterosexual relationships, it was largely because I hadn't questioned what it would look like if I weren't. It took many years for me to realize that my relationships with men were not fulfilling me. I never allowed myself the time in my earlier years to question my own heterosexuality, even though, looking back, there were so many moments to do so. My indoctrination into heterosexuality and heteronormativity was constant and set in motion with rigid boundaries enforced by familial, religious and societal influence. To break away from these deep-seated systems of belief meant a complete disrobing of all that I was taught. Deciding for myself who I was most happy in intimate relationships with was a full-fisted grasp upon a self-actualized identity and one that I hadn't considered could be a possibility for me.

I would be remiss if I didn't note my own unkept, learned violence: the violence that collected in me after it was inflicted upon my body, mind and emotions for years. It sculpted me in ways I was unprepared and, at times, unwilling to unpack. I collected these words, fists, these shapes upon mine and I used them back on people. Sometimes I still use them on people but I am now more present to when I am. It impacts me in profound ways. It doesn't always happen immediately but I see the faces of the people who gave me these broken tools that I have shaped into weapons. My commitment to change and transformation is stronger than my commitment to self-destruction. When working from the rigid binary of "the abuser" and "the abused," the overlap is more common than many of us would like to admit. It is fairly easy to exist in both spaces. In these moments, the need to deconstruct the familiarity of violent reactions and hold oneself accountable becomes increasingly important. Patriarchy, misogyny and sexism have a way of permeating all of us to our core. It is essential that we are all personally committed to not perpetuating abuse upon each other's bodies.

I have found so much strength in just working on transforming my interpersonal relationships. The lessons I have learned through my intimate relationships and friendships have proven paramount over the more mainstream organizing I have engaged in. I have had opportunities to advocate for friends and loved ones who have experienced sexual violence. I have had many chances to lift up the voices of activists who are doing incredible work daily. I have taken the time to listen to and read the words of powerful warriors who are working on the ground while navigating their own daily trauma. I have waded through some of my own trying relationships and have helped turn violated and battle-weary bodies into dynamic and loving companions. There have been countless moments of growth, connection and compassion shared.

I suppose I could spend all of my time attempting to transform or inform, but that feels exhausting to me. It feels much more effective to work within the realms of my own experience and the in margins that are often overlooked (that I inhabit and those that I work to be an ally to), in order to effect change. Maybe this is burnout but it feels more positive than that. So many survivors don't see mainstream activism ever centralizing our lives and we need people to centralize all of our stories. I am present to the fact that as a white, mostly middle class, queer cisgender woman, my experiences are centralized in ways that other survivors' experiences aren't. I am also present to the fact that the white, heterosexual, cisgender woman dominates mainstream anti-sexual violence conversation, activism and is the recipient of much organizational funding. My privilege has allowed me to be invited to many of the spaces I have been in, has allowed me to share my voice in the places I have spoken, but my voice is simply one voice in an incredibly resilient narrative. I find it essential that I acknowledge and utilize my privilege to work for that collective transformation and liberation in the centralization of experiences now overflowing in the margins.

There are the parts that make up my larger whole. There is "what happened to me," there is "who I am," there is "who I lost to become who is here now," there is "who I will be." Sometimes these parts overlap. Sometimes they live out their own lives, calling back to pieces left behind, buried under other bodies—different bodies that wear the same face. They are all mine. I am claiming them. I am claiming my madness, I am claiming my righteous anger, I am claiming my history that pushes me forward. My past informs my present and I won't be shamed for it. While these parts may, at times, carry on separately, none of me can actually be separated. All of it hinges on what came before and all of it can be changed in an instant with what is yet to come, what is yet to dive deep into these bones.

Anonymous

Gender: Female
Age: 60s
Age abuse occurred: 12

MUCH IS IN the news about Catholic clergy abuse, but you hear almost nothing about abuse in the Jewish religion. I was sexually abused by the cantor that trained me for my bat mitzvah when I was 12 years old.

Although I was a deeply religious child, I left my religion after my bat mitzvah, in every way that mattered. It was as if steel doors had closed around my heart, blocking out anything that could hurt me, but also cutting off my faith and my relationship to G-d.

We are often taught that our spirits and our bodies are separate, but I believe that our sexuality is very much tied to our spirituality; our sexuality is the most personal thing about us and goes to our very core and essence. I know now that when I was sexually abused, my spirit was attacked as well as my body. In recovery programs, we call abuse "attempted soul murder." Recovery from sexual abuse for me was healing from a deep spiritual illness, as much or more as it was from physical and psychological damage. That is why it was so difficult to heal from sexual trauma when the perpetrator was a "man of G-d."

I didn't remember the worst incidences of abuse for 25 years. I wouldn't have believed it possible to not remember had it not happened to me. When an event is too traumatic, too baffling for a child's mind to comprehend, somehow the mind closes it off from memory. From the vantage point of an adult, I think this is a very effective coping strategy. I honestly don't think I would have been able to go on living otherwise.

My recovery began by going to a 12-step program for survivors of incest and childhood sexual abuse. Slowly, slowly, by hearing the stories of other survivors and sharing my own, the steel doors around my heart began to open. I finally began to heal, to recover my spirituality, first in the 12-step fellowship for survivors, then by finding a loving and welcoming congregation. At least I was able to find my way back to Judaism, the source of my strength, which had been stolen from me all of those years ago.

Rachael Busch

Gender: Female
Age: 36
Race/ethnicity: White
Occupation: Counselor
Location: Pittsburgh, Pa.
Age abuse occurred: 17
Note: It was through the courage of the clients I worked with that ultimately gave me the strength to put a voice to my own trauma history. For that I am forever thankful.

I AM A STATISTIC. I am the one in four girls under the age of 18 to have been sexually abused. I am a victim. I am a wounded healer. I am a granddaughter, a daughter, a sister and friend. I am a Caucasian female who grew up in a lower-middle class family. I am a lesbian and a devoted partner. All of these descriptions create a picture, but they are general descriptors. They cannot tell the story of what it is like to live life after being raped. I have been a nameless statistic for almost 20 years. My voice was lost in the struggle and I was not able to put words to a personal story of trauma and healing. Now, I am taking that power back to put a face to one story of healing and hope. My name is Rachael and this is my story.

For most of my life, I have struggled with depression. As a teenager, I was looking for an escape from my mental woes. I decided to apply to become an exchange student in the hopes that I could go to another country and reinvent myself. At age 16, I was chosen to go to South Africa. It was a time of political upheaval in the country, but as a teenager I was not afraid of anything. The country was beautiful and I quickly made a close group of friends. I believed that I had made the best decision of my life by living there. That thinking would soon change.

In October of 1992, a few weeks before my 17th birthday, I moved in with the family of a schoolmate. We had become close friends in the three months I had lived there. I started spending time with her group of friends. We spent our weekends hanging out on the beach at a ski boat club. It seemed like a dream come true spending nights gazing out over the clear Indian Ocean as the sun set. A few short months later, my illusion of an idyllic life would shatter.

On New Year's Eve of 1992 into 1993, my host sister wanted to go to the ski boat club to celebrate with our friends. I did not feel like going, but was pressured by her parents to go. When we got to the club, there were many people on the beach all in different states of celebration. My host sister's mother had given us a box of wine. I typically did not drink, but after my host sister went off in search of her boyfriend, I was lonely and missing home. I began to drink. Several hours later, I was feeling the effects of the alcohol. Then, my host sister's best friend walked up to me and my life forever changed. He told me he was looking for my host sister and asked if I would help him. I did not think anything of it and walked down the beach with him. When we were away from the crowd of people, he asked me if I would have sex with him. I laughed and said no. He pushed me down to the ground and when I looked up a group of his friends were there. He raped me as his friends watched. All the while, I tried to fight, but it was futile. He said horrible things to me and his friends laughed as he brutalized my body, mind and spirit. When he said it was his friend's turn, I blacked out.

When I woke up, bloody and battered, I staggered toward a group of people I knew. I could not speak to tell of what had happened. I just cried and a friend thought that I was homesick. When we went home that night, my host sister went to bed. I went into the bathroom and ran the hottest bath and attempted to scrub away what had happened. I was 8,000 miles away from home without anyone to help me. I had only ever kissed one guy in my life before that night. Now, I was physically and mentally in the worst pain of my life without anywhere to turn.

The next morning, my host sister's best friend called the house and wanted us to go back to the club with him. He told her that I had consensual sex with him and she believed him. Now, I definitely could not tell her what happened. Who would she believe, someone she had known for six months or her best friend? I did not want to go back to the club with him, but again I had no choice. He picked us up and took us to the club. A bunch of our friends were sitting around a fire. He asked me to go for a walk with him and I said no. Again, I was pressured to go off with him. When we were down the beach away from everyone, he threatened me to keep quiet about the night before. He insulted me and drilled fear into every inch of my being. I did not believe that things could get worse. Then he pushed me down on the ground and raped me again. Twice in less than 24 hours, I had been raped by someone I had previously considered a friend.

My life spiraled out of control. I was young and scared in a foreign country. I lived there for another six months before I finally got to come home. Every time I saw him or one of his friends, I was paralyzed with fear. By the time I came back, I had worked hard to push what had happened out of my mind. I had again lost my voice and was unable to tell anyone what happened when I came home. I suffered from flashbacks and nightmares. I was afraid of the dark and being alone with men. I did not know how to cope with all the thoughts and only found solace in self-injury. I could not express my pain out loud as my voice had been silenced, so alone I would draw razor blades across my skin. It was easier to self-injure and be able to watch the physical wounds heal than deal with the mental pain that did not heal. I hid this behavior from my family and friends. It was my secret, just as the rapes were.

When I went away to college, my self-injury escalated. It helped to keep the memories of the rapes locked away. One night, the boyfriend of my resident assistant came running out of the shadows toward me as a joke. I had a major flashback and it triggered all the memories of the assaults. While it was a difficult experience, it was the catalyst that pushed me toward getting help. I was a psychology major and went to a professor for help. I began counseling, but could not bring myself to talk about the rapes or even say the word rape as it applied to me. Life was pure hell, and I could not even appreciate the good things I had. I had made a close group of friends at school and I had fallen in love unexpectedly with my roommate. She knew that I was in pain and I eventually told her that I had a trauma history, but then I refused to talk about it with her. (Over the years, my roommate has been there through the highs and the deepest lows, but only recently could I appreciate all that she has sacrificed and done to keep me alive and help me heal.)

I spent the next 16 years in and out of counseling avoiding talking about what happened. I have been hospitalized seven times for self-injury and suicidal thoughts, but still could not find my voice. I felt hopeless and ashamed. I did not believe that anyone else could understand what I had gone through. I kept my voice locked away as the words of a perpetrator who was 8,000 miles away still rang through my head.

One of the strongest factors I attribute to helping me open up about my sexual assault history is the other survivors I have worked with over the years. I had wanted to be a therapist since I was in fifth grade and my friends would joke that I was the only person who never changed my major in college. The more I learned and the more I listened to the stories of others, the more it pushed me to find my own voice. I worked as a rape-crisis counselor during my undergraduate years. I was able to tell the people I talked to about the amazing courage they had in seeking help. At the same time, I felt like a hypocrite. Here I was telling others that the trauma they had lived through was not their fault, while believing deep inside that I was responsible for mine. During graduate school, I spent more time working with people who had experienced sexual abuse. The people I worked with had survived the unspeakable and were able to trust me enough to share their stories with me. I approached my clients with unconditional positive regard, and even when it took them years to start talking about what they had experienced, I stood by them. In my mind, I was looking for the same type of therapist to help me.

I had gone to myriad therapists over the years, but was unable to feel comfortable enough to share my deepest secret and shame with them. As hard as it was to keep this secret from my family, I knew they would always love and support me. When I eventually got up the courage to tell my mother what had happened, I wrote her a letter because I still could not face uttering the words out loud. As I expected, she supported me and loved me. She did not pressure me to tell her details and has let me come to her in my own time. The thought of telling a therapist I barely knew was overwhelming. One therapist I finally opened up to told me that it was no big deal that I was raped; it wasn't like I was in the Holocaust. Another therapist wanted to know every detail of the rapes the minute I walked into the room. The experiences I was having with therapists made me never want to share my assault history with anyone. So, for the next decade in therapy, I dealt with the aftermath of the rapes instead of the actual traumas. I would work on my depression, anxiety, self-injury and disordered eating, but refused to ever let the words of my rapes leave my lips. I knew that I had to keep searching for someone who would listen and not judge me for what I had experienced. As I searched, I continued to shape my own therapy style based upon what I was looking for and what my clients needed.

I have been a therapist for eight years and have heard countless stories of heartbreak from children and adults alike. Whether the abuse had happened a week ago or 30 years ago, it has changed who they were. Their courage and strength makes me strive to be a better therapist every day. Their voices have helped me to find my own voice. I eventually found a therapist that I truly trust and have been able to start dealing with my own rape history. For the first time, I was able to say the words out loud that I was raped. I have been able to experience the feelings associated with my rape history without thinking they would kill me. I have been able to reach out for support from my family and my partner. I have been able to admit to myself that I am a wounded healer and, while I wish I had never had this experience, it helps me work with others. I know the struggles I have gone through and the very long journey of healing this has been. My experience allows me to see life from both sides of the proverbial couch. I know what it is like to be flooded with memories and emotions, to want to die to end the pain. I know how hard it is to ask for help and put your broken trust into that of a stranger. I also know that healing is possible, that it sometimes gets worse before it gets better, but it is worth it.

I am a statistic, but I will no longer be a faceless one. I am an amazing granddaughter, daughter, sister, partner and friend. I am a wounded healer. I have learned from my pain and history how to show empathy for others. I am helping others on their journeys toward wellness. I used to self-injure to see physical healing, but now I can feel mental healing from within. I am a survivor who will no longer be silenced. I will use my voice to shout out, "My name is Rachael Busch. I was a victim, but now I am a survivor. I am the real face of a rape survivor. My perpetrator tried to break me, but I have taken my power back. I will continue to speak for those who have not yet found their voices until everyone starts to believe, to listen, and to care. We are not just numbers on a report, we are real people, and we as survivors will change the world!"

R.C.

Gender: Female
Age: 20s
Race/ethnicity: White
Occupation: Student
Location: Philadelphia, Pa.
Age abuse occurred: 4-7, 24, 27

MY HISTORY OF sexual abuse began when I was about 4. I had a brother who was four years older than me, which means he also had friends four years older who were around the neighborhood. I was raised in the South with six other siblings, four boys and two girls. My sister was 14 years older than me, so she was more of a mother to me than my own mother, who was always leaving my dad because of abuse and arguing. I can't blame my mom because she never really had a life, marrying my father at 16 and having my oldest brother shortly after.

We were all raised Catholic. My father was very strict, and when I was younger, he was an alcoholic doing odd jobs even though he had a pharmacy license. He didn't practice until I was about 12. He is very old-fashioned and didn't believe in friends, talking on the phone or any other "normal" activities children would do except for doing well in school, which was very important to him, and to me as well. He was very racist even though we lived in a primarily black community. I thought that he loved his dogs more than he loved me, and he used to beat me and more my brother. I was terrified if I broke a plate and there were restrictions on what food to eat and the refrigerator. I still have a scar on my left thigh from being whipped by a switch. He told me once that he thought of leaving the family at one point, but stayed and always took care of us when my mom would leave. We had a huge yard and in the back was where my brother and his friends watched me take my clothes off. One time, my brother's friend felt me up and made me sit on his lap. I don't remember (or I blocked it out) how we first had sex, but I remember there was a garden lounge chair seat cover that he laid in the bushes and stuck his uncircumcised dick inside of me. I remember that it hurt so I told him to put it in my ass instead. I didn't know anything. I thought I would get pregnant, but my brother told me I couldn't because I didn't have my period yet. I didn't even know what that was until the summer before I went into the sixth grade.

I felt bad for my brother because of the way my dad treated him, so when he was begging me to have sex with him I would. I never wrote anything like this or acknowledged it really until now, and I feel disgusted and about to cry. The abuse definitely lowered my self-esteem. One of my older brothers almost caught us and stopped my brother by just saying, "What are ya'll doing? Get out of here," when we shared a room. My brother was later moved up to the attic. He was treated differently. He was older but seemed to be treated like he was younger than me and I believe he had some type of mental illness that was never treated. He had friends that would stay the night and they would come to my bedroom and try and sleep with me or touch me and when I told my brother he would take their side. He didn't protect me like a brother should. He got into drugs, and then I got into drugs. I was in rehab by the time I was 15. I always said that as soon as I was 17, I was moving out, and that's exactly what happened. When I was 16, I started dating a guy that was seven years older than me, and moved in with a girlfriend when I turned 17. I remember my dad crying and asking me not to leave him. He was alone. Just like my sisters, who moved as soon as they could, it was my turn.

The guy I was dating was a DJ in the rave scene and also sold drugs. Which meant traveling, staying in all kinds of places, all kinds of people on drugs like ecstasy, ketamine, meth, benzodiazepines, coke, heroin and marijuana. By the time I was 18, I was addicted to intravenously using coke and heroin. When my boyfriend started using heroin more than selling it was when there became trouble. I worked at a gas station ripping off customers acting like I was ringing them up, but keeping the money instead. I supported us. It took me seven years to find a way out, which was with a married man who was an addict, too, but had money and we traveled and did drugs until we got arrested for staying at a beach house we broke into. After I had a couple weeks to think in jail, I met a girl who I stayed with for five years. Still getting high. I waitressed mostly, but I would also steal anything to pawn and purses. I swore that I would rather steal than trick, but I would get sick, so sick, and did end up fucking drug dealers to get well. I saw no way out. I didn't trust my family, even though they grew and tried to help me—including my mother and sister kidnapping me at 22, taking me to multiple rehabs. They wouldn't take me because I was now an adult. I told them that I was on methadone, which is seen as rehabilitation, but is really just a substitute.

After I couldn't take the life I was living with my girlfriend, another girl came along just like me, but with a much more criminal mind, and we went to Florida. I started stripping to support our habit. I felt valueless, empty, only this time I would get paid to do things I had done before. (Nobody wants to grow up and be a stripper. It's done out of necessity.) I remember a man stole my money from dancing one night, and he told me he'd pay me $300 to go to his hotel. Not having any money and knowing I'd be sick the next day (I always had to be inebriated to dance), I went, stupidly. This is where he fucked me and would slap me to keep my eyes open. I discovered my money in his pants, because he was trying to act like his wallet was missing and my rubber-band of money was sticking out. We were arguing, and somehow the cops got called, and I still to this day have no idea why I don't have a prostitution charge, but I thank God that I don't. Thank God they came because he very well could've raped me, or worse, because that was the kind of man he was, and I got the feeling he would have. He was from another country and could've easily gotten rid of me and been back in his country before I was even found.

The girl and I found this psycho guy that let us rent a room out of his apartment. This is where we were introduced to a guy who made his living suing people, selling drugs, and just happened to inherit a good chunk of money from his family. He was also a drunk. He kept a safe on a boat that was beached at a marina, and as soon as we got the chance, we stole the safe, which contained $90,000 cash and a half-pound of weed. The girl's mother drove us, got a hotel room, and tools to crack the safe, and we split it three ways. It was quickly spent on getting out of Florida, two cars, a motorcycle, hotels in Center City Philadelphia, and drugs. We bought ounces of PCP and would drive down South. The cops stopped us because the new car had dealer tags, and they took us and four ounces of wet to the train station, but impounded the car.

Back down south in Myrtle Beach. Buying probably 2 grams of black tar heroin a day, which was $200-$400 a day depending on who we were partying with. Bought another car to get the one out of impound in Philly and picked up the girl I was with, and my ex-girlfriend, which became a bizarre triangle, and this continued until getting arrested by the Avondale, Pa., police. We all gave a different name. My girlfriend didn't have a license so she used mine even though she's like a foot taller than me and Italian. We almost got away when the last thing the cop said was, "Do you mind if I search your car?" Multiple times before we had said, "No," but for some reason she agreed this time, despite knowing there was all kinds of paraphernalia and drugs in the car. I believe this was my wake-up call. I spent almost five months in Chester County prison. The cops wouldn't pick us up for court dates because I later found out that the girl's father was responsible for another cop getting shot. My time there was HELL. I was coming off about a three-bundles-a-day habit (about 30 bags) to nothing except some jailhouse cocktail that didn't do much. I was shitting myself, delusional, trying to take stuff out of the wall and talking to people that weren't there. I was a mess. Tracks up and down my arms, neck and feet. I was 5'3" and weighed maybe 90 pounds. I wouldn't call my family because I was so ashamed of who I was and what I did. I later found out my father hired an investigator to find out if I was alive or not and Avondale being the small town it is had our story in their paper. In jail, I took any kind of program just to get out of my cell. This led me to a parenting class even though I have no children. (Thank God.) I happened to say that I had been molested and raped, and a woman told me that I was abused, and that abuse isn't love. That finally seemed to click and give me a little relief. At least, enough to acknowledge that it happened and I needed to get over it and start my life.

I was 26 when I got locked up in June 2010. I still have a problem with drugs, although now I am trying to quit with methadone, again. I also use Xanax and eventually this is the only prescribed drug that I want to be on and I am fine with that, because after you have lived the life I've lived, my brain is so screwed up I wouldn't even leave the house. I still have dreams of being trapped, running and raped. There was an incident in South Philly where I was out late copping drugs. I was always worried about North Philly and all the stories I was told, but never thought it would happen in my newer, nicer neighborhood. A Spanish guy from the house where I was getting my drugs from was going to drive me home because it was like 3 a.m. and I was so paranoid from the coke that I thought a cop was coming down the street. The guy had to go inside his house to get his keys anyway, so I went inside and he forced me upstairs on his bed and tried to fuck me but settled for a hand job when I told him I had AIDS. My fucked-up head didn't even report the crime. I guess I didn't think anything would happen because I went home and just tried to forget it ever happened. You don't forget though; you just have to stuff it away and go on with life even though you have something that others haven't experienced—and I wish they never do.

My doctor even accepted blow jobs, talked shit about how he wants to fuck me in my ass in exchange for payment. Sex is not the same. It never will be. The only way to fix it is to talk about it and spread the word and maybe it will help others who have been molested and abused. Self-esteem is a big issue, and I believe if I had a chance when I was younger, if my brother didn't take my innocence at 5, I might have had a chance and not have wasted so much time, money and energy living life the wrong way. I don't speak to him really. He has apologized, but in a condescending way, like, "What are you going to do about it now." I just think he's sick and I don't go home except on holidays, if that. I just recently told my sister and she doesn't really talk to me like she used to. She and my mom just don't know what to do or how to help.

I have done some therapy. I have a pair of shoes with red around them and I was told every time I wear them to imagine to take all the pain, suffering and anxiety like it's in a glass and I squeeze the glass and break it and the red ring around the shoes represents the blood and tears I've lost, and now I'm walking away and stepping on all the hurt. Little things like that do help. I'm sure I could do more to help myself, but I guess I'm not there yet. I know they have support meetings, but I'm not much of a talker. I'm learning, I'm just not there. All my innocence was taken and I wasted so much time and energy keeping my secret, which kept me sick. It has caused so much anxiety and I think I'm crazy often, as well as getting stuck not wanting to even leave the house. It's sad that after all these years it's still there, and it will always be in my mind. I just have to find a better way to cope. Even though my brother abused me, I still took up for him. I have always felt the need to protect and make sure everyone else is OK—even at my own expense.

The abuse led me to my relationship with females because of my disgust in men. It's still hard for me to even talk to people due to trust issues. If this never happened, I believe I would've had a shot at life. I have always made good grades getting scholarships and honors—even last semester at CCP, and I expect to continue. My friends from school that I grew up with are mostly professionals already, and I am 10 years behind due to my drug addiction. I have faked a lot of days as I'm sure most people do, putting on that mask to get through the day, like everything is OK.

Now, however, I have grown. I have a new love for life, and myself. I am going to school to become either a radiologist technician or, if I can get in because of my background, an addiction specialist. After 10 years wasted, I believe I am more and want more out of life. Writing this now I feel stronger. I think the clean time I had during jail gave me a new appreciation, even though I would carve myself with razor blades to get some type of relief. All I had was time to think about everything I did wrong and everything that was done to me. There was a girl who was in the cell next to me that I would talk to through the vent, whose story is far worse than mine. She would tell me stories of tricking in Camden, where she was tied up and beaten and somehow escaped. She was released about two weeks before me at 22 and had a son that she wanted to get back to but was found dead in Virginia. I don't know what was different between us that she didn't change her way of thinking and I have. She wasn't ready, and nobody can stop you until you are so tired of how you're living. I now feel after all of this there is a reason for me because there have been many times where I should have overdosed and situations I was in and escaped. If everything happens for a reason, the only reason for experiencing sexual abuse is to reach out and help others in the same situation. I am grateful for the strength that I found and know there's more to life. I have H.O.P.E.—hold on, the pain ends.

M.D.H. and L.J.F.

* * *

M.D.H.

Gender: Female
Age: 33
Race/ethnicity: Caucasian
Occupation: Employer relations and graduate placement
Location: Boston
Age abuse occurred: 21

IT'S NEVER BEEN written down or otherwise recorded, certainly never this way, never in a complete fashion, never remotely comprehensive of the countless details. It's true what they say, I suppose: The devil is in the details. I can certainly relate to that.

The devil was entirely, irreversibly and ever-present to darken my days and dwell in my dreams—even now, despite my decade-plus battle. The battle of a lifetime. Consisting of one event, one night, the ultimate irony belying the millions of shattered pieces, pieces that make up memories, memories I don't want but must place, places I'm forced to go in my head in order to piece the night back together. To get back there has proven extraordinarily challenging. To get back *there*, to that time and place when life as I knew it would end and never be the same, ever again.

You took my life, you took it by force no matter what the law states, or what lawyers might've said, or hell, what I took the lead in convincing myself of for fear that I would be called a liar. I don't regret my decision, albeit clouded at the time, to not pursue a legal course of action. I survived the atrocity only to find out there was not necessarily any peace, reconciliation or justice within the justice system. In law school, I learned just how unfriendly rape law could be to someone with my particular experience and the accompanying circumstances. Knowing all that I know now, it still strikes me as the right choice.

I know what you took from me, and that indeed you took by force. Some days, those two words, that one tiny little phrase, bear such enormous meaning and weight. It was so heavy at times I thought the fight futile and the odds all but against me forever. I couldn't even stomach portions of the whole wretched truth, let alone swallow the ugliest reality I'd even been forced to accept.

After I was drugged and raped by you, a man I knew but not too well, everything stood still. It was as if my world clock, governing all feeling and movement and thought and action, simply froze. Often I find myself reviewing exactly what I might scream, if I could safely encounter the devil who raped me while unconscious and voiceless and choiceless. I've written it down countless times, but on not one single occasion has this provided any relief. Nor any sense of resolve or regaining of my center that was lost when the demons were loosed upon me. Nothing will replace the innocence. That too, was stolen from me.

You left me for dead in the dark, all alone, to navigate through the poisonous wake of your eternal shadow. You took everything from me that night. And I do mean *everything*.

Afterward, it was morning—at least the light would have suggested morning. In the cloud of it all, I somehow moved from the darkness and seclusion of the small hot berth of the giant yacht to the deck above toward the light. Though I moved my legs to walk, it was as if I remained paralyzed, the world continuing to rush and race all about me.

So many obstacles cluttered the path ahead of me; so heavy and dense was the mental fog that I had no center, no self, no recollection of what had happened. *Two beers consumed, no hard drugs or the like.* Or so I'd thought. So was my intention.

Something powerful drove me out of that awful scene, away from the nightmare and toward the light, the powerfully blinding, harsh and refracted Sunday morning light. It was as if someone but not me had witnessed the scene unfold, witnessed the crimes and the theft and the wrong and knew of the power that'd been robbed from one—silenced all the while—by another: the Taker, the Rapist, my Rapist. In the minutes that followed after my consciousness was restored, the Witness lent to me her Presence of mind, her Power to move, her Power to find the light above.

I knew what you did though I smothered it and hid it and denied it and fought it and suffocated it and ignored it and minimized it. I knew it all too well but found every imaginable way of refusing to let it in to my mind, or my life, or my truth. I know what you did to me, though it took years of my young life to recapture even the smallest details. It took a bitter, brutal, internal battle of the most dreadful kind. It literally sickened me to review the possible scenarios. With so few concrete, linear details from that night, I continued to think I must have blacked out. But how? One beer at the bar that night. Maybe two.

Things were drastically different then, shortly after I turned 21, when we often drank to excess. Every night was a near replica of the last, partying hard and often, typically until dawn, and with infrequent pauses in the action. At first, it was exciting to be far from home, removed from the watchful eye of any authority figures or rules or curfew; it was glamorous and novel. I shared this life with my brother, N, and the closest girlfriend I'd had in a long time, C. I wish I'd never left N at that bar. I wish I'd stayed in the comfort and safety of his big arms and his ever-protective reach. I wish I'd never left N and C because maybe then I would never have had to reveal the horror to N, the horror that he would undoubtedly internalize and live with and shoulder for an eternity.

What haunted me then cannot possibly compare to what haunts me now. At some point I could no longer run from the truth of what you did. Of what exactly was done to me that night, of how clear the signs were— all be they scarce.

I remember the pants I was wearing; they were black. The next morning, they were unbuttoned and unzipped halfway. You did that to me. You left me like that. You didn't even move the pieces back together or attempt to recreate the illusion of normalcy. You just took what you took and disappeared when you were through. The bra I'd been wearing was left unhooked in the back and you did that to me. You left it undone. My head was pounding and it felt as if I'd swallowed a mouthful of sand or cotton or both.

I don't know for how long I lay there, the sheets crumpled around me, damp and disgusting, the air dense and stale. Recycled and dead is how I felt. Because of you. It was merely the beginning.

I knew I had to check one more thing prior to zipping and buttoning those borrowed black pants, dirty with repetitive nights out and layers of sweat absorbed from the hellish South Florida summers we mostly spent biking and dancing and drinking. I knew I had to reach down my own pants, and feel for the presence of a substance, the existence of which would provide me with a definitive and irreversible set of facts. It was the only way I would live with and own the truth of what you did to me.

Like a record on repeat or an old VHS tape on "pause," the image, half-frozen, blinks and twitches as if jolted by an electrical current too weak to move it forward to the next scene, to that moment, that time consisting of no more than a minute or two or three. The image, the motion of my own hand moving and searching for the truth and finding it; the indescribable dread that lasted a lifetime in that isolated cavernous hellhole of a prison, when I found a truth I still wish to this day I never had to search for. The remnants of you all were over me down there, the truth everywhere, despicable and unavoidable. The stench of you all over me. The smell of your body fluids in and on me. The evil, the darkness, the truth.

IT WAS ONLY in hindsight that I began to seriously question my inability to distinguish those who might be bad from the good, those who might take advantage of rather than protect me, and all the in-betweens. It was amazing that I survived through the years under such a thick layer of profound innocence, that despite my lack of worldliness I somehow managed to reach my 21st year (relatively) unscathed.

It wasn't arrogance or invincibility I carried with me then, considering my dominant parental figures' impact over the years preceding. It was far more elemental, basic, almost guileless. All the same, these traits were part of the innocence that was lost when stolen. It had never been the case that I went out alone, or even alone plus one. Every night but for that *one*, my brother was always nearby. Always. Not that night.

It started with me feeling tired. Not into the party scene (for once). Not interested in drinking much. One beer. Maybe two. It was a bar we frequented. That I remember. There was a yellowish light, and everything was open-door, open-window due to the soaring Southern Florida temperatures in those summer months. Fans on the ceiling perhaps. Live music perhaps. Decidedly uninterested in the scene. Tired. I shared my plans with C and N, separately as I recall, and planned to leave alone for our boat. I wish I'd never left N. I wish I'd stayed forever in the safety of his reach.

It was much farther on foot to our boat than to yours, which lay on the opposite side of the same Intercoastal Waterway. You must've planned to walk me away from it all that night. I know this only now that I've discovered and reclaimed the truth of what you did, only now that my memory is restored sufficiently to recount the "must haves." These were my saving grace. These details, however foul and painful and sick and inexplicable, they were literally all that I had. For years and years, I clung on to these for dear life; and without them, without the self-blame and shame and denial and isolation and excuses and drinking and hatred and anger and all of the endless ocean in between, I would have never found my way to owning the truth. The truth is plain, though not simple.

And in the immediate aftermath of the rape, there was nothing but paralysis, confusion, denial, disbelief. I could scarcely recall a thing in sequence. I was sure of nothing I thought I'd been certain of just hours before. You drugged me with a Corona on the deck. You took me down below to one of the berths facing the bow. It was small, it was hot, it was black. There is nothing but one single flash of a memory, a passage of time I will never be capable of describing with accuracy. No such thing exists. This one single incalculable moment is literally all I could reclaim from the time in between my first sips of that Corona and the following morning waking up alone and half-clothed. I own this all now. But I fought against accepting this foul reality. You stole the words from my mouth with which I could've screamed and the air in my lungs upon which I could've relied to fight you off of me. You took these things all at once. And in the time it took me to type this one sentence, another woman will endure this nightmare.

I intentionally save this flash of memory for last, as the mere thought of it consistently leads to a feeling of absolute loss of self-control, as if I were suddenly submerged and drowning in an endless ocean. I remember the oppressive heat and the awful weight of your body on top of mine. I remember dampness, unbearable humidity, an indescribable thirst. I remember there was no way of moving my body and there was no way to speak. An utter state of paralysis. My body was not my own. My limbs felt unattached, severed. My voice was nonexistent, as if even my soul had escaped and taken the air I'd been breathing with it. And then I heard you say, "What? You don't like it? You don't like my sex?"

And then silence. Blackness.

* * *

L.J.F.

Gender: Male
Age: 25
Race/ethnicity: Caucasian
Occupation: Small-business owner
Location: Billerica, Mass.
Relationship to survivor: Boyfriend

I AM DATING and building my life with a woman who was raped more than 13 years ago. Living with a rape survivor has so far been as difficult as it may sound. But being there for M has also shown to be very rewarding.
M and I met at her front door while I was working on her lawn. We were instantly fixated on one another. We spent nights under the stars, in the rain, in each other's arms. M and I started staying together a few months later. About a month into spending each waking moment by each other's sides, M woke in a panic, covered in sweat, confused and lost. Instantly, my first reaction was to settle her. She grabbed on to me and wouldn't let go for minutes straight. I soothed her and we went back to sleep. This happened several times before a discussion came up because of the concerns I had expressed. The first time M described the horrifying assault in deep detail, I could not bear to hear it in its entirety. To hear what someone had done to such a sweet, caring, beautiful woman was heartbreaking. It still is heartbreaking. I decided it was time to disclose the physical violence I endured for years at the hands of my mother, who decided that was the best way to deal with her and my father's divorce. M felt my pain, and I feel that this connection brought us closer.

The pain I feel for M in my heart and soul is far more painful than your average injury or loss. This pain runs through every sense of my body. And they are multiplied when M shows signs of Post Traumatic Stress Disorder—night terrors, fear of confrontation, a loss of self-confidence and, most of all, self-resentment. I believe M has in some way blamed herself for what she went through 13 years ago. I think that the blame and other side effects of the assault haunt our relationship more frequently than we both know. M's emotions and how she expresses herself have been drastically affected by the assault she survived. She has developed some issues that involve confidence, beauty, trust and emotional freedom. Physically, we have never once had an issue—the passion is the strongest we have ever known. However, M tends to run when we have a disagreement or when her emotions become overwhelming. I believed her actions stemmed from a fear of rejection or injury. When M and I went through a difficult period of time connecting and communicating, we agreed on couples therapy. (We had always had our own therapists, but never went to together.)

We began going to make sure things stayed in the "honeymoon stage" as long as we could. It was like preventive maintenance. A few months in to therapy, we discovered that the assault M faced 13 years ago was a large part of the disruption in our relationship, and played a role in why we could not connect when in conflict.

Recently, M got emotionally involved with a co-worker. She began lying to me and spending the majority of her time with another man. This went on for almost five months until I caught her in the act of making plans with this individual. My first reaction was to ask her to pack her things and that things were over between us. I then remember the constant struggle she was undergoing due to the assault. M begged me to stay and promised to eventually fix things and be more open and honest with me. This took a lot for me to stay, as I am not one to feel taken advantage of and then forgive so easily. However, I kept M's healing in mind. Maybe she was confused or torn or even worse—needing someone else. M lied to me for several months, but I stayed around because of how special I knew she was. I stayed because M loves me and had opened up to me more than anyone in her life. I stayed because M needed me and I needed her. Here we are, together, and in our eyes, forever. Enjoying each other, continuously asking questions, constantly falling in love.

M and I have been to galas and banquets to support her and fellow survivors and future survivors. We donate when we can, whether it be money or time. The Boston Association Rape Crisis Center (BARCC) has played a huge role in M's success in healing. I am more than happy to continuously be a part of that as well.

M had an awful, life-altering experience, but if I abandon ship when times get tough or worse, then I would be letting her down, and I would be letting me down. I need M and she, in my opinion, needs someone just like me who can help cope with her challenges and her past damages. Together we make an amazing team and I believe she needs a team. Whether her team consists of her possible soul mate, therapists, family members, herself, or all of the above. M has never once given up. To this day, she is still putting an enormous effort into healing. Though I have been through pain with her, maybe even because of her choices made during our involvement, I love M. As long as she puts in the effort to heal, be honest and help me understand, then I will continue to remain by her side. M was assaulted 13 years ago, but we have a lifetime to share consisting of much more time to learn and grow together. I believe M's survival played a role in molding who she is today. That's the person I fell in love with and that's the person who deserves my time.

Woody*

Sex: Male
Age: 67
Race/ethnicity: White
Occupation: Change agent/interventionist for corporate and government **organizations**
Location: Chicago, Ill.
Age abuse occurred: 8-16

I WAS BORN on Oct. 11, 1944. At that time, sexual abuse was something only spoke of in whispers so the children wouldn't hear. In some respects, my sexual abuse began on the day I was born since my father was a drunk, worked long hours and did not have much of a role in my life. I was raised mostly by my mother and grandmother, who both hated men and were loud and outspoken about the repulsive and idiotic things that men did. My sister and I sat and listened to these stories as children, and lived with a father, uncles and male cousins who were almost all drunks and validated what we heard. I believe this made me question my masculinity while growing up. It made me hold myself in contempt as a young boy, thinking I'd grow into a man who would be held in contempt along with all the others I heard about. To a great extent, that is exactly what happened. Overcoming that self-contempt and gaining the respect of others is the story of my recovery.

My father thought that making me a man required me to defend myself from physical abuse, so when he came home at night he would pummel me as he encouraged me to defend myself. My father was 6'1" and weighed in at close to 300 pounds. He was a mountain of a man, and nobody ever intimidated him except his mother, who regularly emasculated him and brought him to tears, in my presence, during our weekly visits. My mother did little to protect me from my father's physical abuse, and visiting my grandmother on weekends was not optional. My mother's first husband died when she was pregnant with my sister, and I don't think she ever got over that loss. Consequentially, she was cold and intermittently physically abusive to me. By then, I had learned not to cry when she hit me—unlike my sister, who cried even before she was hit for the first time.

My grandmother, my mother's mother, was a saint to me. She gave me unconditional love, wisdom and affection. Without her, my rage would have been inflicted on many people rather than just a few.

The neighborhood I grew up in was mostly Italian, mostly first and second generation, with a Jewish segment that was slowly migrating to the suburbs. As a person who really had no religious affiliation, I really did not fit in. And as a young child, I did not have a lot of friends. I was small for my age and had amblyopia (blind in one eye). Because my mother made me wear an eye patch as therapy, I bumped into a lot of people in my kindergarten class. The lack of depth perception that comes with vision in one eye made sports like baseball and football impossible. A gym teacher used to make fun of me, saying that my position on the baseball team was "left out."

The first incidence of sexual abuse occurred several times by a young man who took me as a vulnerable and needy young boy of 6 or 7 into gangways between buildings for oral sex. As a child, I never told anyone about it. In fact, for years, it was a memory that was merely translucent.

There was also an adult woman who would stop by in her car and take me into it for make-out sessions. I remember that she was blond and had large breasts.

When I was 10, two men named Jim and John threatened to beat the crap out of me unless I had oral sex with Jim, who was my sister's boyfriend. Somehow, the word got out about what had happened, and my father came to me one night and asked me about the incident in a very caring and gentle way. He was not gentle and caring with Jim or his father.

However, that did not end it. Jim caught up with me. He outweighed me by 100 pounds, and started to beat the crap out of me. Fortunately—and to this day I believe it was an act of God—the fullback on the high school football team came along and broke Jim's nose with his elbow.

Around the same time, there was a young man who did not have any friends. He was not very bright and worked at a newspaper stand in the subway. He tried to befriend me by offering me books and money. When we walked down the street, he would touch my penis momentarily. To this day, even when my wife touches my penis in the same way, I get a creepy feeling.

My sister became sexually active after that, and since I knew she was having sex with several guys, she took me into her bed. I remember mounting her but not anything else.

After that, boosted by a growth spurt, I started muscle building, boxing, learning martial arts, and obtained .25- and .45-caliber handguns. I also became an expert at throwing knives. I also became a member of a street gang known as the Counts. We had gang fights on a regular basis and when blacks began to move into the neighborhood, we had fights almost every day. We also did a lot of vandalizing and did a few random robberies. I was picked up by the police 17 times during my early through late teen years.

People knew I carried my .25 in my back pocket and with a lot of practice, I became an excellent boxer. Unfortunately, I took my anger out on more than a few people who got in the way. They were often bigger than me but I was fast and hard to hit.

Yet, despite all of this, I remained psychologically and emotionally vulnerable to predators.

Lydia became my first real girlfriend in the seventh and eighth grade. She had dark hair, beautiful eyes and was very smart. Lydia's family was very protective of her, to the point that she was not allowed to participate in activities or socialize very much. So our entire relationship was on the sneak. After school, we made out at her house. It would be more accurate to call it frottage since Lydia backed up against the wall and I rubbed our genitalia together until we were both sweating and I had stains on my pants. We also were able to ditch school a few times with each other and have a few random interactions in gangways. On the day I told her I loved her, she lay down on the couch and invited me to get on top but then her brother came home. She successfully snuck me out. I knew, eventually, we would get caught and I did not want to bring that on her or to face her brother, who was a golden-glove boxer. Lydia did wonders for my self-esteem. I still remember the intense feelings I had for her. She showed me that I had a capacity for love and was lovable.

My alcohol and drug use began to emerge as I moved onto high school. I was able to obtain alcohol fairly easily and began to drink regularly. I met a couple of gay musicians who convinced me, with alcohol, drugs and a new Lincoln convertible, to make out one time.

One time, a few of my buddies and I were walking down the street and ran into a carload of guys from an older, rival gang. We shared the territory and generally stayed out of each other's way. But tonight they were drunk and they decided to pick a fight with us. My buddies backed down but I snapped and decided to accept their challenge. Something inside of me just exploded and I backed up against the wall and started swinging and kicking until five guys were down on the ground. That day changed my life because I knew I had the power inside to put everything into a desperate attempt to survive. Of course, I could have simply backed down and said we were outnumbered, but that thought never crossed my mind. I understand why people become professional boxers. It may be brutal, but it is better than murder or assault.

Meanwhile, I met someone I'll call the Fat Man. He was a friend of a woman who owned a beef stand in town. He lured me to his place with liquor and great stories about his accomplishments. He weighed in at about 400 pounds. He pimped me out to a group of middle-aged men for several months until it was discovered and exposed by his business partner, who happened to be one of my peers. Fat Man had convinced this young boy to invest in an ice cream parlor, but after too much unwanted frottage, my peer had enough and backed out of the business arrangement. In a last-ditch effort to convince my peer to try some male-on-male sex, the Fat Man told him about me. When my peer confronted me, I was speechless. I quickly became persona non grata to all my childhood friends.

When I graduated high school, I was depressed and not ready for college. The sexual abuse was over, but the scars remained. I dropped out of college after one year and went to work in a factory. Bored, I tried to go to auto mechanics school but was a failure as an auto mechanic. Finally, I landed a job as a foreman with a plastics company. They are still around today. The owner was a real professional and tried to help me along. I started to believe in myself. I worked hard, made some money and got married to the girl next door. We both just wanted to get away from our parents. Her mother never let her forget she was an orphan and owed her good life to her. Mine were still angry about the wasted year in college. I ended up quitting, thinking I could go into sales but I failed at that. My bruised ego could not handle rejection.

I was unhappy with my marriage and did not see a way out, so I volunteered for the draft during Vietnam to get away and then go to college when I got out. In boot camp, I learned that my wife was pregnant while on the pill. I literally drank my way through the Army in Germany where they had great beer, good wine and not much to do. I took a few college courses and discovered a career direction in Human Resources.

When I was released from the Army, I went to college for one semester and worked at the school. Living with my mother-in-law was not working out so I got a regular job at a manufacturing company. They nurtured me like I was their son. I was promoted seven times in just three and a half years and found my voice and calling. I was an advocate and a change agent. That became, and still is, my primary identity. Up until then, I still had a street corner identity. I finally was able to forgive my father and establish a relationship with him.

At the same time, I started to smoke weed on a recreational basis. Now with two children, I began to feel the pressure to follow the Church's teachings and began to think that my mother-in-law was running my life via remote control. My wife and I had terrible verbal fights, and our sex was dutiful and limited by the Church. I met a woman at a workshop and never tried to conceal our affair. My wife and I divorced.

I went to therapy and found several mentors in that area. It helped me understand, but I was never really honest about my drinking or sexual abuse.

Another marriage, to a woman 10 years my junior, ended in five years. Up until then, my life was focused on my career. But as it advanced and the stress increased, the only tools I had to deal with it were drugs and alcohol. It got to the point where they only made it worse.

After that, I went on a 10-year binge. I worked as a janitor to the president of a nationally recognized consulting firm. It was like a roller coaster, and I did not know who I was.

I ended up in a drug and alcohol treatment center in Colorado and my life began to turn around with the help of AA, NA and psychotherapy. I wanted to give rather than take, and I knew I needed to make amends to specific people as well as to the world in general. I worked at an inpatient psychiatric unit for a year, and then worked for the CDC for three years working with HIV patients. I was commended for identifying the change in the epidemic toward women being infected, went back into consulting, civil service and the Red Cross—and finally into an 18-year relationship with the love of my life, who is a gifted psychotherapist.

She accepts my faults, appreciates my gifts and is able to give and receive. She is the partner I always wanted.

Many open AA groups discuss the high incidence of sexual abuse among us and even get into their stories. I was finally able to stop minimizing my abuse: I lived in 26 different cities trying to run away from my problems, and was married four times. I was fired at least 10 times. I wasted my talent, millions of dollars and hurt a lot of people along the way. But with a lot of hard work, humility and patience, I have been able to establish a relationship with two out of three of my children.

I continue to make amends on a daily basis and I understand that taking care of myself is the most important thing I need to do. I am still somewhat of a loner but push myself out into social settings. Oddly, the thing I love most is facilitating groups. Somehow, that puts me into a different mindset and I am comfortable with people.

Recovery from sexual abuse for me is about letting the light shine on the wound and being able to reclaim the innocence that was taken from me. Thankfully, our society is making progress with this problem. However, we need more focus on the most vulnerable amongst us—on a proactive and not a reactive basis.

Janelle Adamska

Gender: Female
Age: 28
Race/ethnicity: Eastern-Euro-Celtic-Native mutt
Occupation: I work at your local supermarket and lift heavy things. But in my time not working for the man, I am an artist working for my own womanness.
Location: Philadelphia, Pa.
Age abuse occurred: 6; 8; 28

SMOKING TO INHALE, I try to remember to breathe. Not breathing = not feeling. I'm really good at not breathing. See, when I was a kid, I could just make myself stop, but I learned early that the body is resilient and will force you to breathe again and again. Time passes and you're back to where you were before. Now, I'm staring at a blinking cursor on a numb-white, digital representation of a page, a space with no sense of feeling or touch, trying to figure out how to keep breathing without carcinogenic aids, trying to think of how to tell you about how I was touched, all the while knowing you will feel the paper my story's on and be able to put it down. These words were waiting and will wait despite the persistent marking of time: 62 blinks on my computer screen; 22 years to quit my denial; and, if I'm lucky, one moment when one reader will bear witness and no longer acquiesce to the pull of a culture that allows, denies and rewards the pervasive paradigm of sexual subjugation.

I was raped when I was 6. Now, I know what image must come to your mind. It wasn't the creepy man in the white van peddling candy with a nefarious grin. It wasn't a dark shadow in a dark alley. It was two seemingly normal, neighborhood boys just budding with their adolescence. I don't know what they were thinking when they looked at 6-year-old me. I've often wondered why they couldn't see that I was horrified or why they didn't think they were hurting me or why they wanted to hurt me. A big lesson for a little kid to take in, but I learned that some people will not see you or care to see what they are doing to you if they are getting off.

You don't need to know the dirty details of my days in a doghouse. I won't indulge you with the full scoop, mainly because I'm aware of how titillating descriptions of sexual acts can be, even when speaking of them in terms of abuse. I am not comfortable or consenting to you getting any visualization of my degradation.

I was fine—until I wasn't. I had gone all these years unable to admit what kind of effect my own history with sexual abuse had on me and then, quite suddenly, the things that were previously numb awoke in a screaming sharpness. My previous survival tactics of gas-lighting myself failed: *It wasn't that bad. It wasn't as bad as what happened to my mother. It wasn't as bad as that story on the news about that one girl in that one city so far away. There wasn't any blood. It wasn't that big of a deal. I don't remember.* But I do. Those intoxicating illusions of denial no longer fix what those young men broke, and there have been times when I could think of nothing besides the rubble.

The pieces would be more easily picked up if my experience were an anomaly, but bad things happen all the time and, even still, nobody talks about it. 1 in 4 girls. 1 in 6 boys. Silence. Amongst my friends, it's easier to count those who haven't than to try to quantify how prolific the problem of sexual abuse is in our culture, internationally and throughout time. I'd rather count those who haven't. It's a smaller number, a nicer number, and a lucky number. I have experienced inappropriate boundary-crossing from trusted individuals of the male gender numerous times since I was 6. I know that any gender can commit abusive behavior. I have known both females and males who have experienced rape or molestation. I know a few that have experienced the horror of "stranger danger." I know people who have felt the dread and despair after having someone they love and trust be blind to their individuality and choose instead to see them as an instrument for selfish ends. I know what it's like to be shut down by a mother, shutdown by a clergyman, shutdown by friends and lovers. *Don't talk about it. No big deal. Keep going. This is what happens. Don't put yourself on a cross; it's too high. Stay down. Stay quiet.* They wanted my silence. I gave them that for far too long.

Once I fully realized the broken pieces within myself, I began to see the cracks everywhere. When I've been dismissed for speaking out against the things that offend my identity and trigger my memories, my ability to validate my experience has been limited. When this is done by partners and whole social circles, it makes allowances for the spectrum of abuse to continue. The stories of other survivors have only made me louder. It's through this vocalization of things laid mute that I have been able to survive the outfall of my useless defenses. I feel I must speak because I walk out my door in the morning and am constantly reminded of my "sexual usefulness" by men on the street, jokes told by friends at bars and in the work place and in reflections of my femininity in every ad to sell everything. In a few turns of the page, I will be triggered again with images, bodies, women—me—hips splayed, two-dimensional, to be acted on, all with the suggestion of a gaze that is not my own. If I listened to all the cues around me, I might begin to believe that that is all I am. I can't believe that because it would mean that I have to accept that I will be used again. I must have faith that there is a way to change the cultural climate that allows small, everyday abuses committed by nice, normal people through language and image to escalate to rape. It's not about simply saying "no" in the moment. It's about each one of us saying "no" to these things every day, no matter how small the instance.

Since this is a people problem, we need to examine why this happens. Why have most of the people that I have met been abused? Why is the male body used as a weapon statistically more than the female body? Why do we think about sex and the bodies of others the way that we do? Is it biologically hardwired, or are we sentient beings who are able to think, reason, read the rights of another person's person as more important than our wish to act upon them? Is it a joke? Are we reading the signs? Is that the problem? Are we taking to heart the seemingly permanent availability of women's bodies in our visual culture? We are all visual creatures. We all take in our surrounding environment and make decisions about how to act on it. There is no one answer. But certainly, numbers tell us it is a human cultural dynamic that is a painful problem stretching far and wide through time that has been excused, downplayed and flat-out denied. We must examine our consciousness and be willing to eradicate our own abusive behaviors in order to ensure that we ourselves are not enabling or committing. We need to confront our friends when we notice abusive language and behaviors. That's what friends do: Hold you accountable for your failings and successes in the journey to be healthier and happier on this earth. We can go to the moon, but you know what they say about running away from your problems. This problem belongs to everyone.

Charlie S.*

Gender: Male
Age: 64
Race/ethnicity: White
Occupation: Retired
Location: Boston, Mass.
Age abuse occurred: 60

MY ORDEAL STARTED in 2007. I met a woman on an online dating site. I'll call her Robin. During our dating process, she told me that her husband of 30-plus years came home one day and told her he was leaving. This devastated her so much that she ended up in the hospital for about a month with depression and other medical problems. She was put on different medications and underwent therapy.

This happened approximately six months before we met. As our relationship progressed, I felt compelled to just be her friend before anything else. In time, we talked about taking our relationship to the next level. I knew she was still vulnerable and we both decided that if it were to happen, that she would make the first move. We were both comfortable with this.

For the first few months, we did the usual things couples do. We went to dinner and the movies. We played games, went to the beach and talked about our backgrounds and families. I could always sense a feeling of uneasiness on her part when it came to talking about her daughters, who lived out of state. She also felt betrayed by her husband and expressed her feelings in not-so-nice terms about him. I focused on being her friend and supporting her.

Eventually, the night came when she said she was ready to be intimate. We didn't rush into it. We talked for a while to make sure she was making the right decision. She was convinced she was. Afterward, she seemed fine yet we waited a couple of more weeks for that time to come again. In time, she told me how comfortable she felt with me and said she believed that she loved me. She had mentioned me to her daughters and said our relationship was "friends with benefits."

By this time, she and her husband were in the process of divorce. She told me she had papers that would "make her husband pay" for what he did to her. She had also hidden $50,000 to keep it out of the divorce settlement. This woke me up!

In December 2007, Robin went to visit her daughters for Christmas. I drove her to the airport and we made plans that I would pick her up when she returned and we would go out to dinner. I planned to talk with her about her emotions and actions when she returned. From the moment Robin got in the car on New Year's Day 2008, I knew she wasn't the same person.

Evidently, her husband had visited her daughters before she got there and Robin was under the impression her daughters had been "brainwashed" by him to take his side in the divorce. She was so upset she vented her anger toward him the whole ride home. This was a prelude of what was to come, another sign that clouded my better judgment.

When we got to Robin's house, she handed me a soda and went to take a shower. Within 10 to 15 minutes, I was very groggy. Robin returned and forced herself on me. When she was done, she expressed how much she needed that and how good it felt. She said if I wanted to satisfy myself, I could have her. I realized what was happening but couldn't believe it. I repeatedly asked her to get off me, but she kept telling me how good I made her feel. Still dazed, I finally pushed her off.

It didn't dawn on me until later that she had drugged my soda with some of her medications. I wanted to leave, but Robin insisted we go out to dinner. I said I wasn't comfortable with what just happened and left.

After the assault, I experienced fear, anger, embarrassment, sleeplessness, eating disorders, and waking up every day not wanting to do anything except stay in bed hoping it was all a bad dream. In time, I pulled myself together and fought back. I sought counseling and was diagnosed with post-traumatic stress disorder. Through my support group, I've been able to help other survivors, mostly females, through their ordeal. I've been accepted into RAINN's National Speakers Bureau program, and with family and friends I was able to help put together a Public Service Announcement regarding sexual awareness. Along with two female survivors, I was interviewed on Current TV and spoke out against Sen. Todd Akin's "legitimate rape" statement.

Rape is one of the oldest crimes in the history of mankind and yet we're still in the infancy stages of how to prevent it. I often ask myself how we make the general public more aware of these assaults and what can be done to prevent and overcome them. Female victims are too often stereotyped. Too often, they go to the police and are told they were "asking for it" or they were "dressed too provocatively" and there was nothing that could be done. Talking with female survivors, I've found the misunderstanding of rape by police and the fear of being killed by their assailants as the two most prevalent reasons they did not come forward earlier than they did. When I reported my assault to the police, they bluntly told me nothing could be done. This is why I empathize and relate with those female victims.

Since my attack, I've been a strong advocate for sexual-assault awareness. Many other survivors have done similar good deeds. Since we have the means and the ability to make changes, then we have the responsibility to take action.

If we don't fight back, the predators win again.

Anonymous

Gender: Female
Age: 26
Race/ethnicity: White
Occupation: Medical field
Location: Philadelphia, Pa.
Age abuse occurred: 15-16

2000: I started dating a guy when I was 14 close to turning 15. I had only kissed one boy one time before him so having my first boyfriend was a big deal for me. It was the beginning of my sophomore year and I was embarrassed of never having a boyfriend. I always had crushes but I never thought they would like me back. I did not think much of myself. This guy was my older brother's friend and I saw him all the time. He would hang out at my house many weekends. We innocently dated a few months and then broke up. After we broke up, we stayed in contact for months, mainly through email and instant messaging. We started hanging out again. He stood me up for a date twice, which should have been a sign of his lack of respect, but I let it go even though I was hurt by it.

2001: About five months after breaking up, we went out on a date and he was all over me. His best friend, who was older than him, drove us to a secluded park and he got out of the car and left us in the backseat, which made me extremely nervous. All we had done was kiss and make out when we had dated. And we had not seen each other so when we hung out for the first time in a while, I was surprised that he was making out with me heavily and immediately trying to unbutton my pants. He shoved his hand down my pants. I was panicked and frozen. He did not put his hands inside me but did not remove his hand from my pants right away. After that failed attempt, he got out of the car and was whispering to his friend. They were both standing at the trunk and I was still in the car. I felt uncomfortable. I was nervous but I still liked him and I just thought he was a horny guy and I did right by stopping him.

Not too long after that night, we started dating again. Everything was going good and normal.

After a few months, he started pressuring me into taking our relationship to the next level. It came to the point that that's all he would talk about. I did like him and care for him but I kept saying no.

One night, we were both drinking and he would not take no for an answer. I would say, "No, not yet, wait, I'm not ready." I had my period and had a tampon in so I was using that as an excuse, too (pretty sad that i had to use that). I was almost passed out. He started to try to have anal sex with me because he did not have a condom and wasn't about to risk a pregnancy. All I remember is being face down on my bed and being really confused. I truly believe that if he had a condom he would have had sex with me no matter what, and despite all my efforts to say no and stop him. Thank god he was so wasted drunk, because he was unsuccessful with the anal sex. I was still a virgin so that gives me chills to think of my first sexual experience being face-down drunk for anal sex because "No" just wasn't good enough to him.

He was going away to college and I tried to break up with him. I did love him but I feared him cheating on me. I thought I was being a good girlfriend by allowing him to go out and experience the world and not be tied down. He promised me till he was blue in the face that he loved me and only me and he begged to stay together. I loved him and believed him. After him being away in college for a few months and him coming home most weekends we took our relationship to the next level. We did love each other, so I don't regret that. I just wish he didn't pressure so much.

Before that even happened, I told him repeatedly that I could not handle it if we did have sex and he cheated on me. I would be crushed. As it turns out, that's exactly what he did but just failed to tell me until later.

He would come home mostly every weekend. We were in love and I was happy. But he started to get really pushy with sex, like it was expected on demand. I felt pressure to keep up because of low self-esteem. He was my first and only boyfriend and I did love him. He would brag to his friends about stuff between us, some true and some made up. That bothered me. I remember one time, he was pressuring me so bad to perform oral sex that I ended up in tears after being forced to do so. Another time, he pressured me to have sex with him seven times in two days. (Looking back, I'm thinking he is a sex addict.) Do you know what seven times in two days does to a 16 year old? I was sore, and was glad when he went back to school.

2002: As months went on, we started to grow apart. It's hard to have a long-distance relationship in high school. I stayed faithful but was hanging out with friends more.

The night of my junior prom, he came down and we went to the prom and then to the after-party. We did have sex, and then I wanted to hang out with the whole houseful of people and friends. He did not want me to. We started arguing because he felt like I was ignoring him a lot of the night—which I kind of was because we were growing apart, and not to mention the girls were making a million group bathroom trips. So I did leave him alone a lot but with a lot of other guys. He was also angry because I was not really drinking at the after-party and he paid for me to. We spent the majority of the night upstairs arguing.

At one point in the middle of the night, after arguing for a long time, I was sitting on the floor hugging my knees in silence, saddened by the fighting. He was kneeling on the floor not far from me. He came over to me for sex and I said no. He started pulling my shorts down and I pulled them back up. He put his hands on my shoulders and pushed me back hard. I hit my head on the floor and it hurt, and I immediately started crying. I grabbed my head with my hands and in the midst he pulled my pants down and began to have unprotected sex. He was much bigger than me and in really great shape. The weight of him plus my shock left me to put up no fight. I thought he would stop since I had said no and now I was crying and I thought for sure that when he saw my reaction he would stop. He kept going. I was shocked and numbed. I turned my head the opposite way as far as it would go and stayed frozen that way until he finished. I rolled over, pulled my pants up and went to sleep. He laid next to me and we both slept right there on the floor.

When I woke up the next day, I was exhausted from being up all night, and I kept thinking, "Is what happened true? Was I raped by my boyfriend, who I love?" I remember sitting on the sofa with him the next day, waiting to see if he would say anything or address it or apologize. My brain kept dismissing it. He never spoke of it and neither did I.

After that, the dynamic of our relationship changed. I never said one word about it and neither did he, but he became much more aggressive. He was always sweet and kind to me before, and then all of a sudden his demeanor toward me changed. I pushed what happened in the back of my mind, but looking back I can now see why I behaved in certain ways after.

One time, we were alone at his house and he wanted me to take a shower with him. I was frozen in fear and said no. He was cursing and calling me a whore and took my pocketbook and threw it out the front door and said, "Get the fuck out."

Another day, we took a trip to an amusement park with my brother and his girlfriend. When they were having fun on the water park, I refused to get in my bathing suit and I sat on the bench, miserable. They all thought I was weird for doing that, and even I didn't realize at the time it was all because of what he did to me. I didn't want to run around in a bikini in front of him.

Our one-year anniversary came up and I couldn't bring myself to have sex with him. I had to drink beer to have sex with him. I hated beer and he poured it in shot glasses and was making me drink it. He literally sat in front of me pouring shot after shot of nasty beer, which I gagged down. He wasn't even drinking.

We broke up after I kissed my best friend at the time. I was honest and told him the next day. He strung me along a few months. He would be nice and then would be nasty again. I knew the relationship wasn't a stable one, but I thought since I lost my virginity to him, I had to try and make it work. I was 16 and in love and thought I would marry him someday. He was pressuring me to perform oral sex on him but I wouldn't, and was hesitant since we weren't together. He promised me he would get back together with me if I did it. Once, he tricked me at a party into doing it and then he left me there crying and begging him to stay.

After being broken up with him for a few months and newly dating my best friend, my ex showed up at a store where I was and was harrassing me to kiss him and get back together him. I turned away from him to look at a rack of clothes and he grabbed my butt pretty aggressively. I turned around and pushed him, but as I was turning around he grabbed me in the front really sexually as if I was his to take.

I have not seen him since.

2005: I got in contact with him three years later by phone. I sent an email saying to call me. He did right away. I was not strong enough to fully confront him. I danced around the subject. I never used the word "rape." I focused mainly on "If you told me you had cheated on me, then we wouldn't have even stayed together and then nothing would have happened." That was not the focus but that was easier to talk about. He was being nice on the phone saying he loved me, blah, blah, blah. He said he thought we just had sex and that he wouldn't want to do anything to hurt me. That helped for a while but I never understood why I still felt the need to confront him until just recently, when I read that it has to do with reclaiming control. He still had the control even in that conversation. He led the conversation and I wasn't brave enough to say what I needed to. He never validated me or took any responsibility.

Every so often, my thoughts would be consumed by this and I would panic and not sleep good for days.

2007: I heard that he was now a cop. I was in the hair salon and my 3-year-old son was getting a haircut. The hairdresser went to my high school so we were chit-chatting and she was telling me what a few people were up to, and he was one of them. I could not breathe. I panicked. That is the day I told my dad and my mother-in-law about the rape. I felt like I could not even function. I was consumed by that for a while. Now, every time I see a cop car, I panic and my heart skips a beat.

I have recurring dreams that I run into him as a cop and he rapes me again because he feels he is above the law. I know this isn't the case, and I feel like it's time to confront him. I am strong enough now to say things I couldn't before. I want to face my fear of him doing it again.

I will no longer be afraid.

2011: I sent him numerous emails trying to get in contact with no response. I got the nerve up to call the police station where he worked. It was a 15-minute conversation of me almost begging him to meet with me. He said he didn't know and that gave me hope that he may have a conscience after all. I was in tears getting off the phone because I was so close to having this be over and my attempts had been failed. That same weekend, I drove to the station. I wasn't going to talk about this there but I thought if he saw me he would know I was serious. Another failed attempt. I sent a few more emails pleading for him to meet me. I had made a goal when I turned 25 to do this. My time limit was running out as my 26th birthday approached. I tried one more time by getting the nerve up to call the station. This time went even worse by him plainly saying no and hanging up. I burst into tears. I sent my email with the information I wanted him to read. I knew by sending this he can no longer respond to my emails since that would be incriminating. I had to do it because I wanted him to understand and read my perspective.

I am now left feeling that I did not accomplish my goal. I do not have closure and peace. I do not have hatred or even bad feelings for this person. Date rape has severe consequences because the victim most often doesn't get the proper help or validation. This has caused me to have trust issues since it was a betrayal of trust by someone I knew and loved.

All of this causes issues in subsequent relationships. I have flashbacks and panic attacks that I can't control. I have thought about this a lot over the years and really would just like this person to give me acknowledgement of the wrongdoing and an apology. I do matter. I did matter and I deserve the respect from the person who did this.

Diata*

Gender: Wombyn
Age: 25
Race/ethnicity: African-American
Occupation: Teacher
Location: Philadelphia, Pa.
Age abuse occurred: 5-12

MY FATHER WAS a revolutionary of sorts. I can recall him preaching and praying passionately in some of Washington, D.C.'s most impoverished and neglected neighborhoods. Ramshackle houses and project buildings long deserted by humanity were the areas targeted by our church for "street ministry." Essentially, church was set up in the street, or in barren, abandoned parking lots. I was very young then, maybe 8 or 9. I can remember the green, broken glass and crumbs of concrete that somehow broke off from the curbs and sidewalks.

Loud speakers propelled the scratchy sounds of prophets screaming for redemption, and the band kicked a gospel beat for the people to move to. Ministers laid hands on the otherwise washed-up, hopeless and faithless ghetto masses. And there was my father, reaching out to these men, women and children. I have memories of pride as I sat in the metal folding chairs set up for the street congregation. I straightened the wrinkles in my pink dress and smiled as two white observers beamed about the efforts of my father. I beamed, too. I saw that my father had a genuine heart, a spark within him for his God and his people.

But somewhere along the way, things went awry for my father—a man who had honest hopes to be a successful and moral human being. Somehow, he fell short of the call. At some point, he fell and fell hard. He buckled under the pressures of the system that sought to rob him of his manhood. He lost the battle to retain his self-worth as a man of color, struggling for meaning in a society that hated him. He understood that the upward mobility he desired was continually being flaunted in his face, and all the more vigorously kept from his reach. Eventually, the demons that haunted his past could no longer be ignored. One day, he woke up, and God wasn't enough to sustain him. He realized that his plan for a happy life of church and family wasn't enough to erase the bitterness of his reality.

And somehow, this hatred for society translated to hatred for his life and his family. I am unsure of the process from trauma to abuse—victims becoming victimizers. What about my father's consciousness allowed him to take a negative path instead of "fighting the good fight" for what he wanted? What about the struggles he had made him want to prove the destructive stereotypes about black men correct? Why did he turn on the only people who loved him—his children?

An unfortunate truth I hid and suppressed for what I thought would be forever is now at the forefront of my consciousness. For years, my father sexually abused me. The statistics for sexual abuse and rape are outlandishly high considering how "hush-hush" the topic still is. Victims are still stigmatized and shamed despite the efforts of social organizations and the media's attention. Somehow, this disease continues to spread. My question is: Why? And how? How can someone feel entitled to take what does not belong to them?

It has taken me until adulthood to speak kindly, to look honestly at my father as a human being and not a monster. Today, I realize he suffered vastly in his personal, professional and social life and was unable to cope with the pressures of his large dreams that soon became deflated. I also suspect that he was sexually or physically abused in his youth. In no way do I excuse his behavior. Nor do I tolerate his constant denial and dismissive attitude toward his role in my abuse. The mere thought of him still makes me angry; to hear his voice mirrors rusty nails on a chalk board. But I understand that forgiving him is a part of my healing.

I used to feel nothing; I was numb to the experience. It is natural for the body to go into shock when pain and trauma are so great that it may threaten to take us out or to drive us insane. But later, I felt anger and hate so intense that nothing could parallel it. Today, more than anything, I pity him. I feel sorry for the shame, guilt, regret and disgust he must feel. He has never admitted the abuse took place, let alone apologized for his monstrous actions against his daughters. He may never admit it, but I know what he's done haunts him in his dreams.

I will never be sure of the reason he did it. I can only infer based on the research I have conducted through family members. Understanding that the abuse was *his* problem and not mine was a huge step in the process of my healing. The process is hard, treacherous and unfair. But there is a lesson and a reason for all experiences. It is up to you to find out the mystery. Above all, know that you are beautiful, powerful, complex and worthy of everything good. You can heal yourself today and move forward a little lighter and a bit more strong. We have to speak out to save our children, particularly our young girls, from suffering what plagued us.

Cassy Byrne

Gender: Female
Age: 22
Race/ethnicity: White
Occupation: Northwestern University graduate seeking employment
Location: Chicago, Ill.
Age abuse occurred: 18-21
Editor's note: *Cassy's story is much longer than most in this collection. We felt her detailed narrative was worth presenting in its entirety.*

MY NAME IS Cassy Byrne, and I am 22 years old. While I was at Northwestern University, I became a victim of repeated sexual assault, and I am sharing my story publicly for the following reasons:

　　1. To give a detailed first-hand account of how sexual assault, in its variety of forms, can—and does—occur in the real world.

　　2. To give fellow survivors a name for what happened to them (understand that we, as a society, are typically not given a comprehensive—nor accurate—definition of what sexual assault actually is, and for this reason, many survivors end up suffering in silence for months or even years without knowing why, which means that they are unable to find support when they need it most).

　　3. To give those who are unfamiliar with sexual violence an inside look into (a) all of the complex issues that are interwoven between sexuality,

violence, relationships and abuse, and (b) the various ways in which the psychology of a victim can respond to said abuse.

4) To dispel widespread myths and misconceptions about all of the above, and in doing so, generate a safer, more understanding and more informed environment for sexual assault survivors and friends to cohabit.

Snow White Loses Her Virginity

Flashback to April 2009. I am 18 years old, a freshman at Northwestern University, and a total loser with no friends. Not that I'm complaining; it was kind of fun for a while. I had been waiting my entire adolescence to be On My Own. In retrospect, it would have behooved me to have had some sort of a support system around me for when life started throwing me curveballs.

One of my favorite On My Own activities at the time was going to the movie theater alone, and Saturday afternoon was the perfect time to do it. On this particular Saturday afternoon, I went to see a French film called *Paris 36*, and as I was leaving the theater, I saw a man sitting on the benches in the lobby, staring and smiling at me. I gave him a half-hearted, polite smile back and briskly left the building, put on my headphones and started walking home. I had gotten to the end of the block when I saw the same man I'd seen sitting in the theater jog up beside me and start saying things. I paused my music and started trying to assess this man's level of danger to me. He told me he was a grad student at Northwestern and claimed to have seen me many times in "the language building." I was a Linguistics major studying two languages, so it wasn't implausible. He told me his name—Doc*—and I reluctantly gave him mine. We walked and talked together for a while. His jovial demeanor led me to believe that he was not an immediate threat, but I remained skeptical and kept my responses short and guarded.

He invited me to see a movie with him. I declined. We soon came to the junction where we had to part ways. He suggested that we go for coffee sometime. I said, "Um ... yeah ... I mean, I'll probably just see you around?" (After all, he'd allegedly seen me on campus before, so no need to be hasty in making plans.) At this point, I was just trying to end the interlude in any way that I could; no stranger had ever pursued me to this extent before, so I was in rather unfamiliar territory. Then he gave me his number.

I took it, figuring I didn't have to ever use it. But then he asked me for mine. I was thinking I could just give him a fake one, but I surprised myself when my real number ended up coming out instead. Oh, well. I supposed I could always just ignore his call when it came.

As soon as I got home, however, I got to thinking, and I realized that this could very well be my *one, single chance* to lose my virginity! At last! OK, just to put it into perspective, I had never been in a relationship before. I had barely even *kissed* a guy (only once outside of Spin-the-Bottle and high-school theater productions—so my track record didn't fill me with much hope for a sex life. I had also been "the fat girl" all my life, and didn't realize at the time that fat girls could get laid, too. So as I was reveling in the irony of the fact that one week prior to this encounter with Doc, I had written an entry in my diary about coming to terms with the fact that I would probably be a virgin for eternity, I started growing continually excited by the prospect of actually having sex for the first time. (I was never much the romantic type, so I really didn't care *who* I lost my virginity to, as long as the job got done.)

Besides, men were always complaining that women took sex "too seriously," and I definitely did *not* want to embody that horrible persona of a girl who could not distinguish "sex" from "love." Unfeeling, emotionless sex, with no strings attached; that's how I heard that all the men liked it, and so that's the way I was determined to like it as well. Besides, if I actually cared about finding a man I could trust before having sex, wouldn't that make me an uptight, sexually repressed prude?

A sad—and dangerous—state of mind to be in, I know now, but welcome to what it's like to be a teenage girl.

Doc and I met up at Starbucks the next day and did the typical getting-to-know-each-other routine. We talked about family, school, general thoughts about the universe. I learned that he was 26 years old, born in Iran, studying engineering. He was an atheist, too—like me. We spent a large chunk of time decrying feminism. (I realize now, in retrospect, that I should have considered the things he said during this portion of the conversation to be "red flags." But at the time, I thought that "feminism" was just that horrible thing that men didn't want women to have anything to do with, so I just adopted that mindset and pretended that it was something to be proud of.)

After a while, we started discussing movies that we liked, and I mentioned some movie he'd never heard of, so we decided to rent it at Block-buster and proceeded back to his place to watch it. I was on my period, but I wasn't sure of the protocol regarding when to bring up that fact, so I continued to wait. While we were sitting on his couch, watching the movie, he made some weird attempts at kissing me. I don't know, it was really weird, and it just wasn't working. At one point, he got frustrated and exclaimed, "Are you *shy?!*" I replied, "I'm … inexperienced." He probed, so I admitted to him that I was a virgin. His choice response was, "First time's the best time!"

Now, not even I was too virginal to not know *that* was complete hog-wash. But we started making out anyway. This was also the first time I had ever made out with anyone, and I knew that I had no idea how to do it right, but I tried my best. After awhile, he got frustrated with me again and growled, "Explore!" and attacked my lips once more. The hell if I knew what that was supposed to mean. Anyway, we got to second base and everything, but I didn't feel like I was enjoying anything that was happening. He was just so rough with me … but I assumed he knew what he was doing, so I didn't say anything.

Then, I told him that I wanted to wait until my period was over to have sex. He said he didn't mind that I was on my period, but I insisted that it mattered to me. He continued to try to get me to "put out" by making very leading moves, and I had to continually stop him from going too far. Eventually, he drove me home, and that was that.

At least, for the time being.

Starting the very next day, I began starving myself.

I experienced the onset of this illness for the first time as soon as I became aware that the loss of my virginity was imminent, and from that moment on, sex continued to be the trigger of my episodes in one way or another. Sex is not the trigger for every person who suffers from anorexia, but it most certainly has been for me.

In the first month-and-a-half of my being sexually active, I dropped around 30 pounds due to starvation. It was pretty bad.

About a week later, I lost my virginity to Doc. I don't remember much, except for that it was incredibly painful and bloody (and that he tried to convince me beforehand that it wouldn't be). At one point during the sex, I asked him to try to be gentler, and he said that he would try, but he didn't really. But who cares? I had finally lost my virginity! And I felt awesome!

Really, I did. I felt all empowered and capable. And sexy. (Although, that could have just been the eating disorder talking.)

Looking back on it, I wonder how I could have evolved sexually from there if only I had stopped seeing Doc after that night. Moved on to someone else. Someone more respectful. Someone who listened. Someone who cared. How would that have looked? How would *that* have felt?

Partner Rape

Things proceeded pretty favorably for the next few weeks. The sex was enjoyable, although much of it was "angry sex" because we didn't actually get along very well. But in a way, it was special. I didn't really have any friends yet at school, and this was the most intimate relationship I had ever been in. The combination of those two factors made me feel as though I had created some kind of a retreat—a sort of "home away from home"— for myself. A place that I *thought* was safe. But then something happened. And it took me two-and-a-half years to figure out what. It marked the beginning of the end for me.

It was the first night that I had slept over at his apartment. I woke up the next morning, and he was hard. We engaged in light-hearted conversation about what we were each going to do that day while he retrieved a condom from his closet. I was so excited, because, of course, I was someone whose sexuality had just been awakened for the first time, and so my libido was at an all-time high. He climbed into the bed, looked at me, and said: "Roll over." I was totally unprepared. I assumed we were just going to do it doggy-style. So I rolled over. The next thing I knew, he had penetrated me anally. No lube. No warning. I *screamed*. One of his hands was pulling my hair, and the other was around my neck while he pounded me. I was in so much pain that I couldn't breathe, and I felt like I was going to pass out. At one point, I said, "Wait! Wait! I ... need a breather." He actually did stop. I turned over, and he asked me if I could breathe. I told him I was done with that for the day. He was disappointed, but proceeded to have vaginal intercourse with me.

When I went to wash up afterward, I discovered that I was covered in so much blood, I wasn't sure if I could go home right away. The feeling of isolation and fear that I felt in that moment as I examined the wreckage that was my body is still palpable to me now. I used his shower—still in a complete daze—and when I emerged, he asked if I wanted to get some breakfast. I told him I didn't eat anymore, and he called me stupid. Then, he took me home. And I could not sit down or attempt a bowel movement without excruciating pain for at least three days.

The next night I saw him, we discussed oral sex over brandy. I had always sort of been turned off by the idea. From what I had experienced of our culture, it seemed to me that blowjobs had become more important to men than vaginal intercourse, and that really ticked me off. Still, Doc really wanted me to do it.

While we were standing in his kitchen that night, he retrieved some yogurt from out of his fridge, and as he fed me a spoonful of it, he spread it all over my lips and chin, while giving me this sick, perverted look. I had seen enough pornography to pick up on the innuendo. Needless to say, I was really creeped out. I just didn't feel ... good. There was something about the way he was looking at me. After we had sex, we played some music for each other. He was really obsessed with the song "Caribbean Blue" by Enya. Played it on repeat while doing the stupidest dance. I can't listen to that song anymore; it really sets me off.

He started pressuring me to have anal sex with him again. I told him repeatedly that I didn't want to, because it had hurt too much—not just during, but for days afterward. So then he asked me for oral sex—as if it was the *least* that I could do, if I wasn't going to take it up the butt. I reiterated that I would rather not do that, either. But he told me that he wouldn't have sex with me again unless I went down on him. I still seemed unsure, so he kept bargaining with me. I eventually assumed the position, muttering, "This is so bad" and I attempted to give him a blowjob. It was challenging. While I struggled with it, he upped the ante: "I'm not going to fuck you again unless you take it all the way to the hilt."

The bastard.

Well, I tried. And I gagged. He had his hand on the back of my head, so I asked him to please remove it. He got all defensive, but complied. I kept trying, but I kept gagging, and with tears coming out of my eyes, I told him that I wanted to stop, that I just couldn't do it. He huffed, "Fine," got out of bed, went to his computer to replay that stupid, insufferable Enya song for the millionth time, and proceeded to act like I wasn't even there. Feeling an unprecedented amount of shame and inadequacy, I threw the covers over my head and really did try to disappear.

The next month or so of our affair continued just as tensely. He continued to pressure me with regard to anal. He said that if I did it, he'd "like me better." I said that I didn't care, that I never asked him to like me to begin with. So he said, fine, and that I'd just have to "deal with the consequences." He was always so good at *ignoring* me when he wanted to get something out of me. Neglect was one of his most powerful weapons of manipulation. But I didn't understand any of that at the time. I just wanted to feel wanted and worthy, and that's precisely what made me such a vulnerable target in his eyes.

I was also coming home every night after seeing him with intense bruises all over my lips, breasts, arms and legs. I felt branded. For a while, I thought that I liked it. His abuse felt so much better than his neglect, and those were really my only two options. I also didn't have any frame of reference for what sex was *supposed* to be like, and not many of my friends had been in casual sexual relationships, so I didn't know what was or wasn't "normal" behavior. On some level, I knew that the wounds were signs of something bad. But for the first time in my life, I felt like something was *happening* to me. You know, a Real Event. And I think that's what kept me so involved, despite the constant warning in the back of my mind. I kept thinking that this was something life-defining and significant.

I was right.

As time went on, I began to feel completely paralyzed around him. I could never ask him for anything, out of fear that it would give him leverage to bargain with me. (A fear that still plagues me to this day in all of my intimate relationships.) I also could not achieve orgasm during sex, and that bothered me. When I first expressed that concern to him, he seemed eager to rectify the situation. But after hours and hours of digital stimulation, he came to the conclusion that it was my fault, that the problem was in my head. So that shut me up. Indefinitely.

Eventually, the strain of it all really got to me. I was tired of feeling unwanted and unworthy. I couldn't take the constant pressure of anal sex beating down on me—it was a *constant* battle, and I felt like whichever way the pendulum swung, I lost. I could either satiate him and endure unbearable pain, or I could deny him and feel the sting of his neglect and frustration. So I ended it.

He got angry and defensive. Asked me if he'd hurt me, told me casual relationships didn't have to "end," that we could still hang out and not have sex. (Oh, yeah? A clear manipulation.) I told him how I felt about the anal situation, how it made me feel guilty and worthless. He said, "What's *with* you?! Why are you being so *negative* tonight?" I was just trying to be honest. Then, he said that when I came back to school after summer vacation, maybe I'd feel differently. Just to placate him, I said, "OK, we'll see," and hung up. I felt so relieved to have gotten myself out of that mess.

Depression and a Second Helping of Abuse

That summer, I turned 19, and I had my first depressive episode. I didn't know what it was at first; all I knew was that it was scary. I had never felt so hopeless, so worthless, so *lifeless* in all of my life. I ceased to find joy in anything. I didn't want to go anywhere or do anything. I wept uncontrollably on a daily basis, curled up in the fetal position, shaking violently. And the worst part was: I had no idea why.

Well, I had *some* idea. I noticed a pattern in the thoughts that seemed to trigger these episodes the most (though, at the time, I didn't know what a "trigger" was). The thoughts that kept pounding in my head had to do with the fact that I felt worthless to all men. I hated myself so consummately for not being able to perform certain sex acts. I felt like a complete and utter failure as a woman. It made me not want to be alive. These were thoughts that I could not escape, because I was reminded of them *everywhere*. Sex is all around us, and you never realize just how pervasive something is until you're trying to avoid it. So I went on loathing myself and further hard-wiring into myself the feelings of worthlessness that Doc had first instilled in me. I knew that this was why I was so unhappy. But I didn't know that I was ill until I got back to school in September, and I started perusing the Internet and discovered that what I was experiencing were symptoms of clinical depression. But even though I'd figured it out, I remained in denial about it for over a year. On the bright side, I ended up finding a real group of close friends around this time, and that was a welcome and comforting distraction. It gave me something to care about and devote my time and energy to.

However, a lot of the time I still wound up having to ditch all of my commitments for those all-too-frequent "bed days" when you just cannot bring yourself to face the world. And even when I did manage to make it to my classes or to my various social engagements, it was hard to not be triggered by the slightest mention of sex or sexuality. I would sometimes have panic attacks while sitting on the toilet, because the sensations of defecating were reminiscent of anal penetration. Often, I would randomly feel a "ghost penis" inside of my vagina that sent me into paroxysms of trembling and tears. The combative action that I took most frequently in response to that feeling was to shower repeatedly, but I could never seem to wash it out.

One night, while I was home for winter break, I decided to send Doc a Facebook message. It was a cry for help, actually. I needed to know more about what had happened to us—to me. I was obviously still struggling with trying to understand it all myself, and the process had quite literally made me sick, so I thought that because he was more experienced than I was with all things sexual, he would know what to say to pull me out of this. I made sure not to make it sound as if I was blaming him, only that I needed an explanation for the things he said and did to me. His response was surprising and hurtful. He seemed irritated and told me that I wasn't the first woman to complain to him like this. (Like what? Like maybe he should stop raping us?) He then accused me of getting caught up in "the land of romantic-marriage-type relationships," and followed it up with these maddening, immortal words: "YOU HAD A EXTREME SEXUAL EXPERIENCE AND YOU CAN BE PROUD OF IT. And you don't need to tell your top secrets to any body else."

It's easy now for me to roll my eyes and feel enraged. At the time, it really affected me. I didn't know anything about sexual assault, the plight of a victim, the profile of a perpetrator. What I heard when I read what he wrote was: *You're just a silly girl. Get over it. Or better yet, embrace it. You just don't know good sex when you have it. You should be thanking me.* But the subtext was actually: *I'm a repeated sex offender, and maybe if I put you down enough, you'll blame yourself and not tell anybody about what I did to you.* If only rapists would be so direct.

I was so enraged by what he said that I responded a little less sensitively this time. He answered by calling me on the phone, and we wound up talking for hours. For some reason, I came to the conclusion that he wasn't malicious, just daft, and that he may have been experienced, but he wasn't experienced with women who were *inexperienced*. So I decided to brush off my grudges and give him the benefit of the doubt. (Sigh.)

When I got back from winter vacation, I sighted Doc in the Starbucks where we first had coffee (it's the same Starbucks that triggers knots in my stomach whenever I pass by it, and I can't ever bring myself to go inside it now). I felt paralyzed. I couldn't think, I couldn't make eye contact, I couldn't hear anything but my accelerating pulse. My entire body was trembling. I just stood at the register and placed my order until I worked up the courage to look. He was standing outside the window now, his back facing me. Was he waiting for me to come out? There was no way he hadn't seen me. I panicked. I started calculating escape routes, wondered if the Starbucks employees would let me run out the back. But when I turned to leave, Doc had vanished again. I wanted to cry for some reason. Why hadn't he spoken to me? Didn't I at least deserve a "Hello"? I was so upset that I decided to text him: "So we're both trying to avoid each other then?" According to him, he hadn't seen me at Starbucks, and he insisted that we see each other that night. I stopped responding, so he called me. I ignored his calls. His persistence continued until I caved in and started taking his calls. (I'll admit, I was a little flattered by the unrelenting attention.) I agreed to have a "talk" with him, but I made the mistake of letting him take me back to his place to have it. I did all of the talking. He just laid there, sprawled out on the bed, trying to seduce me. After I had said all I'd wanted to say (and after he had characteristically ignored all of it), the whole situation seemed kind of futile, so I had sex with him against my better judgment. We had officially resumed our affair.

And that's when the abuse spiraled out of control.

Over the course of the next couple months, he began to reveal to me his preoccupation with sadomasochism. And not in words. He started constantly choking me during sex (and sometimes before sex, as foreplay)—so tightly and prolongedly that it would hurt me to swallow for days afterward. He would grab me and smack me—he even walloped my ass once, leaving deep, unsightly bruises all over my cheeks. He liked covering my eyes, my ears, my mouth, pinning me down so I couldn't move, leaving me defenseless. He got off on making me feel genuine pain and humiliation. One time, we decided to use these plastic handcuffs that he had, but it didn't take me very long to figure out that he was more interested in making me yelp and watching my wrists bleed than he was in actually restraining me. Another time, he bit my top lip so hard that it went numb, swelled up, and left an ugly red bruise that I had to cover with dark lipstick for weeks. And as he was doing me, he would crane his head around, a full 180 degrees, and stare at himself in the mirror—I kid you not, for the *entire duration*—because I apparently wasn't enough to hold his interest myself.

His efforts to make me feel invisible were so thorough. I stopped feeling like a person entirely. I was just a vessel for his pleasure, and I accepted it, because I had no choice, I was so beaten down. I had tried telling him how the way he treated me made me feel, but it was like he didn't believe me. He was *convinced* that I secretly liked it; he'd tell me that "other girls like it," and that his job was to "bring it out of me"—even though I told him again and again how much it turned me off. I couldn't accept that it was just a miscommunication, because I was constantly struggling against him. The problem was, that's exactly how he liked it.

He also continued his attempts to sodomize me. He would try to physically force my head down onto him, and when I struggled, he yelled: "Come *on*, don't waste my time!" He then began anally raping me. I would scream, and I would cry, and I would push against him—but he just held me down and said, "Shh ... shh ..." as he thrusted. He did always stop ... eventually.

Now, I know what you're thinking. Why did I keep going back? But it was so hard to believe that I was being abused. "Victim" seemed like the antithesis of everything I thought I was. So I hid it, even from myself. And I *tried* to like it. He convinced me that there was something *wrong* with me for not being into it. I already felt worthless, subhuman, and ashamed, so the only way I could see to stop feeling those things was to try my best to obey him. It was my attempt at reclaiming my agency over the situation, I guess. And believe it or not, this is the kind of mentality that keeps hundreds of thousands of people in abusive relationships *all the time*. Judgment won't fix the problem, but creating a safe space for victims to talk freely about what happens behind closed doors just might.

One night, it all became too much. I completely broke down on him. And maybe it wouldn't have happened if I hadn't been tipsy, but I had come to realize that it was so much easier for me to be with him after a couple of drinks. That slight disassociation helped me get through it. I had had some vodka, and he tried to penetrate me anally again. When I fought back, he caught me in a stranglehold and ordered me to jerk him off, saying that only then would he let me go. I struggled *furiously*. He was just too strong. Eventually, I threatened to elbow him in the balls, and he hesitated for a second and let me go. And then he yelled at me. He actually *castigated* me for taking it so seriously, for always ruining his fun. "It's just role play!" he argued. How was I supposed to know that? I started weeping, telling him that I was so depressed, that I could not remember what it felt like to be happy, and that I needed his help.

He looked at me like I was crazy, and after hearing me out, he confessed that he thought I was just too emotional for him, too insecure, and too much work for too little reward.

So I was at my lowest of lows. I picked my clothes up off the floor and dolefully started putting them back on. He asked me where I was going, and I told him I was leaving, that I didn't want to be a chore, so it was over. As he drove me home, we kept talking about what had gone wrong. He claimed to not have known that I didn't like it. I said that I distinctly remembered telling him so—on at least three separate occasions. He then declared that he could only remember me saying it once. "Wouldn't that have been *enough* times?" I replied. But he maintained that it was all just one huge misunderstanding. And I didn't know what else to think besides: Yes, he *must* be right.

When I got out of his car, I said, "I'm sorry ... for ..." but I didn't know how to finish the sentence, and he just waved it away. Then he told me that I could call him anytime I wanted. As soon as I was out of his sight, I erupted into tears and wept all night. When I woke up the next morning, I felt as if someone had died. (Possibly me?) I couldn't get out of bed, so I didn't. I checked my phone, and there was a text message from Doc: "Sory for last night. I misunderstood u and did the wrong role play." I thought about that for a long time and ended up blaming myself, yet again, for what had happened. I concluded that I just didn't understand the rules, and that I should have known better.

The next day, I wrote Doc a ridiculously self-deprecating Facebook message, apologizing for being a "whiny, needy, stupid little bitch" and thanking him for "trying to tolerate me." I took full responsibility for not realizing that the abuse was a "game" (rather than blaming *him* for not obtaining consent before initiating it). And then I went to New Orleans for spring break with my family. It was the most depressed I could remember being. I was in a constant state of crying, and the distance didn't lift my spirits the way I thought it might. When I came back to campus, Doc started texting me, pressuring me to come see him. I felt completely resigned to this vicious cycle that I couldn't seem to escape. Naturally, I caved.

He picked me up that night. On the way back to his place, he stopped to get some food, and while I sat in his parked car, I considered making a run for it. Let *him* feel rejection and isolation for a change. But I didn't, because ... where would I go? This was the only Place in my entire world, it seemed. Everything else that had ever existed for me was from another *life* ago. So I sat tight, and I waited for him to come back for me.

Once we were in his bedroom, I reminded him that I was on my period, and he said, "I know. I like blood." Then he attacked me. He had sex with me in that way that I hated—right after I had explicitly asked him not to—where he would wrap his arms around my head, bury my face into his chest, and just pound, inhumanly. I started crying and pushing against his chest. That, of course, didn't stop him; it never did. So I screamed at him to stop. He did. And he yelled, "*Why* do you *always* have to *ruin the sex?*"

I guess I had some fight in me on this particular night, because I retorted, "What, you'd rather I wait until you've *come* before I tell you I don't like it?" And then he yelled, "Yes!"—without a *hint* of irony, I assure you. I was appalled by what I was hearing. I had always assumed that there was some shred of humanity in him, and that he just hid it really well. He had never spelled his malice out so bluntly ever before, but that's apparently what I needed in order to figure it out. The fight escalated, and at one point, I smacked him in the jaw. I was kind of disappointed by how weak the blow was, but his reaction was priceless. He actually tried to argue that he didn't deserve it, that he had done "nothing" to me. I laughed and explained the irony of the situation to him, and he then tried to deny that he—a *self-proclaimed sadist*—had ever caused me physical pain. I was beyond delirious by this point. Hysterical. I said, "You plead ignorance every time you want to avoid the problem!" And he said, "That's just how you want to interpret it."

I realized then that this conversation—the one I had been trying to resolve with him for a *year* now—was utterly futile. As I was clearly giving up, he decided to try to be cuddly and sweet with me. I shoved him off the bed in disgust, and when he got up and I shifted up onto my knees to reset the balance—*he cowered.* I know, I know, it was wrong of me to be forceful with him (and I certainly am not condoning it). But the feeling I had in that moment, when the power seemed finally reversed—when finally *he* could feel the fear he made *me* feel (if only for a moment)—was so spectacular that I couldn't help but revel in it.

Eventually, I walked out on him, but he told me to wait so he could give me a ride home. I allowed that, and the whole time he was getting dressed, he tried to make it seem as though this ending was his idea. It was pathetic. And for once, I could see that clearly, that's what he was all along. That night and the next morning, I felt *ecstatic*. I had ended it, and I felt sure that it was for the last time. I wasn't happy, but I felt this *energy* that had been dormant for so long. It was mostly fueled by anger, and I could tell that's all it was, but I was resolved to hold onto it for as long as possible.

That summer, I turned 20. I also started working out, because I had heard that exercise is supposed to help deal with depression. I worked out—all day, every day—to the point where it was seriously excessive.

Unfortunately, it didn't help. I was still having depressive episodes every night, and sometimes even during my workouts. I surmised that this might have had something to do with why I was depressed to begin with. I felt that I was playing right into the hands of the societal beauty standard that had driven me into having body image issues in the first place—and moreover, the thought of being even *more* attractive to my rapist made me sick to my stomach.

Date Rape

Back at school, I finally moved into an apartment off campus. I tried to keep up my exercise routine, but since I was out of my parents' house, my anorexia was able to thrive uncontested, so I could barely do 20 minutes of yoga a day without feeling faint. Unhealthy, I know, but it sure made me look amazing.

And I wasn't the only one who noticed. There was a man who worked in the student union who was pretty keen on me. Grumpy* had been hitting on me for about a year already, but starting the September of my junior year—he started laying it on really thick. I thought that, even though I didn't want to have sex ever again, maybe sleeping with someone else would turn Doc into a distant memory for me. So one afternoon, Grumpy suggested we get dinner sometime. I gave him my number, and he called me that night. I learned that he was 34 years old, divorced with kids, working two jobs. One of his kids was a daughter, which made me feel relieved, because I thought that that would have conditioned him to be more respectful toward women.

I was wrong.

The first night we spent together, he was having some trouble maintaining an erection, so he tried to get me to have anal *and* oral sex with him. I said no. Then, at several intervals throughout the remainder of the evening, he said things like, "Ugh, I wish you'd sucked it!" He also made a lot of comments, suggesting that I had so much to learn, and that he was going to "teach me." It was the same condescension I received from Doc on various occasions, and it really made me feel uncomfortable and small—and somewhat threatened.

We talked on the phone a couple of times after that night. During one of our conversations, he kept ragging on me about the oral sex thing, saying, "I really wish you'd done that other thing that I like ..." So I bitterly and disingenuously replied, "Sorry." He replied, "It's all right, I'm not going to rush you." How considerate. That comment *really* ticked me off. So I angrily answered, "Well, if you're only staying with me because you're hoping I'll change, then that's not a very good reason, and you know it." His brilliant response? "Oh, quiet, woman! Don't start with that!" (Where do I even begin to unpack that one?) As soon as I hung up, I crawled up into the fetal position and had another typical breakdown, replete with tears and suicidal thoughts. He called me back twice that night. I didn't answer.

The next night we saw each other, I asked him to pick up a bottle of Captain Morgan's on his way to my place (as I wasn't old enough as of yet to buy it myself), and I said I would pay him back as soon as he came over. We started having sex for a while, but I really wasn't feeling into it. I stopped him and took a couple of swigs of rum, and he commented: "Yeah, baby, drink up. Maybe if you get drunk enough, you'll do something *else* ..."

So much for "I'm not going to rush you."

The next thing I knew, I woke up alone and naked at 5 a.m., my makeup smeared all over my face and my sheets, both my pillows mysteriously out of their cases. I had the worst hangover I had ever experienced in my life, and there was vomit all over the bathroom floor. But the worst of it was that there were two blurry, brief snapshots of memories playing and replaying in my head: one of his penis in my mouth, and the other one of me running to the bathroom with the intention of puking. That was it. That was all I could remember.

I texted Grumpy and told him that I totally blacked out and was wondering what in the world had happened. It took him three days to call me back. When he did, he told me that I started going down on him (he didn't mention the level of coercion or force that it took to get me to that point, but I can imagine), but that I had to stop as soon as I began bawling and talking about my abusive ex-lover.

The next day, I went by the student union to give him the money he said I still owed him, and he insisted that we needed to talk. He said he'd call me later. I told him not to bother, but he was determined to. When he called me, it was just to say that he really enjoyed me sucking him off the other night before I stopped.

In the midst of all of this drama, Doc texted me. I distinctly remember entertaining the thought that I kind of missed him. I tried going out into the real world and having a sexual experience without him, and that was a complete disaster, too. At least Doc was capable of not talking about blowjobs for five seconds. And the more I thought about it, the better I managed to convince myself that everything that had been wrong with my relationship with Doc was my fault, that he had only been trying to help me explore my sexuality. So I decided to text him back.

I told Grumpy I no longer wanted to see him. When he asked me why, I said that it was because I couldn't give him what he wanted. He essentially hung up on me, but a couple days later, I saw him at the student union, and he said that he missed me. I explained very thoroughly how the way he was pressuring me to give him head made me uncomfortable, but he just tried to deny that he had been doing any such thing. I got frustrated trying to talk sensibly to him, so I just walked away.

The next day, I ran into Doc. We had a nice, light-hearted conversation, and started texting again. Which led to us seeing each other again. And to be honest, it felt different this time. Mostly because I had come to the conclusion that I was a terrible lover, that I brought absolutely nothing to the table, and so I figured I would just let Doc do whatever he wanted to me— no matter how it made me feel—because I figured I owed him that much for all the hell I'd put him through.

I sunk even lower into depression during this period. I remember distinctly feeling as though I was the embodiment of the walking dead. The only time I ever felt remotely alive was when I was with Doc because I had been reduced to nothing more than his sex toy. I had no other purpose.

I've always considered this phase of our relationship to be one where he didn't actually rape me, but that's only because I stopped fighting back. He had drained all of the fight out of me by this point, and I was just a hollow shell of the person I used to be.

Someone else came into the picture around this same time. I met Happy* through my student group. He was a grad student as well, a self-proclaimed feminist, and we had been good friends for almost a year by the time we slept together. As soon as we got to his bedroom, he started making a move to go down on me, but I stopped him. When he asked me why, I said that it was because I wasn't comfortable reciprocating. He said that that was fine, that he just wanted to make me feel good. I said, "Then just fuck me." So he did. I ended up walking out on him for no good reason that night. I still to this day don't understand why I did it. Maybe I was afraid to be with someone who would treat me with respect. Maybe I just wasn't ready for it. Maybe I didn't think that I deserved it. Who knows.

Alas, I felt guilty about what I'd done, so the next time I went over to his place, I naturally brought him a homemade pie as atonement. But before that happened, I saw Doc for one last time.

He told me to get on top of him, so I did, and I rode him till he came. Then he turned on the porn channel on his TV and made me watch it, making comments like, "Ooh, yeah, that's such a great position, we should do that, it's so relaxing, mmm . . ." It made me feel sick. I suddenly wondered what I was even doing there, with this man who made me feel so terrible and objectified and shamed me for not being kinky enough. I just closed my eyes and waited for it to be over. At one point, he asked me to give him a massage, so I did. And I stayed the night and hoped he would have sex with me in the morning (because that was usually the routine, and he hadn't even touched me all night), but when we woke up the next morning, he ignored his morning wood and said he had to leave to go to an appointment.

I left and cried all the way home. Suddenly, the words that my best friend (and confidante) had uttered more than a year ago popped into my head. In the beginning, when Doc had first begun to sexually abuse me, she had said to me: "Cassy . . . you will know when you've had enough." As I walked home that morning after seeing Doc, it became all too clear to me: I had had *enough*. It really was over this time. That was indisputable. So I skipped all my classes that day because I was too busy lying in bed listlessly and falling apart.

And that was the last time I ever slept with Doc. (No, *really*.) I still ignore his calls and refuse to acknowledge him when he approaches me on the street.

A week or so later, I slept with Happy again. He was incredibly sweet and respectful, which was still throwing me for a loop. But at one point, we were laying in his bed, talking, and I saw that he was hard. He started stroking himself and he gave me this look, and I just knew what he was going to say before he said it: "I know you're not into it, but... I really wish you would taste my cock." I scoffed and turned away from him. He quickly realized I was genuinely upset and said he was only kidding. I still couldn't look at him. So he stroked my arm and said, "I'm not going to force you to do anything you don't want to do. You know me. Have I ever been that kind of person?" I concurred that no, he wasn't. So he said, "Then why would I do that?" But I didn't know how to answer that. It was such a good question. Why would anyone do that? I still don't know.

We lay in silence for a long time. Eventually, he fell asleep, but I just stared at the wall for hours, wishing I could just be someone else. Why did I have to be me? Would I ever be able to satisfy anyone? It seemed that no matter how much I gave, men were always going to be pushing me for something more. Sex was going to be a constant tug-of-war for me, forever. Why couldn't I just be enough? We had sex again in the morning, and it was very pleasant. But I couldn't un-know the fact that he couldn't accept me the way that I was, and I hated how much I resented him for that.

Needless to say, he never called me after that. I understood why. After all, it was completely his prerogative whether to sleep with me or not. And in a way, it was kind of refreshing to meet a guy who wasn't going to just continue seeing me with the intention of trying to change me. But what hurt was that he completely wrote me off. I had sent him a few scattered, platonic text messages over the next couple months, but he never replied to them. It seemed to me as though I wasn't just useless to him as a lover, but I was useless to him as a friend as well. (We are now on friendly terms.) This realization didn't help. I once again resolved to never have sex again, and continued to break down at every opportunity, because I apparently wasn't worth a single, solitary damn.

Relationship Violence

After winter break, when I returned to campus, I began frequenting the Starbucks in which I had first met up with Doc, because I was hoping I would see him pass by. I didn't want to start up again with him, but I had this unshakable, nonsensical desire to see him, watch him. I was fascinated by how positively normal he looked, just walking around in downtown Evanston, Ill. No one seemed to understand as they passed by him that he was dangerous—a sadistic criminal—and I felt like I was the only one who knew.

There was this regular at Starbucks who took a liking to me. Bashful* was a 39-year-old graphic designer and "rapper" with a patch of short, yellow dreadlocks on top of his head. He started chatting me up, and I was very short with him. Whenever it got to the point when I had to adamantly request that he leave me alone, he would pull the line, "I just want to be friends; it's so hard to find friends in this town." which quickly escalated into, "What, you don't want to make friends? What's wrong with you that you don't want friends?" (I learned later that he had evidently been banned from several coffee establishments in the area on the grounds of having repeatedly sexually harassed women.) I told him straight off that I wasn't interested, that I hated sex, that I wasn't any good at it, that I had a long history of sexual abuse, and that I didn't give blowjobs.

And somehow *none* of this deterred him.

I wasn't flattered; I was annoyed. He badgered me for my number over and over, and I refused him again and again. We continued to run into each other all over town for the next week or so—I was almost convinced he was stalking me. After a while, I got exhausted from the pursuit and gave him my phone number, figuring that it would only take a night or two of actually being intimate with me for him to realize I had nothing to offer him. At least he offered to do a liquor run for me, which was the only upside.

I went over to his place, and we started talking and drinking. I remember him saying something like, "Man, I can't *wait* for you to get drunk—you're so insecure and shit!" He also mentioned that his drug dealer (Dopey*) and another friend were coming over to bring him some "herbs" and would stay for a while to smoke it with us. So that happened. Dopey turned out to be really attractive and exponentially more charming and interesting than Bashful, so I spent most of my time on the couch talking to him.

Needless to say, I ended up getting *thoroughly* crunk. So crunk that I somehow found myself sitting on Bashful's bed alone with Dopey, making out. I remember entertaining the thought that maybe the three of these men were planning to gang-bang me or something, but I was too intoxicated to make my body catch up with my thoughts enough to make a run for it. Things started escalating, and I noticed how not in control of my body I was. My panties eventually came off, and Dopey was poised to enter me when Bashful knocked on the door. We scrambled to make it look like nothing had been happening, but Bashful took one look at us and he knew. He started screaming at Dopey and kicked him and his friend out of the apartment—but not before Dopey managed to get my phone number. Throughout all of the commotion, I stood alone in Bashful's room, terrified. I didn't know if this man was violent, and somewhere in my mind behind all of the cloudiness that the drugs had created, I was aware that I had just committed one of the worst cardinal sins of dating. I could only think of one way to avoid retribution for my actions, so I undressed and climbed into his bed and waited. (I remember hearing Dopey, as he was leaving the apartment, say to Bashful, "Hey, man, respect. Respect, man. Respect.") Bashful and I had sex, and I felt terrible afterward. I was more paranoid from the drugs than I ever had been before and I could feel my hangover coming already. At one point, after Bashful went to sleep, I tried to make a run for it—I grabbed the bottle of Malibu that I had paid for and left the room, but panicked once I noticed there was a night guard working at the front desk and I was underage. I went back, but the door had locked behind me, so I called Bashful, and he opened the door—confused as to why I had left in the first place—and we stayed up all night yelling at each other.

Dopey texted me a bunch after that, and we ended up getting together. In the texts, he had told me how "fun" he thought I was, so I figured I couldn't ever let him see me sober. It took us over a month to actually have sober sex for the first time, and looking back on it, I guesstimate that over the course of the nine months we spent together, about 84 percent of the sex we had was when at least one of us (usually both) was inebriated.

At first, it was really fun. He was incredibly charming upfront, and I was always drunk, so that really took the edge off.

It didn't take long for me to discover that Dopey had just as much of an anal fixation as Doc had. Right after I refused to go down on him, he tried to pressure me into having anal with him. I said that we could *try* it, and it was the first time I had ever experienced it with lube, but the pain was still too much, and I couldn't bear the physical flashback that brought me back to being raped by Doc, so I told him to stop, and he did.

Before we saw each other next, though, I felt that I had to clear up my boundaries explicitly, to give him a chance to think critically about whether he wanted to continue our affair or not. So I sent him the following text message: "Listen, I just want to make sure we're clear on my boundaries. I'm not going to change my mind about anal/oral, so if that's not okay with you, I don't want to make you come all the way over here just to be disappointed. It's your choice, and I wouldn't hold it against you if you're not getting the sexual gratification you need from me and decide you don't want to keep seeing me. But if you do want to, I need to feel secure in that you're not going to try to push me past my limits. It's fine whatever you decide, but please, be honest, that's all I ask."

He said he definitely wanted us to keep seeing each other. Who knows if he had really thought it through, but at least now, he wouldn't be able to claim ignorance if he tried to take advantage of me.

The next time we got together, I learned that he had a "fatty fetish." Like, it wasn't just that he preferred "women with meat on their bones"— he actually watched porn of morbidly obese women. I didn't know how to feel about it at first. Was liking me solely on the basis of my body type really any different in theory than *rejecting* me based solely on my body type?

As soon as he picked up on the fact that I was anorexic, he would encourage me to eat whenever he was around. It still wasn't terribly healthy, because he did tell me that he would prefer that I put *on* weight (and that's sort of just as uncouth as telling someone to lose weight, if you think about it), so I ended up *over*eating and that's sort of just the equal/opposite problem as starving oneself.

But being with him really altered my self-image in an unexpected way. When I would look in the mirror, suddenly I was seeing myself through the eyes of someone who was *more* attracted to fat women than to skinny women, and so instead of thinking of myself as beautiful *despite* my body, I was thinking of myself as beautiful *because* of my body. And it was a really nice change.

On the other hand, I started getting a sadistic vibe from him. He was so hard to read, though, because he was constantly backpedaling and changing his views based on my reaction to whatever he said. But one thing I remember vividly was when we were sitting on my bed, listening to some music. He turned to me, and with a sick, twisted smile on his face, he said,

"Do you like sex and violence?" I totally froze. I panicked, my heartbeat accelerated, and I couldn't speak. I only had the wherewithal to shake my head. He could tell that I freaked out a bit, so he apologized and said he shouldn't have said anything. I tried to just forget about it, but I felt really afraid all of a sudden. Like, here I thought this might be someone I could begin healing with, but what if he turned out to be just another monster?

A few times during sex, he even put his hands around my neck. He stopped doing it each time I removed them. But just the thought that he wanted to do that to me—and that he didn't ask first or anything—made me feel uncomfortable. (Even to this day, when a man I'm sleeping with even so much as *asks* if I'm into such-and-such-a-thing-that-traumatized-me, I can't help but go into "fight, flight or freeze" mode. I'm getting better at dealing with it, but it's a huge internal struggle every time.) I stifled that fear for the time being. After all, I could've just been being paranoid, and he hadn't actually done anything to hurt me—yet.

As time went on, I learned more and more about him. He revealed to me in confidence that he was an illegal immigrant, that his mother had abandoned him when he was just a child, and that he slept on the floor of his stepfather's flat, where he lived with his little brother and sister. He also mentioned that his stepfather charged him for storage. I felt so deeply for him when I heard all of that, that I offered him my bed to sleep in whenever he needed it, and said that he could keep some of his stuff in my room because I wouldn't charge him (and my inner girl squealed *so hard* the first time he ever left his flannel pajama bottoms at my place—it was just the most adorable thing that had ever happened in my *life, OMG*).

At first, he was very careful not to take advantage of that offer (he said he wanted to "respect my space"). But one night, his stepfather kicked him out, and so he brought all of his stuff over piece by piece and somehow wound up living in my apartment. It was never an official transition. I didn't even realize what was happening until it occurred to me that he had essentially "moved in." It was so clever. Especially when he got fired from his job. I said that I would support him while he found a new one. The thought occurred to me that he was just using me, but I convinced myself that I was only suspecting that because of my trust issues, and told myself that perhaps it was time for me to just relax for a change.

As for the sex, it started triggering me on a regular basis. He only really liked doing it from behind (which I had negative associations with), and he was always chastising me for touching him too much, but he never gave me the affection I needed in return to console me for the sex I didn't enjoy. Once again, I was too afraid to ask for it most of the time because I had been conditioned by Doc to keep my needs to myself.

It wasn't as if I refrained from trying to communicate my feelings at all to him. It's just that every time I expressed even the slightest feminist thought (e.g., "We're supposed to be an equal partnership, we should both be making compromises"), he would reply with a harsh, "Chill out!" That would always make me retreat into myself to fume in isolation.

It was an effective silencing technique that he utilized often.

But when I was drunk, I really loved being with him. Looking back, I feel as though liquor was the adhesive for our entire relationship. And at the same time, its demise.

One night I skipped a concert I really wanted to go to so that I could spend time with Dopey. It turned out to be a very ironic mistake. My roommates were home that night, and right as Dopey and I were about to have sex, he said, "Be quiet, though, because you're really loud and I hate that." He could tell that comment made me a little bit despondent, so he amended: "I mean, I hate that they can hear us." So we started doing it doggy-style, and he took his phone out to videotape me. I tried to keep the noise level down, but some moans still managed to escape. He got really frustrated and said, "Come *on!*" and cupped his hand around my mouth, pounding into me angrily and repeatedly shushing me. I was immediately triggered.

He was getting off on oppressing me. He was getting *angry* at me for enjoying myself, so I simply stopped enjoying myself.

So I just closed my eyes, held my breath, and waited for it to be over. Afterward, I curled up into a ball, trembling and silently weeping, and I guess he just decided not to say anything.

That night when we had sex, he "accidentally" put it in my ass, and I had to run to the bathroom to cry.

About a week or so went by, and I guess he started to pick up on the fact that my episodes were actually indicative of something, so he started trying to pull it out of me.

One afternoon, we were sitting on my bed, taking about movies, and he asked me if I'd ever seen *Eternal Sunshine of the Spotless Mind*. I had. He asked me if I would ever do that—erase someone from my memory. I immediately thought of Doc, and said yes, I would. He asked me why. I said, "Because I'd be a different person." How, he wondered. "I'd be happy." We kept talking, and he kept probing. He said that maybe, if I talked about it, I'd feel better. That I'd realize that what happened to me wasn't my fault, and that it wasn't personal. I told him that realizing that doesn't make the trauma go away. Then he told me, "Maybe that's why I'm here—to help you." But I told him I didn't want that to be the relationship. That I didn't need him to sit there and tell me how to feel, that I needed to go through my process if I was ever going to heal. He said, "I understand." And I said, "Thank you. That's all I want from you."

The conversation moved on, but I could feel the tears coming, so I just proceeded to pound the beer I was drinking to try to achieve enough numbness to the point where I wouldn't care anymore. It didn't work, so I eventually excused myself to the bathroom so that I could weep in private. When I came back, he asked if I was OK, and I lied and said I was.

He said, "I *need* to fuck you in your butthole."

I replied, "Then you'll have to find yourself another girl."

So he said, "I guess I do, in that regard."

I felt like he was just kicking me while I was down, so I said, "Fuck you," and got really moody and quiet. He got fed up with my attitude and got up to leave—and that's when I realized that I had to tell him. I wasn't going to allow this to happen again. I had lost Happy because I hadn't spoken up, and now I was going to lose Dopey the same way.

So through choked tears, I said, "I was anally raped, OK? Repeatedly." He said he was sorry, but started leaving anyway. Said that he needed to "get his mind off of that now." I started crying harder and told him that he *should* see someone else, because I knew I wouldn't be able to sexually satisfy him. He said that he *was* sexually satisfied, kissed me, and left. I erupted. I wept for literally five hours straight. It was scary. I couldn't believe that he would break me down like that and not even stick around to pick up the pieces. When he came back that night, he said, "I want to apologize to you about earlier, what I said. I didn't mean to offend you. And I'm sorry." I said it was OK, and we dropped it. Of course, it wasn't OK, but I was so emotionally drained, I didn't know where to take it from there. That night, before we went to sleep, he said, "Just don't fall in love with me, OK?"

What the hell? Where did that even come from?

I asked what he meant, and he said that he cared about me, but love was just a touchy subject for him right now and he didn't want to "break my heart."

After that, we went back to being adorable together. He even started kissing me in public, which was weird. But OK, I figured I'd just go with the flow.

But then weeks later, he brought a movie over for us to watch together that was set in prison. I asked him if there was any anal rape in it and he said, "No, but if you're into that, there are a couple of websites we could look at."

?!

I responded to that by asking him why he had to be such an a-hole.

He laughed and asked me why I couldn't be more "open-minded."

That made me furious. I reminded him that I'd *had* anal sex. He asked me how it was. What?! "You *know*," I said. "You already know—I told you!" And he said, "Geez, chill out, look, I'm sorry if you had a bad experience or something." I couldn't believe what I was hearing. Why was he acting like I hadn't told him? I was in shock. He then told me that he didn't remember me telling him anything and apologized for his "bad memory." More shock. So he said, "What—were you raped or something?" Yes, I said, repeatedly—"I *told* you!" He said he was sorry that happened to me, and that he wished he had been there to "kick his ass."

A week later, he dropped the L-bomb.

I didn't know what he meant at first. I assumed he just meant that he "appreciated" me for taking such good care of him (after all, I was giving him a place to sleep and paying for all of his expenses, which became a huge issue over time, and it eventually got to the point where whenever I refused to pay for something he wanted, he would punish me for it emotionally).

I hesitated and reciprocated the sentiment.

One afternoon, we had a big fight that came out of nowhere. He said he felt like a burden on me and said he was going to leave—but at the time, I didn't want him to. We ended up confessing our "love" for each other, and started saying it on a regular basis. We also sort of established ourselves as an actual "couple." I'd never had a boyfriend before, but I thought that it would be a good experiment—especially since I had been so wounded by casual relationships in the past, that I thought maybe this would help. Maybe "love" would help.

For a while, it was really nice. But man, my depression was really starting to bum him out. It was around this time that I realized that it was no way to live. For the first time, my illness was affecting someone *else* and not just me. I knew I needed Real Help if I was going to be in this relationship. But I didn't know how, or if I was ready. So I just upped my dosage of alcohol for the time being.

Eventually, I was able to bring myself to make an appointment with the university's counseling services. The intake that I had to do over the phone was so stressful, I locked myself in the bathroom with a glass of wine in the middle of the afternoon crying while I regaled the staff member with my story. When I went in for my appointment, they told me I'd have better luck at the Women's Center, because they specialized in sexual assault trauma and would offer me more sessions. But the strength that it took me just to do that first intake was so draining, I decided to put off calling the Women's Center.

I started drinking *biblically*. I would start drinking as soon as I woke up each morning, and I kept drinking until I passed out each night. It became a routine. Drunkenness became the closest state to happiness that I was capable of achieving, and so I needed spirits in order to keep my spirits up.

Throughout all this, Dopey continued to tell me that I was enough—more than enough—and that he loved me.

Pretty soon, it was July 4th—the day before my 21st birthday. My friends and I were having a BBQ get-together, and at this get-together, there was this girl who Dopey clearly was into. She spoke Spanish and was, like, three times my size. I knew that Dopey was instantly attracted to her, but I tried to stifle my inadequacies as much as possible so I could enjoy my night. As the party progressed, however, I got more and more drunk, and Dopey spent all of his time sitting on the couch, talking to this girl. At one point, I asked him to dance with me to a song that was playing, and he refused. I was really inebriated, and really wounded, so I went into my friend's apartment to cry. A bunch of my friends found me, and it was kind of embarrassing. Eventually, the girl came up and saw me, and I drunkenly pleaded with her not to sleep with my boyfriend. She said she would never do that. I told her that I trusted her—it was *him* I didn't trust. She went back outside to tell Dopey I was in the kitchen crying, so he came inside and retrieved me. He told me I was being ridiculous for feeling threatened by that other girl, that I had "nothing to worry about," and so we went home and had really rowdy sex. I woke up the next morning, on my 21st birthday, with a hangover. All Dopey said to me about the night before was, "Take it easy on the alcohol, OK? You get really emotional." I still felt that I had had every reason to cry.

The next time we fought was when a friend of mine from out of town was staying on my living room couch. When Dopey and I went to bed that night, he looked really upset, so I asked him what the matter was. He said, "I just don't feel satisfied in certain aspects." *UGH*. I couldn't believe we were having this conversation *again*. He would say it was OK, but then he'd just bring it up again. I scoffed at him, rolled off onto my side and said, "Aagghh, I want to kill myself."

He said, "That's very selfish of you to say."

"But I'm telling you that that's the way it makes me feel," I replied.

He paused for a moment and said, "You're not for me."

It was such crap. Mere hours before this, while we were out on the town together, I mentioned to him that he was my first boyfriend, and he said, "Hopefully, the last!" I didn't take that comment seriously, but come *on*, what was with all the mind games? How could he build me up like that just to tear me down?

I asked him, "Can I tell you something true? The sight of an erect penis really frightens me." That took a lot of strength for me to say. My track record regarding talking to men about the effects of my sexual-assault trauma was not very good, and I was so ashamed of the reality of the situation to begin with, that most of the time, I kept it bottled up inside of me.

His response? "Then you should find yourself a lesbian."

Rage. That is an insult to all lesbians and sexual-assault survivors everywhere. That's just not how sexuality works. So that made me really upset. Eventually, *he* broke down crying, saying that the problem wasn't me; he just missed his mom so much. This was a classic Dopey defense. Every time we fought, he'd play the abandonment card. It took me a while to realize it, but his entire search for a girlfriend was really just his way of trying to fill a mother-sized hole in his heart. Or maybe it was all just a clever ruse to evoke sympathy from people so they would give him what he wanted.

Whatever it was, I fell for it. Hard.

Especially this time.

I ended up giving him head.

I went under the covers to do it, because I knew that was the only way I'd be able to manage. I asked him if he was about to leave me, and he said no. "Even if I can't do this?" I asked. Again, he said no. I could only hope that he meant that, because as far as I was concerned, my life was on the line—or what was left of it, at least. I still felt humiliated as I did it, and immediately afterward, I spiraled into an *insufferable* depressive episode. I jumped in the shower as soon as it was over and wept. When I went back into the room, before he could say anything, I invoked "tiredness" and asked if we could just not talk about it. He agreed and went to sleep.

But I couldn't sleep. I was having a complete meltdown. My thoughts were cacophonous and disturbing. I sat on the floor with my computer and tried to distract myself, but I couldn't focus on *anything* except the unrelenting, abusive racket inside my head.

In the morning, he left to go for a bike ride. I started thinking: Maybe if I could just make myself get *used* to giving head, it wouldn't be such a big deal anymore. It wouldn't ruin my relationships anymore. It wouldn't be the cause of my self-loathing anymore. Maybe this could be my chance to heal, I thought. But just the *thought* of doing it made me fall apart.

About a week later, I decided to go down on him—of my own accord. I thought that if I did it without him pressuring me, maybe I wouldn't feel so awful. I was able to face him afterward at least, so that was a good development.

A little while later, though, he said he wanted to do it doggy-style, so we did, but he was really rough, and I cried throughout most of it. He didn't notice, and I couldn't bring myself to stop him. I kept hearing Doc's words in my head, admonishing me because if I ever stopped a man before he came, I'd be "ruining the sex" or "taking it too seriously" and I should just learn to "relax." After I emerged from the bathroom, where I had gone to stop crying and recollect myself, I asked Dopey timidly if it was alright if we set some time aside sometime to work on my ever-elusive orgasm. I was so unbelievably nervous to even bring it up. He said absolutely, that he was sorry he had been so selfish, he just didn't know what to do, and he said we could try it any time I wanted. He said he needed me to walk him through it, though.

The problem was, I wasn't sure if I could. I didn't really know *what* I liked because I was in a constant state of dreading the things I knew I *didn't* like—and that was all that sex had ever been for me. I was always on defense. I had never been given the opportunity to explore my sexuality *for myself;* I was just being constantly dragged along for the ride.

That night, I still cried myself to sleep. The embarrassment I felt for being so afraid to tell him how I felt completely consumed me. I was so ashamed of my reticence that stemmed from the words of Doc again, rattling around inside my head, telling me that I was "too much work," "high-maintenance," "not worth it." I *knew* that these were ghosts that only existed in my head. But I had no idea how to release them.

Soon it was finally September, so classes had started up again (it was my final year at Northwestern). I also ended up going to the College Feminists' BBQ that month and speaking with a representative from the Women's Center about getting myself a counseling appointment, and I was able to do an intake that same day. Finally, I was going to be getting Real Help.

The lows got even lower and more frequent, and the highs became even fewer and farther between. Dopey started verbally abusing me on a regular basis. Whenever we had an argument, he just resorted to name-calling (mainly "bitch" and "cunt"), and then, of course, he'd always apologize later and tell me he didn't mean it.

He also became irrationally jealous and started accusing me of cheating on him with every guy I spoke to. I started actively trying to take some time apart from Dopey during this stage, but every time I brought it up, he would threaten me with violence and self-harm/suicide. By this point, I was suspecting him of harboring some mental illnesses of his own, and he seemed clearly to be on hard drugs again. But I had no idea what to do about it—especially since I was always caught in the crossfire of his episodes, which made it extremely difficult for me to react with compassion. What's more, he always managed to hide his abusive behavior so well from everyone outside of our relationship. The only times he would lash out at me were when we were alone. It was my word against his, and he was such an experienced manipulator. I didn't stand a chance. He also seemed to wait to pick a fight until we were about to leave to go someplace. Like this one time, I tried to justify certain post-traumatic behaviors I was exhibiting by telling him more about my rape, and he said, "You weren't really raped. If you really hadn't wanted it, you could have stopped it." As soon as I heard that, I told him we *needed* to break up—that I simply couldn't be with someone who thought like that. Unfortunately, we were on our way over to one of my friend's apartments for a shindig when we had this conversation, so the argument was cut short, and thus, forgotten after a while.

The next morning, he actually had the nerve to ask me for a blowjob. I told him I had promised myself that I wasn't going to go down on him again until he reciprocated. He said he would have reciprocated right then and there if I hadn't been on my period. (How convenient for him.) And then he continued to plead for a blowjob until I felt like I had no choice. So I did it. It was a pretty low moment for me, considering everything he had already put me through. Pretty soon, we started talking seriously about oral sex and why he refused to go down on me. At first, he said he was just "bad at it." I assured him that I would never know the difference, since it had never happened to me before.

The next time we talked about it, though, he said he just didn't like the way my vagina smelled, and he told me he wasn't going to reciprocate oral unless I started douching.

The next time we fought about it, Dopey said he didn't care that I'd started douching, that he just didn't want to do it. So I told him that if that's the way it was going to be, I was never going to go down on him again. He said, "Fine, then can I get it from someone else?" I said, "Yeah, but we'll have to break up." For some reason, he *still* wouldn't accept those conditions. I was so confused as to what he was even holding onto. Our relationship had gone to complete and utter waste. Why didn't he just *let it die?*

I was 100 percent certain that I was going to break up with him. I just told him—sure, go fulfill your sexual needs elsewhere. Sleep with whomever you like. His response to that was just to give me the finger. (What?! He'd been asking for my permission to do that for months; why was it that when I finally granted him that, he acted as if I was being unfair?)

He completely spun out of control. He called me "weak" for "giving up" on us. I told him that he couldn't hold me hostage in this relationship without my consent, to which he retaliated by saying that I couldn't break up with him without his consent. He kept insulting and threatening me, but I continued to hold my ground so strongly that he finally realized I was being serious, so he resorted to crying and accusing me of "breaking his heart."

I could only get him to agree to *one week* of separation. After he left, he sent texts to me the rest of the night, saying he was going to kill himself, that he was drinking himself to death—just trying to guilt me into changing my mind. I replied, but mostly denied him. (And boy did it take everything that I had.) Still, I cried all night, feeling such an immense amount of guilt for putting him out on the street in the middle of the night in the cold. As a result, I didn't have a restful sleep that night either.

He came back over the next morning to pick up some things that he needed. As he was leaving, he told me he loved me. I responded with, "Take care," but as I was about to close the door, he propped it open with his hand and repeated the words, expectantly. I didn't say anything. He looked as if he was on the verge of crying. I embraced him and told him I just needed some time, and that I did care about him a lot. He nodded and left, despondent. As soon as he was gone, I wept. It wasn't the *depressed* kind of crying, but the *grief* kind of crying. I was mourning what I knew was the end. I could feel that it was over. There was no salvaging this wreckage of a relationship. It was really over. He ended up stopping by later that day, saying that he had been thinking, and that he was sorry for all the hell he'd put me through for the last few months. He promised me that there would be no more suspicions, threats or insults. I wasn't sure I believed him. I mean, we *always* made up after a big fight. He *always* promised me that things would be different. And then, inevitably, a few days later, it would hit the fan all over again. I couldn't trust him.

Days went by, and he wouldn't stop calling me. I told him that we were supposed to be on a break. He got all defensive and hurt, told me I should just go screw "my new boyfriend." I knew he was just trying to manipulate me yet again, so I tried to brush it off. Unfortunately, he always managed to weasel his way back in (he still had all his stuff at my apartment, so he was always able to find an excuse).

By the end of the week that was supposed to be our "break," one of my friends invited me over for drinks. She told me that she had heard from her roommate, who had heard from a mutual friend, who had heard from *that girl* from the July 4th BBQ, that Dopey had cheated on me with her—months ago.

I went home that night, put all of his stuff into garbage bags, and moved them to the storage unit in the basement, so he wouldn't have any legitimate reason to come into my apartment ever again. I knew that I had to do this if he was ever going to really leave.

The next morning, when he called me, I told him that I knew about how he cheated on me, that his stuff was in the basement, and that we were over. He tried to justify what had happened—saying that it was only because we had been fighting and he needed a place to sleep one night—and when that excuse didn't work, he said that it was "only a blowjob"—and when *that* excuse didn't work, he said he only did it because she told him that I was cheating on him. Such complete and utter lies.

I hung up on him, and I felt ecstatic. It was a tremendous weight that I had finally escaped out from under. My counselor, all my friends—everyone was so proud of me. And so was I. The next day, after counseling, I decided to buy a bottle of champagne to celebrate my newfound freedom. I ended up going a little overboard and drinking the entire thing. As soon as I realized I was *too* drunk, Dopey called. I wouldn't have answered it, but I was so inebriated that I did. He asked me if he could meet me somewhere to talk. He said he just needed to explain himself. I said no, but he kept badgering me, so I agreed. I knew it wasn't going to change anything, and it would've been nice to end on friendly terms with him—and did I mention I was drunk?

I went to the place we had agreed to meet, and he wasn't there. I ended up waiting—in the Midwestern cold—for a ridiculous amount of time before I decided to go into the nearest building to warm up. That's when I got a call from Dopey saying he *just* got out of work. I told him I'd been waiting for an hour. He said he was sorry and that he'd be right there. When he got there, he asked if we could go for a walk. I told him that wouldn't be necessary, and to just say whatever he needed to say and be done with it. He told me that he knew he *really* messed up, and that if he had known he was going to lose me, he never would have done it, and blah, blah, blah.

He even asked me then if we could spend just "one more night together." I laughed in his face. It was true that that sort of tactic had worked with me before (the only times I ever enjoyed having sex with him were when he was trying to make something up to me after some huge blowout we'd had), but it wasn't going to work this time. Then he beseeched me to at least sit with him for a while on the rocks by the lake. I asked him what the point of that would be. He said, "I need to walk away from this knowing that I had this time with you, that I tried." I guess I was touched, or I took pity on him or something, because I ended up granting his request. We sat on the rocks for hours. He broke down weeping, telling me how much he regretted what he did, how he was going to miss me, and he enumerated all the things he loved about me. He said he'd been sleeping in the storage unit the past few nights (a lie; he wasn't there the night before last when I threw all his stuff out).

I was being careful to keep my armor up throughout all of this. I knew he could very well just be trying to manipulate me some more, but I couldn't believe some of the things that he was saying. He told me that he realized now that he hadn't been showing me that he had my best interests at heart, that deep down he just wanted me to feel happy and free, that he would never forgive himself for making me feel trapped and controlled, and that even though he wanted me back—and that he was going to keep trying and trying and never give up—he really just wanted what was best for me, and if leaving him was going to make me happy, then he knew he'd have to accept that.

He also declared that the problem with our relationship was that he wasn't trying hard enough, but now that he had a new job, he was going to work hard, save money and prove to me that he could be independent and responsible. He then tried to reassure me that he was never after me or my money.

We held each other for a long time and cried.

After a while, he said he really wasn't looking forward to sleeping without me that night. I suggested that we could just sit out on the rocks all night together and watch the sunrise, if he wanted. He said that sounded good, but that we were going to need some beers and blankets. We went back to my apartment for those supplies (I didn't let him in, though, of course), and then we ended up sitting out on the beach together, drinking and snuggling.

I really felt that this was the right thing to do. I didn't want our relationship to go down in flames; I wanted this beautiful, peaceful, perfect end. We had been through so much together, after all. I didn't want us to go from being lovers to rivals in an instant.

Eventually, he tentatively tried to kiss me. I received it well, and then we started making out feverishly. It was kind of awesome; there was this burning desire that had never been there before (probably due to the fact that it felt a little risky and dangerous, and that he was so determined to win me over, but I didn't care about all that—it just felt *so good*). We ended up making love on the beach. He even made a move to go down on me at one point, but I stopped him because I was still spotting a little bit from my period, and I didn't want him to have to endure that.

After a while, it got way too cold, and I asked him if he just wanted to go back to my place. He said, "That is *entirely* your decision." Boy, did I love hearing that. I told him, "All right, we'll go up to my room—but it's just going to be this *one time*." He nodded in understanding. He even paid for the snacks that we got from 7-Eleven on the way back. When we got to my room, we made love again. It was pure passion. He asked me if he could take me out to breakfast the next morning. I told him I would love that. Then, we fell asleep in each other's arms.

The following day, we did end up going out for breakfast, and he did in fact pay for the meal. I was impressed by his initiative and by the fact that he actually followed through with something for a change, so I asked him if he wanted to accompany me to a movie I'd been looking forward to seeing for months, and he did. After the movie, we went back to my place for mimosas and Scrabble. I even ended up not going out with my friends that night like I had planned, because I was just having too good of a time with Dopey. I wanted to milk this weekend for everything it was worth, because he was being so wonderful to me. We made love again and watched another movie together. After that, though, we got revved up to have sex again, but from behind this time. When he entered me, it hurt, so I started crying. And then I realized: Wait a minute. We're not even *together* anymore; I don't have to put up with this! So I asked him if we could just stop and do something else instead. He reacted so sweetly and said, "Of course we can. We don't have to have sex."

He pulled me into his arms and I immediately erupted into tears. He asked me why I was so sad, and I said I didn't know. Then he told me that he loved me, and I said, through choked tears, "I guess I just . . . finally feel like you do." He held me tighter after that and said that he was all mine, and that he was going to try 120 percent to be perfect for me. I responded to that by reminding him that in the morning, it was going to have to be over. He said that he realized that. So I thanked him for the past few days. He thanked me too. Then we fell asleep.

The next morning, I had to wake up early to go to work. When we said goodbye, he told me he'd love to take me out for dinner sometime. I told him we needed to start small. He agreed, and then he left.

Even though things quickly turned to bollocks again after that, I still don't regret having done it. It was the most romantic weekend of my entire life, and while it didn't make up for the past, it gave me something nice to remember him by.

A few nights later, he asked if he could come over and "hang out." I said that I had a lot of homework to do, so we could only hang out for a little bit. When he showed up, he was high out of his mind. I had always hated seeing him like that. It was so not sexy. And he was always so much less considerate and less interesting when he was high. Needless to say, he was really getting on my nerves, so after a couple hours, I said he needed to leave so I could get back to my work.

He got all defensive and started acting all entitled to stay the night. Well, I was having none of that. I kicked him out, and then he kept me up all night sending me these really angry text messages, thanking me sarcastically for making him sleep outside in the cold rain.

Another night, he got angry that I hadn't invited him to hang out with me and my friends, so he started texting *them*, and that's when I realized this mess could potentially spin out of my control and affect other people's sanity and safety, not just mine.

The next day, when he called me, I told him he really needed to stop and just leave me alone.

He continued trying to guilt me into seeing him, threatening that he would seek revenge, trying to find ways to get his foot back in the door. I probably would've caved if it hadn't been for my counselor telling me again and again that my safety should always come first, and that if I felt the need to call the police about his harassment, then I shouldn't hesitate.

Of course, I couldn't bring myself to do that. He was an illegal immigrant, and I just couldn't do something like that to him and his family. I decided to just block his phone number instead. When he figured out I'd done that, he got a new number and started harassing me with that one, so I had to block that one, too.

He continued harassing me and even stalking me. He would go to great lengths to figure out where I was, and would habitually come by and throw pebbles at my window. To this day, I feel a jolt of terror every time I'm sitting in my room and I hear a sound reminiscent of a pebble hitting my window. Because of this, I kept the blinds closed all day long and kept all of the lights off each night. And every time I heard a skateboard or a bicycle go by, I would panic and hit the floor. I also cut off my alcohol consumption entirely, because I realized how vulnerable to attack it made me. I needed to stay sober, so that if I ever ran into him, I'd at least be thinking clearly. Eventually, I knew I had to tell my roommates about what was going on, because what if he came to the door while I wasn't there and told them some lie about why he had to come inside?

It wasn't fair that I had to live in such fear. It wasn't fair that I had to feel so unsafe *in my own home*. But that's how terrorism works. He was a terrorist, and I was a victim of terror.

It took many months for his stalking behaviors to calm down, and while there hasn't been an incident in a long time, I *still* don't feel safe in this town. I stopped feeling safe here the first time Doc ever raped me three years ago. Luckily, I'll be moving to a new environment at the end of the month, so from here on out, it's just going to be a clean break. A fresh start.

Healing

I'll admit that I made a lot of poor decisions over the past few years, and I know that my self-esteem was embarrassingly low—so embarrassingly low that it alone is enough to make me cringe at the thought of anyone reading my story. But I think it's worth noting that so much of my opinion of myself was *derived* from being traumatized, and the longer I went without support, the more vulnerable I became to attack.

If there's one thing I want you to take away from this, it's that *coercion is not consent*. If you haven't noticed, this is a pretty big issue to me. I know that it's hard to conceptualize nonviolent instances of sexual assault, since the image of rape that we've been spoon-fed our entire lives is one depicting physical manipulation, not psychological. Hopefully, though, after having read my account, you can see how *coerced* sex can be just as traumatic as *forced* sex—because, really, there's no distinction in the mind of the victim; they're just two different ways of dispossessing a person of their right to say "No." And when "no" is not an option, "yes" is meaningless.

Basically, there were five significant components to my healing process, and so I will delineate them for you now.

1. Counseling. I started counseling in September 2011. Before I was raped, I had always sort of looked down on therapy. I had it in my head that people should be able to deal with any and all of life's crises by themselves (but that was before I had ever experienced anything that I just couldn't handle on my own), and I hated the idea of paying someone to listen to me talk about my feelings. I still have reservations about the latter, actually, and if my university hadn't provided free counseling services, I may never have used that resource.

After being in counseling for nine months, all of my pessimism about the value of therapy has vanished. My counselor gave me an invaluable kind of support and validation for my experiences, and just being able to articulate the words after being silenced and shamed for so long was so unbelievably beneficial to my mental health. Sometimes, all survivors of trauma really need is to be allotted the freedom to say the words.

Moreover, because I was hyper-aware that every week, it was my duty to report back to my counselor about what had been happening with me lately—my feelings, my progress, my life events and whatnot—I found myself acting more responsibly in life. All of a sudden, there was someone else there who wanted to make sure that I was taking care of myself and actualizing the strength that I knew had to be buried deep down inside of me somewhere. And with her help and unending support, I managed to find it.

It was a little strange sometimes to catch myself thinking things like, "If I do this, how will I explain it to my counselor?" But I found that that train of thought actually helped me make smarter decisions. If I couldn't justify certain choices to my counselor—who truly *did* have my best interests at heart—then was it something I should really be doing? This mindset helped me to start asking myself the right questions and to think much harder before I acted on my impulses or resignations.

I've learned that the list of things that have triggered me over the past three years is extensive. I'd like to share it here so that you can get a better idea of how intrusive they really are to a person's day-to-day life:

Vaginal sex, anal sex, oral sex, doggy-style, being choked, being slapped, being spanked, being grabbed, being held down, being bound, having my ears, eyes or mouth covered, being videotaped, simply being asked to partake in any of the above activities during sex, overhearing conversations that mention any of the above activities, comments made about how good/bad I am at giving head, being shushed during sex, the phrases "Take/suck that dick," "Good girl," "Suck it," "Come on!!" or any variation of "I wish you'd suck my cock," being told I take sex too seriously, being told to "chill out," being called "worthless" or "useless" (even if only in jest), being pressured, threatened, guilted, intimidated or blackmailed into partaking in a sexual activity, or otherwise being raped, masturbating (yes, you heard me right), defecating, getting high, watching rape scenes in movies or television, watching sex scenes in movies or television, seeing pornography (still or video), certain rap lyrics and entire songs in general (e.g., Cam'ron's "Suck it or Not," Enya's "Caribbean Blue," Lovage's "Sex (I'm A)"), the taste of neat Captain Morgan's Spiced Rum, the taste of Blue Moon Belgium White Wheat Ale, victim-blaming or threats of rape (even when not directed at me), certain penetrating looks from men on the street or in bed with me, the sight of a man stroking his penis while making eye contact with me, certain physical characteristics that remind me of my rapist/s, actually seeing one of them unexpectedly in passing, walking home alone at night, the sound of a bicycle or a skateboard passing, the sound of small objects hitting my bedroom window, the sound of my phone ringing or vibrating, walking by certain locations.

2. Support Group Counseling. In February/March 2012, I attended a free support group in Chicago for student survivors of sexual assault. I had always been interested in the dynamic of group therapy, because I thought that it would behoove me to actually be *around* others who had experienced similar trauma and who were on the same path to recovery as I was.

What I discovered there was sensational. We actually were discouraged to go into the details of our stories, because the point of the program was to focus entirely on healing, moving forward, and leaving the past in our past. The counselors took us through various exercises that were meant to get us in touch with the way sexual assault had impacted our identity, our day-to-day lives, our intimate relationships, our self-image, and much more.

It was so therapeutic to find out that not only was I not alone in having experienced this trauma, but I also wasn't alone in the way that I was coping with it after the fact.

By the end of the eight-week program, I was feeling so rejuvenated— I felt like I was *alive* again.

On the last day, we were all instructed to write a letter to ourselves, stream-of-consciousness style, and the counselors collected them and said they would be mailing the letters to us at some undisclosed point in the future. I received mine not too long ago, and I'd like to share it with you now, for emphasis:

Dear Self,

First and foremost, I hope you are doing well. I hope that you feel as good—if not better—now as you did when you wrote this. You should look back on this day as a culmination of days when your strongest hopes were actualized (or starting to actualize) and your darkest fears were thwarted. I believe in you. I believe in the good in you and the strength in you. You have tremendous untapped power that you're only starting to discover, and I am proud of the progress you have made. Just look at us! Did you ever think we would feel hope again? Happiness? Will to live? And now we do. That is meaningful. You may not believe in God, but Lord knows you believe in moving forward. Change. Progress. Personal integrity and growth. Now go forth and prove it. Do it with COURAGE. CONSENT. CONVICTION. Those are the 3 C's. Don't forget them. Remember everything you did and learned in group; remember how good it made you feel to find communion and support and THE TRUTH. What happened to you will stay with you, but it won't define you forever. Stay strong. Remember your convictions. DON'T LET ANYONE MAKE YOU FEEL WORTHLESS. Because you are worth so much. You're all we have! Take care of yourself, survivor.

— your Self.

3. Good Sex. Another game-changer for me was meeting a man who showed me that sex didn't have to be terrifying, humiliating or painful. He was *so conscious* of the language of consent, and he made me feel as though the way I was experiencing the sex was actually important to him. He was so patient, kind and forgiving. He let me sit in the driver's seat. For the first time ever since I'd first become sexually active, I wasn't thrown in the back—or tied up and locked inside the trunk—while I was taken along for the ride. This man wanted me to actually *be there*.

And what's more, he didn't reduce my worth down to whether or not I gave him head. He still wanted to have sex with me, regardless. It gave me the space and freedom that I so desperately needed to explore my sexuality for myself—and because of him, I have almost entirely conquered my fear of oral sex.

No matter how much good, consensual sex I will go on to have in my life, this man that I met just as I was beginning my journey to recovery will always be the man who restored my hope, and who showed me that what had destroyed me *wasn't* Man, and it *wasn't* Sex—it was *Abuse*. But there *are* good men, and there *is* good sex, and because this exceptionally good man never once gave up on me, I know now where to direct my anger and what to look for in a healthy, consensual relationship.

4. Affirmations. During Northwestern's Sex Week in April 2012, there was a talk called "Sex After Rape," which briefly discussed a book that sounded pretty interesting and relevant to me titled *Urban Tantra* by Barbara Carrellas. The book took an approach to tantric sex as a form of healing. The quote that first piqued my interest was this one: "Healing sexual abuse through sexuality begins by peeling away the layers of armor we have built up to protect ourselves from further abuse."

I read it cover to cover. It was a very emotional and cleansing experience for me. I found that what it really did most was help me to repair my broken relationship with *myself*. By recalibrating my regard for my sexuality from one of shame and embarrassment to one of marvel and love, I managed to heal the wounds that I had brought upon myself for so many years.

All of the self-loathing, self-blame, self-inflicted punishment—reading this book helped me finally forgive myself for all of that and begin again.

Not to mention the fact that it provided me with a bevy of useful affirmations that I recite to myself sometimes before embarking on sexual ventures, to help keep me grounded in my body, in my sexuality, in my self.

Now, that is not to say that I no longer have triggers, or breakdowns, or doubts. I still do. But the difference is that, now, I also have hope. And knowledge. And most importantly, the power to change and to heal.

5. Advocacy. In April 2012, I was on the planning committee for Northwestern's annual Take Back the Night events. For the first time, I was able to feel the incredible catharsis and fulfillment of speaking out publicly against sexual assault. I shared my experiences. I listened to others' stories. We cried together. We embraced each other. And that's when I decided that I could do so much more. I'm now working 24/7 to combat sexual violence, and sharing my story with you all is just one more step in the right direction.

Because of every counselor, every friend, every lover and even every stranger who has supported me along the way, I do feel strong enough finally to not only survive, but to reclaim the power that has been stripped of me—and to fight back.

Terry G.*

Gender: Female
Age: 40
Race/ethnicity: White
Occupation: Educator, performance artist, writer
Location: Philadelphia suburbs
Age abuse occurred: 7, 9-14

I AM A FEMALE SURVIVOR of sexual abuse. I wear a teal wristband, especially when it's Sexual Assault Awareness Month in April. I also wear a declaration necklace I bought from RAINN in which I can wear one or all four rings suspended from a nylon cord, each one with a word of its own: HOPE, COURAGE, STRENGTH and SURVIVOR. I participate in Take Back the Night events, and WOAR's Take It All Back walk. In the past, I've participated in online rape and sexual abuse survivor boards, such as the Wounded Healer Journal and Pandora's Aquarium. I've called RAINN's hotline. I've gone to individual and group counseling at the Victim Services Center. I've gone to therapy for centuries. I had my first flashback when I was 27 years old—13 years after my last incident of sexual abuse at age 14, eight years after my college sexual assault at age 19. I've been learning to say "I'm a survivor of sexual abuse" for the past 14 years. Despite all these empowering actions I've taken, there are moments when I still wonder if it was really sexual abuse.

When I was 7, my neighbor's daughter, who was 11 at the time, invited me over to play. She had a Shirley Temple doll in a white dress with red polka dots on it. I was thrilled because I loved that doll. After a playing a while, she told me to lie down on the bed. I did, and she climbed on top of me. I asked her what she was doing and she said something like, "Something to make people feel better," or something about first aid; I don't recall. Then she rubbed her body up and down on mine, and asked me to move my stomach a certain way, in line with hers. She asked me not to tell, and I didn't. The first aid excuse made no sense to me. I went over to play again, only she had me take my panties off, and she took hers off, too. I realized this had something to do with what I read about when I found a copy of *Where Did I Come From?* It never happened again after those two times, because I think I mentioned it to my sister, and I think she told someone. I do think that my neighbor's daughter was trying to figure out what was going on, because her mother had boyfriends over at the time, or she was sexually abused herself.

My next incident was when I was at the church carnival. I was 9 years old and I saw a man who I thought was my friend's dad. He said he wanted to show me something and would give me a dollar or 5 dollars. I realized when we were walking that it wasn't my friend's dad, and when he asked me if my nipples were pink or brown and quickly peeked in my strappy top, I knew something was wrong. I didn't leave because I thought, "Well, I got myself into this one." I guess I also had in the back of my mind that he would get mad and chase me if I bolted. I don't know why I continued to walk with him and got into his car with him. I guess we continued to talk, but then I noticed his voice got sort of breathy and I looked at him and I noticed his penis was out. "Squeeze it," he gasped. I merely tapped it. I said, "I really gotta go. You said you'd give me a dollar." He gave me a dollar, and I hurried out of the car. I was lucky I got out of there. Very lucky. I still to this day feel his gasping beside me once in a while, and how the moonlight landed on his penis. I still wonder why I didn't leave him when I was walking with him—for the dollar, maybe? Because of compliance? Obedience?

When I was growing up, I had a very strict Catholic upbringing (Note: I am not blaming religion or the Catholic Church). My mother was physically abusive to my sister and me. My sister, although only two years older than me, was put in charge of me a lot (I had behavior problems and was thought to be slow), and also became abusive. I always was afraid to get another beating. I think that's why I was I was so obedient. My mother and sister seemed to know what I did, and it seemed that other adults would tell them what I was doing, and I would get in trouble. I think I expected people to just hit me after a while, so I did what I was told.

As I said before, my sister was put in charge of me a lot. I think that's why these other incidents happened with her. Because my mother also abused her, I think my sister needed to get her anger out and have some power. I'm betting that she was sexually abused, too. The odd stuff started when I was 9. My sister would say it smelled when we were alone in the kitchen. Then she would say, "It's you. It's you that smells." And then she would make me pull down my panties—she would threaten to tell Mommy if I didn't, and that Mommy would make me do it and would beat me if I didn't listen to her. So I pulled down my panties and she would look around and smell my privates, saying how I smelled bad, that I would get in trouble if I didn't get cleaned up. I think she did this off and on until I was about 13. One time I found out it was the potato barrel with potatoes rotting in a nearby room, and she had said that the smell was coming from me.

When I was about 12 or 13, I was curled on top of my bed in my school uniform. My sister sat beside me and asked me if she could put her fingers inside me. I said no. Then, before I knew it, her fingers went under my skirt, somehow past the panties and inside my vagina. I was shocked. Then she got up, and said, "Don't tell Mommy," before she left the room. I never did. I thought for sure we would both be killed.

After I was 14, the physical incidents stopped between my sister and me, but she still continued to make comments about my sexuality, and out me when I was questioning my sexual preference up until my 20s. Even though I am rebuilding a relationship with my sister now, I still don't trust her. I think because of her and my mother, I worry that people are looking at me sexually and thinking how I'm smelly, ugly, even if my clothes are covering me. I don't like having my underwear off and feeling breezes around my privates and thighs for a prolonged time.

I knew these incidents happened. I never forgot them. I go back and forth in calling them sexual abuse. No one raped me. The only one who went into my privates was my sister—and we were not experimenting; I did not give my consent. To my sister and my neighbor's daughter, I was more of a curiosity. Thankfully, the incident with the dollar man wasn't as bad as it could have been. So I don't know what to call it. I don't know where to put the blame. I don't know where to put my anger. I don't know what do with the fear and shame.

However, I developed symptoms of PTSD when I was 26 or 27 years old. I had nightmares of my mother beating me, but I didn't have a body memory or knew what it was until I was meditating and then I felt my sister's fingers in my vagina. I knew then it was a sexual abuse-related body memory because of that and how I curled up in shame from it. My physical abuse flashbacks, body memories and my sexual abuse flashbacks are distinctly different. I flinch and dodge more when I have physical abuse ones, and I curl up and I feel like gagging and want to scrub myself after the sexual abuse ones.

I was hospitalized for a suicide attempt when I was 21. I was having severe bouts of depression—they are horrible now, but I can fake that I'm OK. With PTSD, it's almost impossible to act like I'm OK in the middle of a flashback, or jumping up from my exaggerated startled response, or getting things done when I'm dissociated. The symptoms of PTSD interfered with my functioning more than depression ever has. The worst thing about PTSD for me is that I had flashbacks and body memories in which I couldn't match them with any of the incidents in this essay. Those unidentifiable body memories have been the most physically/sexually painful. I've racked my brain for years to find out where they came from, and I still do. They are absolutely crippling. Although my PTSD symptoms are not as severe or even serious now, I still have flare-ups, and I still wonder why some of my sexual abuse-related flashbacks make no sense. It is these flashbacks that make me believe I was sexually abused. I know the terror of physical abuse, but the terror that comes from these sexual abuse flashbacks is distinctly different. It's come to the point that it doesn't even matter *what* happened any more. The symptoms of PTSD have wrecked my brain, my trust in others, and my trust in my own mind and my own self.

These incidents, the physical abuse, and the PTSD symptoms have profoundly affected me. Despite me being functional and employed, I haven't been able to hold a financially stable career. I have difficulty with long-term relationships. I go hot and cold with my sexual activity— have sex with people I barely know for a period of time or have no sex at all for another period of time. I also have become doubtful of myself. Even though I wrote in the last paragraph that the flashbacks and body memories make me believe I was sexually abused, I'm wrestling in believing that. Why did I have these symptoms for more than 10 years and I still haven't figured out what happened?

Yes, I go to those survivor events, and I wear the teal wristband and declaration jewelry. I still occasionally vent on survivor message boards. Yes, I go to support other survivors and give them hope, but I also go because I still desperately need that comfort after a flashback of feeling like my body was invaded and my thighs and privates are remembering an incredible pain and awful violation, and I can't get the scum off that's all over my legs that isn't even there. I still need that comfort, even after all these years.

Jordan Gwendolyn Davis

Gender: Female
Age: 27
Race/ethnicity: Multiracial (white and Native American)
Occupation: Freelancer on disability
Location: Philadelphia, Pa.
Age abuse occurred: 18

AROUND THIS TIME about four years ago, I embarked on a road trip from my hometown in New Jersey to a small Rockwellian town in New England, where almost five years before, I was sexually assaulted at a therapeutic boarding facility. A staff member, fed up that I had the gall to report a student who threw a water bottle at me, forcibly pushed me on the bed, berated and then sexually assaulted me. This happened about four days before I was to graduate from the place, which had an all-year schedule and August graduation.

Time was running out to do anything about it because of the state's statute of limitations. By then, post trauma had caught up with me and I had to leave grad school. So, earlier that week, I put up a lengthy Facebook note about what happened (with mixed results from former students), didn't eat for the rest of the week, and then, early Saturday morning, on the last Saturday of June 2008, I got up, dressed nice, and made the trip I needed to make. I picked up a friend and set off for the town where I had lived for almost three years. When I started to approach the town, I got so anxious that I was no longer able to drive. My friend had to take the wheel for the final few miles to the police station, where I finally was able to tell my story. I was apprehensive at first, and even though there was a cozy relationship between the owner of the school and the local police department, the office took me seriously.

Of course, the problems were only beginning. About a few weeks later, my parents, who had been in the dark about my sexual assault because I felt so ashamed, received a call from my old advisor from the school and told them about me coming forward about the assault, even though at the time I told, I was 23 and thus an adult out of the school's control. They were supportive, however. In November 2008, the lawyers from the school sent me a letter saying that I never made a police report, and that they were going to sue me for libel. It took the involvement of the local district attorney to pull up the police report. The school has not sued me, but the case has gone cold.

A year after I had finally reported the bastard to the police, I came out as a transgender woman. Today, I am living in Philadelphia, taking hormones, have legally changed my name and the gender marker on my driver's license, and hope to move to California in a year to get gender confirmation surgery. However, as a result of pre-existing disabling conditions, I am receiving disability payments. My world has fallen apart around me.

In a way, my identities have complicated my survivor status. Last year, I had to go to a motel in Bucks County for the night, and was harassed by police who accused me of being a sex worker. I had told them my survivor status as a tactic to have them lay off of me, and they asked me if being sexually abused led to me being transgender—a perception that is totally false. I had always thought I was a girl since I was born, but sadly, could never come out for fear of being killed. Furthermore, in terms of disability, many of the students at the school (including myself) had various, sometimes disconcerting issues, which have led to many people within this small town to believe that the school administration's word was gospel and that they could do no wrong. And after reading a story in the local paper about another sexual-assault issue at the school, complete with a copy of the lawsuit in the online version, as well as victim-blaming dot-commenters, I suspect not much has changed since I finally came forward in 2008.

However, my experience there, though tragic, helped me realize what a serious problem sexual assault is, and how anybody can be a survivor. Five years ago, I was still dealing with the trauma, and would often make prison rape jokes about perpetrators, which I now regret. Even if justice was miraculously served on the bastard and he actually went to prison, I would still be serving a life sentence myself, and I don't know if it will get any better.

Jannina and Evan

* * *

Jannina L.

Gender: Female
Age: 20
Race/ethnicity: Hispanic, Colombian
Occupation: Nursing major at Nyack College
Location: New York
Age abuse occurred: 8-9

MY NAME IS JANNINA. That is who I am, what I'm called. I am 20 years old as of May 6, 2012, and I still feel like a child. I'm sure in many ways, I am. I can close my eyes and remember it like you might remember the way it feels to breathe. Inhale, exhale and it all comes back. That is how ingrained the memories are.

I was born in N.Y.C. to Colombian parents. They met after emigrating to the U.S. They had me in 1992 and my sister in 1993. We weren't wealthy but we weren't poor, and for the most part I felt I was lacking in nothing. My parents were very invested in my sister and I. We never went to pre-school because my mother said she could teach us herself, and she did. At

3 years old, I could already read and write, and I was convinced I was destined for greatness.

My sister had it all figured out at a young age. She had read a book about a brain surgeon and convinced herself that that was her true calling. I, on the other hand, was far more idealistic. I imagined myself as a princess, artist, dancer or an Olympian—all of which seemed very attainable to me at a young age when I was convinced that all dreams come true. But life had a different plan for me—one that would destroy my soul and yet rebuild it years later much stronger than I had ever thought possible.

My father had a son from a previous relationship back in Columbia. He was raised by his mother in Colombia with my father's financial support, which he would send from the U.S. I was told about my half-brother's existence when I was in third grade. Clearly, my world was shaken. My diary (which I had been keeping since kindergarten) became filled with my excitement to meet my long-lost brother. Page after page of hopes and dreams and activities I wanted to do with him preoccupied my mind. Finally, my dad told me the news I'd been waiting for: My half-brother would be traveling to the U.S. and would be moving in with us.

I was still in the third grade when he moved in. Our meeting was anything but spectacular. He arrived while I was asleep, and in a midnight bathroom break we bumped into each other in the hallway. "Hola," I said. "Hola," he said, and he proceeded back to bed. Instantly, we began to butt heads. There seemingly was nothing I could do to make him like me. He seemed to like my younger sister more, and we spent hours fighting with each other. Don't get me wrong, we had our moments of harmony in which he would show me the correct way to kick a soccer ball and tell me briefly of what high school life was like. I lived for these moments.

I sought to impress him in every way I could, yet it never seemed to be enough. One night, on a drive back from my aunt's house, he fell asleep next to me. Somehow his hand "slipped" under me so it was cupping my butt. At 9 years old, I thought this was a hilarious unintentional mistake done while he was sleeping. I thought it was so funny that I showed my sister who just giggled along with me. Ever since then, every time I drive on this road it will remind me of the night when it all started.

When we arrived home, my brother pulled me aside and pushed me up along the living room wall and whispered in Spanish, "You know what just happened in the car? That was a mistake and it won't happen again. I'm sorry, don't tell dad or your mom." I nodded my head as confused as ever. A strange sensation grew in the pit of my stomach that night; an uneasy shame that I could not place or comprehend. But I said nothing and just tried to fight the strange feeling that seemed to cloud my vision and fog up my mind.

This would become a routine over the next few months. Every car ride would equal his touching. It would start with an innocent back massage, his fingertips caressing my back in what I thought was him finally showing me he actually did love me. But then things got strange. He would let my sister take the front seat and ask me to accompany him in the back seat so only the top of my head would be visible to my parents in the front of the car. My back became my chest, my chest became my rear and my rear became parts of me that I was too young to understand and too confused to refuse. The feelings were so strange. Shame, confusion and yet a frustrating want for my brother to keep on loving me. It was in these moments that he wasn't mean or yelling or fighting with me, and I thought this was what all relationships should be like. I sought it out desperately. Blankets, pillows, towels and anything that could be draped over us became his tools to hide under in order to touch me. I would sit perfectly still, hoping not to get caught and hoping that he approved. I was always seeking his approval. He liked when I stroked the hair on his legs and I often fell asleep in the car with my hand over his shin or stroking his calf.

As the months progressed, the feeling of shame, fear and disgust began to override all other feelings. I finally decided to confide in my older cousin, who was three years older than me. She always seemed to have the answers to my many questions, but this time she seemed confused herself and told me that it wasn't normal. She then asked if I was OK. I had never considered the fact that what had been occurring wasn't normal, and her saying so confused me even more, but I told her that I was OK.

The next day, my father received a call from my aunt saying my cousin had left her textbook at my house and needed to pick it up. When she arrived she told me that my cousin had told her about what my brother was doing and that I had to tell my parents. I felt mortified. I felt as if I had done something terribly wrong and now had to confess my faults. With tears in my eyes, I sat on the living room couch while my parents stared in horrified grief as I told them what had been occurring for the past few months right underneath their noses. My father cried like I'd never seen him cry before, and his emotional state was my undoing. I was so afraid and so desperate to keep what I thought was my brother's love that I wrote a note warning my brother that I hadn't told my parents and that it wasn't my fault, and posted it on the front door so that he would see it when he got home from school. My father angrily took the note down, and I was so hurt that my parents could be so angry at someone who loved me so much. Over time, a lot of it, I would finally see the experience for what it was: sexual molestation.

My brother was sent back to Colombia within the next weeks and I would never see him again, but the repercussions from those months would travel with me for a lifetime.

My relationships with boys from that point on held a tragic cycle. I would befriend them and consider them the "brother I never had." When we would become very close, they would see the opportunity to become more than friends and become physical. I would accept this, thinking it was normal. It took years for me to overcome the sense of shame and guilt that accompanied those actions.

My parents begged me to see a therapist but I told them I didn't need fixing. In reality, I was too embarrassed to talk to anyone. For a time, I tried to forget by pushing the memories away. But everything reminded me of him, and with each memory, the emotions would come rushing back. The guilt came in cycles. I would first blame myself, then I would blame my parents and family for being so blind, and finally I would come to blame him.

I was raised in a Christian home, and this would prove to be my salvation. I sought the Bible for the answers to my questions and the solace for my pain. Verses telling of God's love and forgiveness and healing of the emotionally grieved helped me deal with the pain. It was a verse in Matthew 12 that would really help me overcome my feeling of loss. It says that those who do God's will are considered his brothers and sisters and mothers. I realized that God could replace the hole that my brother had left behind. From that point on, my viewpoint seemed to change, and I was filled with purpose. I felt that I had experienced what I had so that I could one day help others who had experienced the same thing. I felt as if God was helping me overcome this horrifying hardship so that his glory would be shown through my overcoming of it.

I also turned to writing. From a young age, I was encouraged to keep a diary. Writing became an outlet in which to vent out all of my confusion, anger, grief and loneliness. In a way, it seemed that getting it all down on paper would empty me of the emotions themselves.

The song "You're My Little Girl" by Go Fish was given to me on a CD at a Christian girls retreat I attended with my cousin. This song would be a source of healing and joy and would eventually help me feel at peace and regain hope in life. I would close my eyes and imagine God singing the song to me. The lyrics would echo in my head for the rest of my days and would be my comfort when the haunting memories came rushing back. *"The ones you love, they let you down, and I want you to know that I'm sorry. The choices that they made were wrong, you were caught in the middle, and I'm sorry. So when the anger and the pain get the best of you, I know it feels like you're all alone but I am feeling it too. 'Cause you're my little girl, you're the one that I created, no one in the world could ever be like you. When you're crying in the night all you need to do is call me, I'll be there for you, because you're my little girl."*

These words spoke to me and helped me realize I did not have to go through this alone. I realized I could cast all my cares and worry on God and he would replace them with joy and a peace that surpasses all understanding.

Years later, while I was in high school, I would come in contact with my brother again via Skype. We did a voice chat and he apologized for his horrible actions. I did not buy his apology, but somehow, hearing it provided closure. I was able to yell and scream and ask the questions I'd always had, which he answered to the best of his ability. I have not spoken or contacted him since that day and I no longer feel like I need to. That chapter in my life is now closed and it no longer defines me but is just another part of me that makes me stronger.

Today I attend Nyack College. I am studying to be a nurse. I am as motivated as ever to be the best I can be. I embrace life and its hurdles. Trials will come, and we must and can overcome them. It's the lessons we learn from the hard times in life that allow us to grow and mature. What I now know is that there is nothing too big for God to handle.

* * *

Evan M.

Gender: Male
Age: 20
Race/ethnicity: Caucasian
Occupation: Criminal justice major
Location: Philadelphia, Pa.
Relationship to survivor: Boyfriend

I FIRST MET JANNINA when I was in ninth grade; she was in eighth grade at the time. The school we went to, located in Manhattan's Lower East Side, offered grades K through 12, so I would see her around the hallways frequently. It was not until my junior year that I kissed her for the first time, as we sat in the theater watching the movie *Eastern Promises*. In my nervousness, I had led us to the right movie but at the wrong time, and ended up only watching the second half—which I have no memory of.

We did not officially become a couple until the second half of my senior year. We stayed up late talking, and we created a routine time every morning and afternoon to meet up in school, and even met in the hallways once in a while to share a brief kiss and hug before I walked her back to her classroom.

I had already known Jannina was a special girl who was becoming a special woman. She had a light that made people flock to her, and many viewed her as a confidant if not a good friend. However, not many people knew much about her personal life, her family, her secrets and her scars. I remember her mentioning that she had to tell me something one day. I was afraid because I thought that perhaps it was in reaction to something I had done, but I could not have been more wrong. She took me to the school auditorium, to a row way in the back, at the end of the day. We really weren't allowed to be there at that time. She told me about a member of her family, a half-brother, I had never met, and will never meet. I had previously met her sister and briefly met her parents. Jannina loved and admired her half-brother, as he was older, seemingly cooler and wiser. She trusted him, and he betrayed that trust. He sexually assaulted Jannina over a long period of time until she spoke up. Immediately, her half-brother was sent back to Colombia to live with his mother.

Upon hearing this news, I was scared, and I did not know how to react. I didn't know how Jannina wanted me to react. I of course shared my outrage that something that horrible could happen at such a young age to her, and perpetrated by someone so close. I told her that I would never let anything that terrifying happen to her again, and that I wanted her to feel safe with me because I knew that, left alone with her thoughts, she wouldn't be. I found that there was little I could do to try and repair whatever damage her brother left behind.

I never wanted to bring up the subject unless it was being discussed so as not to put her in a bad mood, but when she was talking about it, I felt nervous—like I was being tested for compassion and if I could comfort her appropriately. Some days I did pass the test, others I may have been insensitive and said something I shouldn't have, or worse, said nothing at all. I realized it was not something I could talk her through, and that there was no solution to this problem—only a means of comfort. It was like a disease that could not be cured, only treated. And so I learned how to treat her, how to avoid making her feel a certain way, knowing how to evoke a useful emotional response from her when she was most upset. Since there was no combination of words I could say that would fix her heart, I just closely observed how my actions might affect her, and worked from that.

As Jannina's boyfriend of almost four years now, I have noticed some of her subtle reactions to certain situations, caused by her subconscious need to protect her ego, or even her state of emotion. I do everything I can to avoid putting Jannina in an anxious or worried emotional state, but more importantly I have learned how to bring her back from being lost in her thoughts. She associates yelling with an emotional state that I believe to have been present when she was being victimized. In a particularly loud argument, it might result in her turning inward and being incapable of communication. She hides in what the two of us have coined her "shell," where she can hear and see the outside world but struggles to say the things or act the way she wants to. The method I have developed in trying to help her out of her shell is by gently running my fingers through her hair, just creating a sense of calm and security. Eventually, her body does allow her to communicate and make eye contact, and after some comforting words, she is able to talk again. When she sees, hears or even thinks about something for too long, which forces her to emotionally ball up, there is very little that I can do, unfortunately, other than to be there for her when she wants to poke her head back out of her shell.

Jannina will never fully let go of her scar; it will only fade with time. However, she has taken steps to ensure that she does not let it weigh her down every hour of every day. She found peace in God, in reading the Bible, and asking for a purpose, a sign to make good from this horrible fate. I think that is part of the reason why she will make a great nurse someday (as she currently is studying at Nyack College). She knows she cannot fully detach herself from this piece of her past, so she seeks to heal others— not just physically but emotionally, too.

That's why when I read *Philadelphia Weekly* at the restaurant I used to work at, I immediately tore out the editor's note about *The Survivors Project* and showed it to Jannina. I told her that she could write an essay about her experiences, and by speaking loudly about something that is only whispered in auditoriums at odd hours, actually help others and hopefully make a difference—if only in one person's life.

Becky Perkins

Gender: Female
Age: 36
Race/ethnicity: White
Occupation: Statewide outreach manager for the Ohio Alliance to End Sexual Violence
Location: Monroe, Ohio
Age abuse occurred: 12

I WAS RAPED at age 12 by a young man who wanted to "show me how to be a woman." I kept it a secret until adulthood, when I finally broke my silence, got help, and began my walk along the winding road of recovery. For several years now, I've worked as an advocate for other survivors. Today, I provide outreach and advocacy at the state level. I am blessed but also haunted.

As both an advocate and a survivor, I face an interesting and often frustrating paradox. As an advocate, I know and understand all the reasons why survivors are not to blame and should not feel ashamed. As a survivor, I can still feel a faint but palpable aura of shame surrounding me. As an advocate, I understand why survivors don't often report the crime and that their silence does not render them responsible for what their attackers do to others. As a survivor, I inevitably feel the ache of guilt and regret each time I see or read of a brave survivor taking the stand. As an advocate,

I respond diplomatically when someone in a position of authority speaks ignorant words with careless disregard for survivors. As a survivor, my cheek stings from the impact of those words as if they had been struck upon me alone. Knowledge is power, but the truth is that all the knowledge in the world can never completely erase the visceral imprint of rape.

Being a survivor of rape makes my work more challenging—not because I'm reminded of my own experience, but because I'm keenly aware that the pain and confusion I have known quietly exists in epidemic proportions around me. There are so many people out there who have suffered sexual victimization, but we remain both silent and silenced. What would happen if every survivor felt safe and free to speak up? What would happen if the rest of the world was forced to listen—*really* listen—and felt inspired to act? I'm willing to find out. Are you?

T.A.L.

Gender: Female
Age: 54
Race/ethnicity: Black
Occupation: Formerly a home health aide
Location: Havertown, Pa.
Age abuse occurred: 3-4

IT ALL STARTED when I was about 3 years old, and the scenario was always the same. We lived in a trailer park in Plattsburg, N.Y., in the early 1960s. It was a small trailer park with about 15 homes where most folks knew one another by name. In fact, my parents were particularly friendly with one other couple. There were few black minorities in the park at the time, so that was probably why parents socialized with the Taylors*. Both my family and the Taylors were from a military background and had traveled quite a bit in the service. The Taylors had two sons, one my age and one other who was a teenager, about 17 or so. Every time our parents went out of town, the teenage son, Steven*, would eagerly babysit his brother and me. I only remember bits and pieces, but the situations were always the same.

I remember being in the Taylors' living room for a brief moment while Steven greeted his younger brother and I upon our entry. Steven would then proceed to separate his brother and me by escorting me into the bedroom and locking his brother out in the living room. Time and time again, he would do this. Once inside the bedroom, Steven would proceed to totally undress both of us. Then he would lie on top of me and masturbate all over my genitalia. I remember him being so heavy, and I found it hard to breathe as a result. His chest was right in my face. When he was finished, he would wipe his semen off me with toilet paper. I vaguely remember him putting my clothes back. I do not know what he may have said to me, nor do I remember ever leaving the bedroom. This went on for at least a year— the whole time we lived in that trailer park.

I know I didn't verbalize anything regarding the experience at the time and I know my parents in particular never suspected any wrongdoing— something that caused me great anger when I was older and processing the events. When I was older, I always questioned why my parents never picked up any signals or clues that I was being sexually abused. Surely there had to be some signs of abuse. In the course of my recovery, I concluded that my parents should have never adopted me because of their own immaturity and dysfunction. I lost the innocence of my childhood. And that can never be regained once it is lost.

Because of this initial abuse (and there were other forms of abuse as well), I often "acted out" my symptoms in often inappropriate methods to the surprise of my parents and the adults around me. I often "played out" and repeated the exact same sexual scenarios of the sexual abuse with my young peers as well. I often overwhelmed them because they could not process the inappropriate interactions that took place between us. Because of this, I had a reputation of being a slut and a whore. I was severely bullied and harassed from about third grade to eighth grade. Can you imagine being bullied and harassed verbally and emotionally every day for that many years? I can't even begin to describe the severity of the emotional baggage I accumulated during that time.

The shame I felt about my grade-school years actually overshadowed the actual sex abuse I endured when I was 3. As a result, upon my first psychiatric hospitalization at age 18, the psychiatrist gave me an enormous injection of sodium penathol to get me to talk about my problems. That did not work, and I watched him watch me as a result. That hospitalization was one of many more to come. I averaged an admission once every three years from 1978 through 1996. I was finally diagnosed with having bipolar disorder as a result and was put on Haldol and Lithium. This medication regimen proved not to be effective enough throughout my course of treatment, and in 1996 I was put on Clozaril, Zoloft and Depakote. I'm happy to say that since then, psychiatric symptoms have been in remission. But it was by no means a smooth course of events. While psychotropic medication played an important part of my ongoing recovery process, it would not have been as successful had I not also had psychotherapy with competent therapists who specialized in sexual-abuse issues.

I did not really deal with the sexual-abuse issues until a few years after I was diagnosed with being bipolar. And it wasn't until 1983 or so that I finally ended up with a therapist who specialized in multiple personality disorders that I truly began to dissect the true nature and impact of the sexual abuse inflicted upon me at such a young age. Upon our first few visits, it was clear in her mind that I had Multiple Personality Disorder (now known as Dissociative Identity Disorder, or DID). After about a month or two of treatment, she proceeded to inform me that I had DID. The only thing I had as a reference point was the movie *Sybil*, and I saw no similarities between the character in that movie to myself. But over the course of the next 20-plus years, I learned quite a bit about DID and how our minds can create a "system" in order to deal with extreme trauma in our lives. My system is a unique one, just as I assume that others' DID systems are just as unique to that individual person. "We" went through many trials and tribulations, resulting in numerous hospitalizations, counteracting and intervening destructive abuse behavior by individual alter personalities as a result. We are not totally "integrated" into one personality, but rather function as a collective of personalities, agreeing on a hierarchy of sorts where I am the 'host' personality. I am in control most of the time; my gatekeeper, Carol, controls the interactions of the other alters. We all get along quite well at this point. This was not always the case, of course. But my faith in Christ has given me the additional strength to cope with circumstances that have overwhelmed me, and my faith is an important factor in my well-being.

Recovering from abuse starts with breaking the code of silence that enslaves the victim and often protects the perpetrator. Nevertheless, the abuse needs to be exposed. The victim needs to be believed, needs to find solace in an adult who is emotionally supportive and who will address the issue and report it to the caregiver, police, therapist and other adults who need to be involved. The sooner the intervention, the greater the prospect for healing and recovery. For myself, I initially had to give myself permission to even address and acknowledge the abuse in my own mind. I had to realize it was OK to talk about it and break that code. There are resources out there to aid with dealing with sexual-abuse issues. You are not alone! There are people who will listen to you and believe in what you have to share. Find someone you think you can trust and tell them about your story. Ultimately, you will need to find a competent therapist to help you sort through your memories and feelings about the abuse. It can be a scary process, but a necessary one. Only then will you be able to travel down that road of recovery. You do not have to travel there alone. You deserve to be happy. Take that first step and talk about it to someone who will listen. It's a challenge but worth it in the long run.

I am still in therapy. I probably don't really need it at this point but I like the fact that I can talk to someone who is objective and not judgmental with what I choose to share. After being in therapy for 20-plus years, I see my therapist as one of my best friends with whom I can share anything. However, I will always be on psychotropic medication to maintain my "system" and brain chemistry. The medications have different effects on particular alters, but they help control manic-depressive behavior and bouts of psychotic episodes that have often landed me in the psyche units due to many suicide attempts.

But by the grace of God, I/we are still here.

Tamara Dallaire

Gender: Female
Age: 32
Race/ethnicity: White
Occupation: Paralegal
Location: Warren, R.I.
Age abuse occurred: 16
Note: *I am a proud advocate for survivors of sexual violence and volunteer my time to educate people on this subject for One Voice, a survivor's advocacy group created through Day One, a rape-trauma center in Southern New England. When I'm not advocating for the cause, I am a student at the University of Massachusetts at Dartmouth, where I am pursuing my bachelor's degree in Crime and Justice Studies, where one day I hope to help law-enforcement profile sex offenders and educate those in law enforcement on what can be done to better assist and ensure justice for anyone suffering from the aftermath of sexual violence.*

FOR MANY OF US, childhood is filled with the prerequisite bumps and bruises that normally accompany us on our way to adulthood. I was an exceptionally accident-prone child and, depending on certain circumstances, I am an exceptionally accident-prone adult. My mother was a genius when handling my many injuries as a little girl. She always knew just what to do to make everything better. She would frequently bandage my cuts and scrapes, and then kiss them goodbye while saying in a loving sing-song voice, "See, all gone. Mommy makes it all better." To this day, I can hear her voice say it to me while still bandaging whatever cuts or scrapes I manage to get as an adult, even if she is on the other side of the country in Arizona. What happens though when those wounds are no longer just physical, but emotional? Is there a way to bandage them? Will there be a scar? These are the concepts behind healing from traumatic experiences in life. For me, it was healing from a sexual assault in 1996 and the ongoing "bandaging" of those remaining wounds.

Recently, my husband caught me smiling to myself and asked what I was thinking to cause me to smile. I can't remember what particular moment popped in my head to prompt the smile, but the thought that remained was that I couldn't believe how my life has turned out and how proud I am that I have come such a long way from where I was. I think about it every day, and I am never short of amazed that I have the life I have. Although I'm very happy now, the journey to get here was extremely difficult and at times complete torture. The road to healing from such trauma takes a lot of work on behalf of the survivor, but the fact remains that the survivor will never transition from being a victim to a survivor without a sturdy and patient support system. It's simply impossible for a survivor to begin to heal alone. Unfortunately, being alone in this struggle is why many of us do not heal or survive the healing process.

In order for anyone to understand why I can smile about my journey now, I have to start from the beginning. I had awful self-esteem when I was a teenager. My parents were divorced and my brother and I lived with our father and stepmom. Growing up in a household where I was a teenage girl being raised by a man was definitely not easy, but luckily it got a little more tolerable to endure teenage purgatory when my father married my stepmom, who I affectionately refer to as "Mama." Even though I could talk to her when the testosterone got too much to bear, I could not get past the fact that I believed I was ugly and awkward and very overweight. Unfortunately, predators have a keen ability to "zero" in on someone's insecurities like an expert sniper. It's almost like we have a flashing light on our forehead that says, "I need attention. Nobody likes me. I hate myself. I'm a perfect target." The only people who can see that flashing sign are the predators, much like how only a dog can hear a dog-whistle. My predator may have been young at the time, but he locked into those insecurities the moment he saw me.

Not long after I met this person, he "casually" interjected into a conversation I was having with another young lady after hearing me tell her that I didn't have a boyfriend. At the time, I thought his interest in the conversation meant he had an interest in talking to me, but after many years I understand that predators often do this to gain their victims' trust. About a week after the conversation in question, along with normal teenage flirting, he asked if he could take me out. It was only a couple weeks prior to my 16th birthday, so like any nervous parent of a teenage girl, my father wanted to meet him and make sure he felt comfortable with him taking me on a date. Predators also have a wonderfully charismatic quality that allows people who believe they can't be fooled the opportunity to show what makes them so trustworthy, thus removing any doubts that this person was unsafe. Unfortunately, my parents fell for it also, but like many others before them, this is not uncommon and in no way reflects my parents and their ability to raise my brother or myself.

We didn't date long before the topic of sex came up, and like many other young women at the time, especially those who were born to teenage parents, I was not ready to have sex and told him how I felt. Obviously, he made me believe that he was trustworthy and that my refusal to have sex was understood completely. One week after my 16th birthday, he finally became enraged at my rejection and ambivalence about sex, and forcefully raped me by rendering me unconscious. I was left stunned, in pain, bloody and confused about what transpired.

Predators do not view rape as something sexual, but instead as an act of power. They are also usually raised in somewhat traumatic upbringings that leave them with more questions about life than answers, and this all usually manifests into their warped understanding about how to treat others. There are more times than not when this skewed view comes to light in the form of sexual domination that culminates in rape. My predator grew up in a household where women were seen as only vessels for carrying children and should always be submissive in a man's household. Violence was a daily occurrence, as was forced sex, leaving him to correlate violence with sex as a way to dominate whatever or whomever he believed he needed to dominate. That is why now, looking back, I'm not surprised that I found him casually eating a sandwich in his kitchen after I regained consciousness and cleaned off the blood. He acted like nothing happened because, in his mind, what just transpired was normal.

I understand now that this was one of the many reasons I didn't come forward to my family sooner, because I could not understand why he was so nonchalant about the offense. I thought that maybe what happened was normal and that my teenage fantasy about what my first time would be like was just that, a fantasy. After the initial rape, I endured almost two more months of daily sexual abuse at the hands of a person who told me he loved me. I knew that everything he was doing to me was not only wrong, but criminal, and that this is not how love is supposed to work. Like many young women in abusive relationships at this age, I didn't know that I didn't deserve this and stayed with him because I honestly believed I didn't deserve anything better. I believed I was too fat and ugly for anyone else to love, therefore the fact that I was raped every day didn't register as an unhealthy way for someone to show I was worth the time.

Just before Halloween of that year, I found the courage to break off the relationship. I had started to develop some physical issues from the abuse and was forced to see a physician. It was only then that what happened was revealed to my mother because the doctor could see the physical ramifications of what I endured on a daily basis. At the time, however, sexual assault was still seen as a "domestic issue," and anything legal, such as reporting him to the authorities, was seen as not so much of a crime, but more of a "he said/she said" teenage spat. It was more common then to put the victim on trial instead of the perpetrator by making them feel as if they had wanted this to happen to them. I was too young to understand that our legal system hadn't caught up to society, and the lack of legal recourse caused me to become a shell of what could have been if this predator had never harmed me. I still felt too ashamed to tell my father the awful details of what I endured, and after there was no punishment of my offender or justice for myself, I shut down completely and withdrew from my friends, family and the entire world around me. I didn't know it at the time, but I was suffering from Rape Trauma Syndrome, a form of PTSD, most commonly marked by depression, anxiety and often times suicidal tendencies. My young brain just couldn't handle the psychological pain, so instead of talking to someone, I buried the emotions and tried to ease the pain with alcohol. I would often sneak whatever alcohol was in the house up into my bedroom, lock my door, turn up my stereo, and proceed to drown every inch of myself in a haze.

As one can imagine, life didn't improve much after that. I graduated high school two years later, but not with nearly as high a GPA as I obtained only a few years prior. I didn't care about anything; not myself, my family or my education, and I cared even less about seeking help for what I was going through. The next decade was spent in a loveless and immature marriage to the first boy that paid attention to me after the assault. I fell into a deep and very dark depression, and was addicted to anything that would make the pain go away, whether it was alcohol or pills that I would get from telling doctors that I had some type of "physical pain" that only strong muscle relaxers or narcotics could cure. My marriage began to crumble the minute it began, but by 2006, it was so far in the sewer that nothing we could do would save it. Adding to the mounting tension within my household, was also the fact that my husband never believed me when I told him what happened to me. Not only was he my husband and someone I thought would be there for me, but he was also the only person outside of my parents I had ever tried to tell, in every awful detail, what happened to me. His unwillingness to believe me and try to seek help for me was one of the largest nails that had been hammered into our proverbial coffin that our marriage had climbed into.

The end of my marriage culminated with an attempt at suicide, which was actually successful. I took the remaining bottle of anti-depressants I had told my physician I needed, and the rest of a bottle of Jack Daniels I hadn't finished from the night before. I just couldn't take the pain anymore of living inside a private hell, and I just wanted out. Before I had lost consciousness completely after crawling to my bathroom to try and vomit out the drugs and alcohol, I dialed 911 and mumbled a cry for help. I started to get scared because I was having a brief moment of clarity in which I understood what I did to myself and was terrified with the possibility of dying and going nowhere, therefore I mustered whatever strength I had left to dial the phone. Luckily, I didn't hang up, and the EMTs were able to trace the line to my home and come in through an unlocked door.

Spiritually speaking, it was the most profound and beautiful experience of my life. I had turned my back on any religious education my family gave me because the truth was I couldn't accept that a God would allow someone to violate me and shatter my soul the way my perpetrator did. Before the EMTs were able to get me breathing again, my heart stopped for a little more than two minutes and, during that time, whether anyone who is reading this article believes me or not, I went to a place that was warm, forgiving and peaceful. I regained consciousness as the EMTs were saying, "She's back, we've got her back." I blacked out again and woke up in the hospital with no real recollection of what happened. Due to my inability to understand why I was there, there was still that part of myself that had been marred in shame and thought nobody could or would help me, so I begged the nurses to tell my family that I was taken in for food poisoning. I knew this lie wouldn't last, seeing as the night before I was at a dinner meeting for my work and nobody else that I was with, who also happened to be eating the same meal as I was, got sick or experienced anything I was claiming to have. Even then, I was still too embarrassed to ask for help. I did come to one very solid realization, however, that my marriage was truly over. My husband refused to come to the hospital and told the emergency room staff to call somebody else. Although I was lying in a hospital bed with numerous tubes coming out of my veins, I thought that this could possibly be the beginning of a life transformation. My "do-over" had finally begun.

I may have started the healing process right after the suicide, but I certainly didn't heal right away. I wasn't prepared for the intense amount of work that I would have to do to get to the place I am in now. My mother helped me file for divorce and move in with her. Filing for divorce was probably the easiest part of regaining a life, especially when the real hard work came when I started to see a therapist who specialized in PTSD and RTS, and began to relive the rape and sexual abuse all over again. Staying sober was incredibly hard because all the emotions I had tried to bury so deep within myself were now coming to the surface with a vengeance, and I honestly couldn't handle it. I relapsed twice during this period due to the emotional pain I was experiencing. In the middle of this chaos of attempting to heal, a miracle in the form of a man who would become my second husband emerged. Let me be very clear: I did not want to fall in love with him. But it happened. He single-handedly became my biggest support system. His experience with working in the human-services field, mainly with those affected by trauma, mainly through criminal behaviors, gave him the tools to help guide me through my counseling when certain therapy sessions felt like they became too much to handle and I felt like giving up and retreating back into myself.

For two years prior to our marriage in 2008 and up until today, his love and unconditional acceptance got me to where I am today. He has proven more times than I can even count that he will never give up on me, especially after some hard times when he had seen me at my worst. Some of those times, especially after hitting on different aspects of my assault and its aftermath, got particularly violent, with me throwing framed pictures, punching walls, and even going for sharp objects to either harm him or myself. Even through these times, he never once left or said I wasn't worth the effort. His love got me through therapy, through getting sober (clean since Sept. 8, 2008), and through my trepidation of going back to school. I didn't think I had what it took to go to college to learn better ways of understanding predators and helping survivors like myself, especially those who never got a sense of justice. When I kept telling myself, "I can't," he always said, "You can." My family has also learned from his example on how to handle certain situations, especially when it comes to someone suffering from anxiety, depression or PTSD. Mostly everyone in my family knows what happened, with full disclosure of details, and have been incredibly proud of where I've come to be in my life. That support is crucial for anyone who is either beginning to heal or is in the deep throes of healing.

I've even learned to speak publicly about my experience. I participate in an advocacy group geared toward survivors and the healing processes we go through in the aftermath of sexual violence. No predator ever stops and thinks about the aftermath they leave with their victims, and this is why it's crucial to have programs available to help those who need to begin healing. It's an unpleasant topic, but once the uncomfortable silence starts to break down and people start to really listen, it's invaluable to learn what a person who has experienced sexual violence goes through, and the various ways to help prevent such crimes from happening. Education is what propels us to find more ways for a victim to begin to heal, because without it, no one can ever truly transition from victim to survivor, like I have.

Paul McComas

Gender: Male
Age: 51
Race/ethnicity: White
Occupation: Author, educator and public speaker.
Location: Evanston, Ill.
Relationship to victim: Boyfriend

WHILE WALKING HOME ALONE one muggy night in September 1984, my first-ever girlfriend—a talented theater and music student whom I'd known since she was 12 and I was 13—was overpowered by a male stranger in a downtown Milwaukee alley. I wish I could refer to her as a "rape survivor" rather than a "rape victim"; I can't, because she didn't survive. Six months later, traumatized, desperate and depressed, she took the wrong step—namely, off the roof of the tallest building on the UW-Milwaukee campus.

She was 21 years old.

I suppose that, in many different ways ever since, I've been trying in vain to undo her tragic end.

By re-editing and enhancing the short films she and I shot together in our teens (in which she expertly played, among other roles, a starship captain, a primatologist, and a voodoo priestess), and then screening them at festivals worldwide, I've showcased her early acting talent. By basing the character "Stefanie Slocum" in my 2008 coming-of-age novel *Planet of the Dates* on my girlfriend as she was at 16 and 17, I took the winsome, winning, mischievous girl I loved, and re-imagined her as an irresistible literary character. By bringing healing to the heroine of my 2002 debut novel *Unplugged*—the story of an initially suicidal female musician's fight to recover from a series of childhood rapes committed by her mother's boyfriend—I rewrote my girlfriend's final chapter, in the hope of affirming girls and women like her. Both *Unplugged* and my 20-month cross-country book-store tour for it were, at their core, less a commercial or even a professional enterprise than a ministry, a mission: a plea for victims of rape and other trauma to get help, keep going, reclaim all that is rightly theirs—and never, ever give up.

Then there's my work with the Rape, Abuse and Incest National Network (RAINN). The nation's largest anti-sexual-violence organization, RAINN was founded 18 years ago with the help of musician Tori Amos. The blue RAINN bracelet I've worn continuously since I got it, and will wear for life, symbolizes the fact that this heroic organization and its mission are, like my memories of my girlfriend, a permanent part of who I am. Hence my ongoing efforts over the past decade to help RAINN financially, creatively and through advocacy and outreach.

Appointed to its Speakers Bureau last year and to its National Leadership Council in 2012, I'm now working with RAINN more closely than ever. This helps me as well as helping others, for through the work, I'm finally finding a measure of peace about the tragedy that befell my long-ago girlfriend. You see, RAINN and its affiliated rape-crisis centers don't just educate the public to prevent sexual violence and help victims transition into survivors; they also help the loved ones of those who didn't make it, enlisting our aid on behalf of others. They've saved so many—and in a very real sense, they're saving me, too.

My onetime girlfriend gave me the mission, but my work in rape prevention/education and rape-victim advocacy has given me the means. For that, I am and forever will be inexpressibly grateful.

There is, of course, no way to bring back the young woman I lost—the young woman the *world* lost. The curly-wavy auburn hair; the blue-gray eyes, sparkling with smarts and wit; the frequent wisecracks and the daily surprised-and-surprising observations...all of these are gone forever, have been gone now for 28 years. But while it's true that nothing can ever bring her back, it's also true that nothing is, or ever can be, more important than preventing today's and tomorrow's rape/abuse/incest victims from themselves taking, as she did, the wrong step.

If you have been affected by this issue—or even if you haven't, but nonetheless empathize with those who have—then please, volunteer at your local rape-crisis center, or join RAINN or a similar organization. Reach out, speak out, contribute, help. We possess the means to intervene—and we must. For to witness and work on behalf of these girls and boys, young women and young men, is truly to hand them back their lives.

Jennifer Ann

Gender: Female
Age: 30
Race/ethnicity: White
Occupation: Server/recording artist
Location: Philadelphia, Pa.
Age abuse occurred: 7

ANYONE WHO HAS experienced sexual abuse as a child is familiar with the feelings of insecurity, shame, low self-esteem and a false sense of guilt. I was abused by my uncle around the age of 7. After years of silence, I am finally finding my voice. I recently turned 30 and am just at the beginning stage of the healing process.

Many abusers are someone in the family, a family friend or someone who is looking after the child with the parents trust that their child is safe and free of harm. Children that have been victimized are burdened by the fear of disclosing the abuse, and harbor feelings of confusion with regard to their sense of self. Dissociation and blocking particular memories of the abuse can have a detrimental effect on the healing process. Unknowingly, victims can regress in their recovery, and may likely experience setbacks in their personal and professional lives as adults.

There have been a multitude of challenges in the aftermath of the physical and emotional trauma I suffered. In my life, I've had struggles with addiction to drugs and alcohol. I've had periods of promiscuity, reckless behavior and a lack of self-control. This has made life difficult, and it's hard to break the repetition of these self-defeating behaviors. Rebelling and acting out has been an ongoing characteristic in my personality. Whether at school, work or home, following rules and structure have remained a challenge. Post traumatic stress, anxiety, poor contraceptive practices, impulsive/dangerous behavior, lying, stealing, truancy, social withdrawal and depression have all been major issues for me. I seemed to have no regard for authority figures and often disrespected my teachers, parents, police, bosses and anyone who tried to tell me how to act or what to do.

I have had a very difficult time maintaining any healthy relationship with a man. Many times, my relationships with men have been manipulative and abusive. Because of my uncle taking advantage of my vulnerability as a child, I have been re-victimized because I have yet to let go of the naïve child inside. Re-victimization is very common among sexual-abuse survivors. This is why it is so important to get therapy as soon as possible. The longer the abuse festers and is not treated, the more sick the victim may get and recovery becomes more difficult and drawn out.

After years of this behavior, I became more depressed and volatile at home. I would have frequent crying episodes and tantrums. This was a coping mechanism for me; it was the only way I knew to express my repressed anger and confusion. My parents knew that my behavior was erratic and different from my peers. I started noticing that my friends had more control over their emotions, and my feeling different than everyone else isolated me further. I began creating my own world in my mind, often daydreaming and always somewhere else instead of the present moment. Maybe this, too, was a coping skill. Not knowing the right ways to deal with my emotions, this was a way for me to subconsciously block it out.

A false sense of entitlement has been another symptom for me. Feeling as though I were an exception to the rule, above the law and could do or say no wrong. This only further disconnected me from my peers, family and authority.

I have frequently pushed love away. I run away from sincerity and truth, only to end up with bitterness and lies time and time again. I have often exaggerated, and have had grandiose visions of success and becoming filthy rich and famous. My family would tell me I was living in a fantasy world and that my reality was skewed. However, I always thought it was possible and dreamed of one day achieving the highest level of success. It was the intangible that most intrigued and motivated me. I was repeatedly setting myself up for failure, which made it difficult to succeed and flourish in any of my endeavors. My expectations of myself and others were way off the charts, and I would end up feeling defeated, beaten down and hopeless.

Not only did I continue to hurt myself, but my family and friends suffered also as a result of my behavior. Not understanding or able to put myself in their shoes, I was often labeled selfish, self-seeking, ungrateful and lacking common courtesies. However, I was so wrapped up in my own bubble that I didn't see how inconsiderate I really was. Because of this, I slowly began noticing that my family and friends started to become more and more distant. I was embarrassed to explain how I was feeling, and so I would shut them out, not return calls, not respond to invitations, and often rescheduled last-minute after making plans to get together. I had no regard for their time, as I was always on my own watch. This made those close to me feel as if they were unimportant and neglected. I, on the other hand, didn't see anything wrong with it and honestly thought that they didn't even care.

I am just beginning to reconnect and re-establish friendships that drifted away. I have begun to realize the importance of having a few good friends, and how life seems a little lighter with a good support system. I've learned that to make and keep friends, you must be able to give and take. It's not fair if the friendship is one-sided. It will never survive. Like plants that need water to live and grow, we need friends to help us do the same.

After years of struggling in my daily life, I am finally able to stop blaming myself and take action on the road to true healing. I'm discovering that being around others and staying active is essential to one's happiness and well-being.

For those who have trouble sharing their stories with words, there are so many other forms of self-expression and many artistic ways to show how you really feel. For me, it has always been music. With music, I never feel alone. I have been singing since I could talk, and it has always helped me free my mind and feed my soul.

Exercise and meditation are also other great practices for letting go of negative feelings and aggression. This has helped me greatly since I began making it routine in my schedule. Relaxing, stretching and breathing deeply are also other forms of therapeutic practice.

I encourage anyone who reads this to please help those who have been through this nightmare. Children are the future, and their protection is crucial in fostering intelligent and emotionally sound adults. I have learned that I deserve to be happy and, most importantly, that I am alive and every day is a new start.

Cherish the day. Be free. Love much. Laugh more.

Tanya

Gender: Female
Age: 37
Race/ethnicity: White
Occupation: College-educated professional
Location: Portland, Ore.
Age abuse occurred: 2-4

IT'S HARD TO REMEMBER back when I was an innocent little girl, and often wonder if I ever truly was. My body's and my mind's healing balms blocked out much of the pain, but I was very aware sexually from an early age—a terrible, terrible burden that I will always carry.

The assault on my body, mind and spirit started at what I always thought was age 4. It was 1979 and I was with my mother in Rapid City, S.D., for a meeting with Shaklee, home-based business that sold nutritional bars and supplements. It was a split-level house and I was upstairs with my mom in the meeting with the other adults. Suddenly, a teenager appeared on the shag staircase and beckoned to me to come downstairs to the basement. In my gut, I knew it was bad idea. Until this day, I cannot stand the sight of someone beckoning. My mother scooted me downstairs against my wishes. "Just go play," she said. And so I went.

Before long I was in a closed room with androgynous teenager who I found out was a girl. She told me that she was going to touch me, and unless I obliged, I would have to touch her, too. For a few agonizing minutes, I endured the violation and went home a very depressed and forever changed child. During the abuse, something felt awfully familiar that I would only fully realize many years later.

Never in my life had I been warned about or told what to do if someone violated me, but my spirit knew the right thing. I told my mom. I told her that she must talk to this girl's parents. I begged her to. So what did she do?

She did nothing. Absolutely nothing.

Life carried on and the abuse affected my feelings about myself, it leaked into every fiber of my life and of my being. Throughout grade school, I felt like people knew I was different, violated. I was unable to ever truly relate to the feeling of child-like innocence. The fact that I grew up with an alcoholic ex-marine for a father who treated us kids like his recruits did not help.

I began having nightmares as early as age 5 or 6. They were always the same. I am in a hot-tub-style bathtub in a room with planked wooden walls. There is a man giving me a bath and he is pouring a liquid from a bottle with a green Mr. Yuk sticker (Mr. Yuk was a public-awareness campaign during the 1980s that warned children against ingesting poisons.) The man pours the poison in the water, my vagina burns, he leaves me there, and I die.

For the longest time, these dreams made no sense. I had not, to my knowledge, been to a place with hot tubs enclosed in wood planked rooms. Then, over time, I began to realize that this man was my grandfather and that he had molested me countless times while bathing me as a child when I lived with him, my grandmother and my mother for more than a year while my dad was stationed in Greece. I was 2 years old.

In early adulthood, I found out that my grandfather was a repeat child molester and had molested several immediate and extended family members. I learned that he had also come from sexual abuse.

In an effort to heal, I reached out to several extended family members. My efforts were squelched. I was cut off, criticized, shamed and made to feel like a bad person.

Some things just don't need to be talked about. How dare you ruin your cousin's image of his grandfather!

Rather than fighting back, I quickly realized that this reaction was a result of an even bigger patriarchal system that, on my own, I could not take on.

To this day the feelings are raw and visceral. My body is physically affected when talking or thinking about the violations.

Back in the 1990s, I read *The Courage to Heal* and took identity as a sexual-abuse victim. After four good years of therapy, I no longer identify myself that way.

In a nice gesture of karma or the universe smiling on me, I am happy to share that all of my sexual partners in adulthood have been loving, gentle and kind. I do not have any residual sexual hang-ups from the abuse. I consider myself blessed and lucky. I do have to give myself credit here: I did the work and it was not easy. I faced it head-on like I do nearly everything in my life. And I am better for it.

I am a daughter, a friend, a sister, a lover, and I will no longer allow that experience to claim me as it did for so many years.

Anonymous

Gender: Female
Age: Mid-40s
Race/ethnicity: Native American/Caucasian
Occupation: Scientist
Location: Minnesota
Age abuse occurred: 1-5; 14-16; 22+

IN MY FAMILY, keeping the secret has caused as much or more pain as the abuse itself. The abuser in my family targeted our youngest children, and envisioning his actions makes me feel physically sick. I am still estranged from my entire family after more than a decade because of my decision to stand up to the abuser. My family members tried to destroy my integrity, my sanity, my children's lives and my very soul, and the pain continues to this day. It is a struggle to simply live a normal life in the face of such betrayal from those who should have been most trustworthy. My work now focuses on understanding abusers and those who protect them, and my own tendency to be drawn into abusive relationships.

I have been on the path of survival for decades. Because of that, I know that the best revenge is to live well and develop loving relationships with friends and family. If this is done, people can regain a sense of joy. Each person who finds a way to overcome the pain diminishes the power of abusers everywhere. This work is truly honorable.

But most of us are shamed for telling our stories. I believe the main reason other people try to silence us is because they wish to remain in a state of denial—it seems easier and safer. Another significant reason is that abusers are very good at deflecting the blame away from themselves. If people truly understood the nature of abusers, they would demand that they be held accountable for their actions. Another reason is that abusers don't want to give up their control over the victim.

For survivors, shutting away the truth is like forcing an inflated ball underwater—it always pops back up. It's much better overall to take a direct approach to healing by facing and accepting what happened. Allowing abuse to continue leads to an ever-widening problem that destroys the lives of individuals and their families. Allowing it to continue also perpetuates the cycle from one generation to the next. In order to heal, survivors should accept that what happened was not their fault, but also realize that they are the only ones who can heal themselves.

Here are some suggestions, or healing tools, that I have found useful:

1. Keep moving. Do anything at all you can to physically move. This may involve walking, running, sewing, cooking, fixing the car, playing an instrument, singing, or any activity that keeps you moving. It does not have to be productive. Survivors tend to get stuck in motionless remorse. The shock, grief and depression of sexual abuse can immobilize our bodies, leaving our minds hopelessly spinning or zoned out. Movement brings relief from sadness and creates positive thoughts. If you find that movement is difficult, try focusing your mind completely on one activity at a time, and when that is completed, move to the next activity.

2. Practice your spirituality and sacred rituals. Whatever faith you follow, nurture it each day in some way. A healthy spirit provides the inspiration to keep walking along the right path.

3. Forgive yourself. At first, this may seem impossible to do. However, it is a necessary and vital part of the whole process. Tell yourself, "I completely forgive myself for all the mistakes, all bad choices, and for every single time I hurt myself or someone else." Even though others may not admit to what they have done, you may not talk to them, or they might be angry, you still hold the power to forgive yourself and no one can take that away. Do it now. For me, the hardest person to forgive has been myself. This has been necessary because I have become involved with abusive men who harmed me and my children and I feel guilty because I "let it happen." Although I know intellectually that it was not my fault and lots of people are fooled by abusers, I still find it helpful to consciously forgive myself. In addition, we all make mistakes at times, and sometimes it is necessary to make amends in addition to forgiving.

4. Attempt forgiveness of your abuser. This will probably seem ridiculous and pointless and perhaps not even possible. However, realize that it is not necessary to completely forgive the abuser at all times. You can forgive partially. One day you might forgive them 10 percent, the next day 70 percent, the next day 50 percent. The point is to nurture feelings of forgiveness toward the abuser. The reason for trying to forgive is not for the abuser's sake. It is a way to place yourself above them spiritually and emotionally. If you keep holding onto your anger, it will eat away at you and could make you lash out at other innocent bystanders in your life. So do as much forgiving as you can. This does not mean you have to talk to that person and tell them. You are free to keep it entirely to yourself, or to share as you wish. Abusers won't change their ways unless they do a lot of deep inner work and are motivated by extrinsic reasons. Therefore, do not expect any change from an abusive person. They need serious psychological help from qualified people. The important part of forgiving is how sincere you are.

5. Stop all abusive behaviors. This may include drinking excessively, smoking, abusing pills, over-eating sugary foods, etc. Although it might seem like you need these crutches to dull the emotional and psychological pain, chemical abuse actually causes worse pain. What you are doing when you use chemicals is you are taking away your personal ability to control the pain and giving over this job to something else. And that something else will take more and more from you in exchange for removing the pain. If you develop the ability to control your pain without chemicals, and instead rely on your own inner strength, it is like creating your own internal pharmacy that you can call on for free pain relief anytime, anywhere.

6. Do not allow yourself to spend time with abusive friends or family. Be extra careful in choosing with whom you spend time. Your need for intimacy and closeness is normal, but at the same time, your ability to be intimate with a truly loving person will be impaired by sexual abuse. We tend to recreate more abuse in our lives by self-selecting others who are like the abuser. In some cases, we think that if we can fix this person, we will fix the abuser by default. Especially if we grew up in homes where abuse was a normal way of life, we may have a warped and twisted view of what love really is. We might think someone doesn't love us unless they abuse us. This is very sick thinking, but it is common.

7. Open up to the world. If you shut yourself in, you will be isolated and in more pain. Believe there are people out there who will not abuse you, but who will love you truly and provide the safety, security and warmth you are seeking. Weed out any others who are angry, violent or who treat you poorly. Slam the door on the abusers, but open the door to friends, co-workers and family members who honestly care about you.

8. Finally, and most importantly: Don't ever give up. If you ask around, you will find out that you are not alone and that it is absolutely possible to regain a profound sense of joy in your life and to recover from this disease. You do not have to heal every little bit of yourself to feel better.

It's not hard to find others who have had similar experiences since so many are affected by sexual abuse. What is hard is to get these others to talk about it openly. Nonetheless, it can be very helpful to find a support group who can validate what you have experienced and your feelings. Since I have dealt with these same issues for many years and spoken with many others who have been sexually abused, I know that one day all of your efforts will pay off and your life will be justly blessed.

Appendix:
Advocates Speak Out

* * *

Jackie Block Goldstein, MSW, LSW

Occupation: Associate director and child forensic interview specialist, Philadelphia Children's Alliance

PEOPLE ASK ME what I do all the time, and when I say that I'm a forensic interviewer, they are generally either morbidly curious ("Like on *Law & Order: SVU*?") or totally turned off ("Cool, I like pizza"). Occasionally, I get people who actually ask what it means, and I try to come up with a digestible way to explain that I talk to children who have disclosed sexual abuse or assault after it has been reported to the police department or the Department of Human Services. I take their investigative statements in a neutral, non-traumatizing way that is not suggestive and meets the needs of investigators, so that kids don't have to be interviewed multiple times by people who may not know how to talk to them in a developmentally appropriate manner. I know, it's a mouthful. After all of that, I used to expect that people would remark about the intricacies of doing an investigative interview with a child or the complexity of navigating the competing needs of law enforcement and child welfare. But now I'm pretty much re-signed to the routine response of, "Talking to kids about sexual abuse? That must be so depressing."

Most of the time, I just shrug, partially because it's too complicated to go into (and I'm not sure people really want an in-depth response) and partially because I don't think that I've ever really allowed myself to reflect on the impact that 10 years of forensic interviews with thousands of sex-ually abused children has had on me. Maybe I've done that in part as a cop-ing mechanism—hearing about abuse every day has to take its toll—and maybe it's also because I don't like the exposure, the vulnerability that comes with talking about my own experiences. How hypocritical is that? Sitting down with a 6-year-old who I have known for exactly 10 minutes, I fully expect him to share the most personal and traumatic experience of his life in extreme detail, but I'm not even willing to discuss the impact that hearing those stories has had on my life. So in an effort to practice what I preach, here goes.

I think everyone is a pedophile. Most people meet someone and their initial impression has to do with what the person looks like, how firm her handshake is or what kind of a car he drives. But not me. I know this be-cause while out with my mother, who struck up a conversation with the man standing next to us waiting for his latte, she remarked, "He seemed nice." My response was, "He *seemed* like a child molester!" When my mother pointed out that my reaction was probably a bit extreme, I com-pletely dismissed it and noted that if 1 in 4 girls and 1 in 6 boys are sexually abused before they turn 18, probability is on my side. And this was not an isolated incident. In reflecting on it, it appears that my instinct is always to regard someone with suspicion versus giving them the benefit of the doubt—to assume the worst in everyone until proven otherwise. Before you contact me with a list of great therapists in the area, rest assured, my psychiatrist is aware of the problem. While talking about ways to relieve stress, she mentioned getting a babysitter to watch the kids and going out on a Saturday night. "Get a babysitter?" I asked, incredulous. "How could I possibly relax and go out knowing that someone was in my house sexually abusing my children?" She pointed out that in all likelihood, the 16-year-old girl down the street was not going to sexually abuse my kids, but it was no use. I haven't gone out on a Saturday night since.

I assume that all later-in-life issues are the direct result of a history of child sexual abuse. At the start of every *Biggest Loser: Weight Loss Edition*, I make an internal bet with myself about how far into the show the disclosure of abuse will be revealed. The same is true for *Hoarders, Intervention, Celebrity Rehab with Dr. Drew*, and *16 and Pregnant*. OK, yes, I watch too much TV, and low-quality TV at that (don't take it personally, Dr. Drew)—but that's not the point. Last week on *Today*, they led into the commercial break with the teaser that Justin Bieber's mom was going to come on next to talk about her book and all of the obstacles that she faced as a child. I literally said out loud to myself, "sex abuse," and three minutes later, while the rest of the nation was probably shocked, my suspicions were confirmed as quickly as they had developed. I'm looking for it all the time, and I do believe that for kids who experience abuse and never get any help or support because they don't have the opportunity to disclose in a safe place, that is often the final outcome. It's a huge reason why I do what I do every day. That critical moment, where a child weighs the enormous risk of speaking out, is what tips the scale in the direction of health, happiness, safety and success instead of despair, fear, self-harm and failure. In that moment, I have the enormous responsibility of helping that child to see that people do care, that it can be safe to tell, that help is available, and that a positive life trajectory is within their reach. And what greater motivation could there be to go to work every day?

I wake up every morning at 4 a.m. with my heart racing. Scanning my room quickly and listening for the sound of footsteps, I wait a minute to make sure everything is as it should be before going back to bed. It's gotten better over time; when I first interviewed Maya*, I woke up every hour on the hour with the same routine. Maya was a young girl who was sexually assaulted and abducted from her bedroom one night at 4 a.m. With no signs of forced entry and no offender identified, the entire investigative team, myself included, was desperate to figure out who did this. We all suspected a family member, and in some ways, I think that deep down, there was a part of me that wanted it to be true. If it was her stepfather or her older brother and not a total stranger, I could rationalize that something like that could never happen to me or my loved ones, and then the world would make sense again. But if it was truly a family member, how would Maya ever recover after such a betrayal of trust? As I sat in my office before the interview, I agonized over how I could possibly make this child feel safe enough to tell me what happened. How would I get through the interview at all without completely breaking down? How could I force myself to focus on the mechanics of the interview without allowing myself to truly take in the absolute horror that this child must have felt waking up in the middle of the night with a man standing over her bed before covering her head with a bag, taking her from her house and assaulting her repeatedly in an abandoned lot? I'm not sure how it happened, but somehow we both got through it, and no, I didn't cry. If you're curious, I have never cried during an interview (people ask me all the time)—but I have after the fact. I stayed busy for the rest of the work day and was fine—it wasn't until later that night when I checked the front door of my house to find that my husband had left the keys in the lock that I completely lost it. Crying on the floor of my kitchen, I didn't know how I would go back to my office. While contemplating the logistics behind quitting my job in favor of opening up a bakery in Vermont (which would have been a complete failure, by the way, since I can't bake), I realized that as much as I was struggling to process what had happened, none of this was about me—it was about Maya. She was the one who would have to somehow figure out a way to move on—to go back to sleeping, eating, going to school, putting one foot in front of the other, and do all of this when it seemed like every shred of trust that she had in the world had been taken from her. And that put everything into perspective.

So with that, I'm grateful. Doing what I do has made me grateful every day that my kids are safe and my family is healthy and that I have the amazing opportunity to gain strength through osmosis from the incredible kids and families that come to Philadelphia Children's Alliance. At such tender ages, these children experience horrific, horrific abuse and somehow manage to move on with their lives to do incredible things. Occasionally, I have the privilege of seeing the kids that I have interviewed years later, and in the back of my mind, I expect them to look so broken. Seeing their smiling faces, their growth, the wonderful people that they are becoming reminds me that they are not victims—they are survivors.

To the many children who have shared their stories with me over the years, and to the parents who trusted me with their most valuable possessions—who allowed their children to walk back with me into that room to talk about the things that keep them up at night—and to the countless victims out there who have not yet found their voices: I write this for you. I am eternally grateful for the lessons that you have taught me and for the grace that you show every day by overcoming adversity and fighting relentlessly to get back on the path to the beautiful life that every one of you deserves. You inspire me more than I could ever put into words. I am truly thankful.

* * *

Chris Kirchner, MSW

Occupation: Executive director, Philadelphia Children's Alliance

AS THE EXECUTIVE DIRECTOR of an agency that facilitates a coordinated intervention in child sexual abuse cases in a large urban environment, I am always shocked by the number of reports of alleged child sexual abuse in our community. There were an average of 130 reports per month last year, and we are on target for the same number this year, about 1,600 reports per year. As a result, we don't always have sufficient resources to serve 100 percent of the children in our community who need our services. Right now, we serve an average of 100 children per month, with forensic interviews and victim-support services in a child-friendly environment. We work very closely with police, child welfare, prosecution and medical and mental-health providers in our community to ensure that our response to the allegations does not re-traumatize the child, and is supportive of the caregiver. When I arrive at my office in the morning and check our schedule for the day, that's when the impact of this issue really hits me. Every day, we see three to five kids, and they range in age from 3 to 17. They're both boys and girls, and they come from all socioeconomic levels. Slightly over half of them disclose some level of abuse. Those who do not disclose sometimes admit that something happened, but they cannot bear to talk about it. Some kids don't disclose right away, but have to be brought in a few times to build rapport with the interviewer.

Although I was not sexually abused as a child, this issue has impacted my extended family on both my father's and mother's sides. So, I am reminded of the impact of child sexual abuse at work and at home. I have seen the negative long-term effects of this issue on both a personal and professional level. Yet I also have a sense of optimism and hope that it is possible to stop abuse, and that with proper support and timely treatment, kids and adults can heal.

I have been very impressed by the number of adult survivors of child sexual abuse who have become supporters of our agency. Their experiences are all very different. Most have come to terms with, and are able to speak about, their abuse. They talk about the long road that they have followed to get where they are today. Many were abused long before we talked about abuse in our society. But their common theme is a desire to get this issue out into the open. By talking about their own experiences, and supporting our work, they want to help current victims of sexual abuse to be able to disclose and get help.

I never really set out to make this issue my life's work. It has happened gradually, as I have heard the stories from our children, listened to adult survivors, and truly understood the long-term consequences of abuse when children aren't protected and therapy isn't available. I will continue to do all that I can to prevent child sexual abuse, to intervene effectively when abuse is alleged, and to foster an open dialogue about the extent of this issue in our community.

* * *

Roger A. Canaff

Occupation: Anti-violence advocate, child-protection specialist, legal expert

"SEXUAL VIOLENCE: IT'S a part of the human condition."

As a child-abuse and sex-crimes prosecutor in two jurisdictions, I avoided that conclusion for years. Even after hundreds of cases and a greater number of victims, I didn't want to believe it. I wanted to believe, as most do, that while sexual violence against children and adults is certainly something that occurs, it is a relatively rare event, one that's associated with predictable warning signs to render it avoidable in many circumstances.

To put it another way, I wanted to believe in an ordered universe, in a system of existence, faith-based or not, that would simply make sense to sentient, self-aware beings. We crave that, after all. Human beings can adjust to any reality, and indeed adaptation is the key to mental health in any setting. But given the luxury of reflection and the ability to philosophize, it's design that we long for, even if the design strikes us as rigid or cruel. Chaos is what we fear, and rightfully, because it is random and merciless.

So how can any of us believe that the urge to harm others sexually—to intrude violently or exploitively into this most cloistered of private places—is something that just occurs from time to time within us as human beings? And worse, how can we believe that the phenomenon of sexual abuse is not something that strikes rarely and with fair warning, but with shocking regularity, demonic insidiousness, and in almost all situations within the context of relationships based on trust and familiarity?

It's hard to believe. But it's true.

I have looked into the face of it, the phenomenon of sexual violence. I've seen it in the perpetrators, much more mundane and common-looking than most would imagine, and I've seen it in the survivors, the people I have had the honor of working with as the years slipped by and the evidence in my mind mounted imperceptibly. The numbers alone are staggering, both the research-based figures I am aware of and the ones reflecting my own personal experience.

Against children, the conservative figures for prevalence are 1 in 4 girls, and about 1 in 6 boys. For adults, the lifetime figures are about 1 in 6 women and 1 in 33 men. These figures are far greater than what is seen by law-enforcement professionals. Rather, they stem from confidential victim surveys that have been conducted over time, with surprisingly consistent results.

Even the attempts at getting to the real prevalence of sexual violence through victim surveys fall short of capturing the full reality. Further, what we see in terms of cases reported to authorities is in every figurative sense the tip of the iceberg. Most studies put the rate of reporting sexual violence for adults and children well under 20 percent. When adults are victimized (almost always by an acquaintance or someone closer), the desire to report is usually delayed, if not stopped cold, by a toxic mix of shame, fear, guilt, disbelief and dismay. While the common perception of rape is that of a violent attack by a masked stranger wielding a knife in a dark parking lot, the reality is much different. Most women and men are sexually assaulted not by strangers but by acquaintances, whether known for a few hours in a bar, several months on a college campus or military unit, or by a friend, family member, lover or other close confidant.

The rapists are not usually criminally versatile, objectively scary looking men with masks and handheld weapons. Instead, they are almost always similar in color, culture and social circumstances to their victims. The weapons they use are not knives and guns but alcohol, trust, isolation and shame. They seek victims who either won't report the crime or won't be believed if they do. They exploit the (in hindsight) regrettable choices victims make, such as drinking or using drugs. They seek out victims with disabilities (at a nightmarish rate) or those with real or perceived weaknesses or challenges. So, a woman with a reputation for lying, or for being overly dramatic or emotional becomes an ideal target. "Closeted" men struggling with sexual identity or identifying as homosexual are targeted for their fear of being exposed as such. Women violating culturally embedded standards of decency such as dress, language or sexual behavior fall victim twice, once to their rapist and then again to the community that either rejects them as scheming liars, or shrugs and claims that they reaped what they sowed.

Interestingly, replicated and sound research reveals that most men are not sexually violent, contrary to earlier beliefs that all men are potential rapists due to a pernicious mix of testosterone, intoxicants and cultural influences. In fact, it is a relatively small percentage of men who commit acts of sexual violence against adult peers (men or women), and do so over and over again. The disorderedness that creates the urge to victimize is actually neither common nor necessarily innate. Rather, it is relatively rare but prolific. Abusers rape, and usually rape again and again. The origins of the urge remain disturbingly mysterious.

With child sexual abuse, the dynamics are similar in complexity with the added helplessness and lack of sophistication that defines childhood in large measure. Younger children are held less responsible for choices that predators exploit (such as agreeing to a car ride, or the offer of a gift), but this changes very quickly as the victim approaches adolescence. Even young teens are widely perceived (or can be made to appear) as precocious, savvy seducers getting what they wanted from older "lovers." By the time a victim is 14 or 15, she or he can expect, in most places, to be judged as harshly as adults when it comes to how she dressed, how she behaved, who she kept time with and where she went in the context of her victimization.

As with adults, children are far less likely to disclose abuse the closer the perpetrator is to them emotionally and physically. Biological parents—mostly, but not exclusively, fathers—commit an unexpectedly large percentage of sexual abuse. A child in such a situation, particularly a younger child, or one with a cognitive or physical disability, is not likely to disclose at all. Either the abuse occurs so early in life that it becomes an expected though unpleasant ritual with no context in which to view it, or it very clearly presents itself as something the child discloses at her peril. Child predators are masterful and utterly ruthless when it comes to instilling fear, shame and a demand for secrecy within their victims. Threats, direct or implied, are not only frightening but starkly believable. "If you tell, it's just not me that mom and your sisters will hate. They'll hate you, too."

Indeed, they might. Nonoffending family members in many instances react in ultimately understandable but initially callous-appearing ways. The idea that one's father, spouse or live-in lover could be capable of sexually abusing a child within the same household is often a concept that can't be grasped. Family members may equivocate in a foggy, tortured, uninformed reflex. Or worse, they may secretly acknowledge that the abuse probably happened but curse the child who unearthed it and the shaming of the family that followed. In rare but deeply disturbing cases, a targeted child is abused to the tacit approval of others in the family for a variety of reasons. Whatever the unspoken dynamic, even young children readily sense it. But their insight is usually one step behind that of the predator's. He knew already.

For the few children who do disclose, the process (and it is indeed a process and not an event) is often a tortured one. Disclosure often occurs under the worst possible conditions that render them the most unbelievable victims. Kids who accommodate the emotional weight of sexual abuse sometimes act out in adolescence, engaging in high-risk, unhealthy lifestyles that make them seem as if they are simply out-of-control teenagers rebelling against the needed guidance and authority of the offender rather than his abuse. Other victims assume a porcelain persona of perfection throughout adolescence. They earn excellent grades and noted achievements in a desperate attempt to either win the abuser's mercy, or at least protect the family from public ruin and scorn. Either way, the disclosure, when it happens, is often halting, imperfect and unpalatable to the criminal justice and child-protection systems. It many times falls on deaf ears. The child is not believed, and the abuse either continues or remains unpunished. Worse, many children recant their valid claims once the nightmares the abuser promised indeed come true, and the family is publicly humiliated, siblings are relegated to foster care, and the victim is ostracized and resented.

This is why it's not reported. This is why it's not believed or properly dealt with when it is reported. The obvious question, then, is, "What now?"

With regard to children, the dynamics of child sex abuse must be understood so that the behavior of kids experiencing it can be understood. We must be able to accept and understand what children go through so that our response is not compromised when the disclosures we receive occur. Children of any age are capable of lying about being sexually abused, but the incidence of such behavior is rare, and attempts to create "syndromes" and other explanations to suggest otherwise have never proven scientifically replicable or sound. The vast majority of children alleging sexual abuse are being truthful, period. Most never disclose to authorities. This is changing, but it remains obdurate.

We must also acknowledge and guard against the role that institutions play in both child and adult-focused sexual violence. Institutions can be as formal and traditional as the Boy Scouts and as hierarchal as the Catholic Church. They can be as abstract as marriage or fatherhood. Both types can create fertile environments for sexual predators. But the formal institutions we create, particularly the ones we most venerate, are often the ones that attract, protect and supply those among us who would harm children. This is because institutions, religious, communal and otherwise, often provide predators with the three things they require: a steady supply of trusting victims, a cover for what they truly are (cloaked by the role they are playing) and a bureaucracy that will conceal them or move them when they are detected. The reasons are myriad, but they generally come down to a single concept: The institution, because of its value to the world and to its beneficiaries, must be protected despite what it occasionally generates. The larger and more important the institution, the more it arguably produces for humanity, then the more a single individual—a boy or a girl— is lost as grist for the mill. This is tragically misguided but shockingly common. The Catholic Church, among other major religious institutions, continues to deal with exactly this type of institutional infiltration by predators. More recently, Penn State University has suffered deeply due to an undetected predator within its midst that neutered the great school's leadership—either cynically or simply foolishly—into tragic inaction.

In the wake of Penn State in particular, we should expect many other institutions to be revealed for what they often are: venerable, but vulnerable creations of man that can be used in a ruinous mockery of their design. Scouting, athletic leagues, youth organizations of all kinds—particularly when they involve at-risk youth or children with disabilities—are ones that predators traditionally target.

The good news is that we can immensely reduce the ongoing nightmare of child sexual abuse if we are willing to demystify the institutions we create. We must control them, transparently, rather then letting them blind us and harbor predators in exchange for the prizes they exact. Until we do that, until we learn to value the fate of every single individual touched by the institution as much as the institution itself, we are destined to lose our loved ones to the predators within them.

Additionally, despite sound studies to the contrary, far too many people within and outside of law enforcement believe the myths—themselves gleefully relied upon by perpetrators—that women commonly "cry rape" falsely in order to re-claim their virtue after an indiscretion, or to quiet the concerns of some other lover or concerned party. Does it occasionally happen? Certainly. Is it common? Absolutely not. Is there anything about enduring a criminal investigation, an intrusive physical examination, and the rigors of the criminal justice process that make falsely "crying rape" an attractive option for a shamed or scorned woman? No, and it is nonsense to assert otherwise. Indeed, the usual reaction of a woman emerging from a situation of clear sexual violence is disbelief, self-blame and self-doubt. Cases in which the circumstances are less than clear invite even more of these doubts, and in almost all cases are simply endured and processed as best they can be.

Finally, we must focus on what heals survivors of sexual violence, whether children or adults, most effectively, deeply and completely. Among the most prominent factors is the reaction they receive from the person to whom they disclose. If that reaction is one of sympathy, affirmation and support, the survivor is far more likely to heal more quickly and thoroughly. This is not only the right thing to do; it is also the smart thing to do as well-supported survivors at any age will more readily and effectively interact with the systems that can hold perpetrators accountable. The opposite, though, is also true. If the survivor encounters a victim-blaming, unsupportive response, she is much more likely to heal more slowly and be of less value to authorities seeking a perpetrator.

The restoration of dignity, above all, is what everyone should have most prominently on their minds when they behold a survivor of sexual violence, regardless of her or his age or circumstances. It is that restoration that ensures just healing for the victim, and just desserts for the perpetrator, most often hidden from view.

* * *

Mallika Kaur

Occupation: Staff attorney at Community Overcoming Relationship Abuse (CORA), a domestic-violence agency in Northern California

SOME THINGS ARE TABOO. Rape is not one of them.

Sex sells, and rape is retailed every day—on our sitcoms, movies, daily news—as its sordid shadow. We participate in a very selective telling of the rape story: inextricably linked to passion and/or sickness and/or confusion. Seldom power or patriarchy or choice. It is often conveniently linked to race, culture or religion and seldom recognized as a tool of control, oppression or war.

My own initiation into working with rape victims coincided with the launch of the U.S. war in Afghanistan. First lady Laura Bush told the nation in her November 2011 radio address that "the people of Afghanistan—especially women—are rejoicing" after the U.S. attack, while "civilized people throughout the world are speaking out in horror" on realizing that "brutal oppression of women is a central goal of the terrorists." At the same time, I was struggling with my own realizations about the violence against women in this "civilized" nation, set against the constant message that we should be grateful and proud that we are so much better off than everywhere else (and face only mere aberrations and no systemic problems like the rest of the forsaken uncivilized world).

Having grown up in South Asia, before coming to college in Chicago, I had experienced the feeling of sheer liberation walking down the street without constant stares, taunts and occasional attempted grabs. I had slowly let down my guard coming home at dusk, let my shoulders drop slightly, stopped hesitating to bend down and pick up the occasional autumn leaf, untightened my jaw, and unclenched my fists. Indeed, even walking around the block can be somewhat of a drill exercise for women in many parts of the world. And then I responded to my first emergency room call.

Through our hours of training at Chicago's veteran rape-crisis group, Rape Victim Advocates, we had prepared for this call. My friends and I were now state-certified rape-crisis counselors. We had studied and discussed, in gut-wrenching detail, rape kits, STD screenings, rape trauma syndrome, and even logistical details of carrying some snacks, toiletries and light reading in our blue RVA bags. As I got off the phone with the ER, having learned that the victim was a 14-year-old girl, I clenched the bag into my tight fist, picked up the pace, and set out to hail a cab with resolution. And dread. (Not before first spraying some perfume on my wrist; planning to sniff my sleeve should the stench of the hospital be too much, or should I need something pungent to get myself together.)

Once I finally got through the doors of the ER—after producing my RVA identification and beeper and other 'proof' to the incredulous guard who insisted I was "too young to have been called in by the rape nurse"—I stood in silence. A young nurse finally directed me to the room. Again I stood for a minute, bracing myself for the broken victim. I knocked gingerly. I sniffed at my sleeve. A kind face peeked through and ushered me in. The mother offered me her seat, as the daughter sat on the bed, swinging her legs. I introduced myself, and the mother thanked me for coming. I smiled weakly, almost wanting to ask if I was in the right place. The mother felt bad because her shift at work just let out a few hours ago, and so this was the earliest she could bring her child in to the ER "to get checked." The child, neatly dressed with a large school backpack lying next to her, asked me if I'd like to help her with her homework. I barely hid my incredulity. The mom explained that her daughter was not going to school for the rest of the week "given everything," but she must keep up with all the work. "Her sister will get her all updates and the homework," she explained.

If it hadn't been for the training at RVA, if it hadn't been for the repeated lesson of being present for the survivor and not for myself, if it hadn't been for the instructions to neither judge nor to project, if it hadn't been for Nissa and Kavitha, my sisters-in-training with whom I spent countless evenings processing my own prejudices around such violence, the next hour would have been absolutely impossible. For I, like most other people I know, had received most of my education about rape victims from films and from my obsession with *Law & Order: SVU*. The bloodied and crawling victim, the psychopathic abuser, the centrality of fierce law enforcement, the enraged and often inconsolable family member.

We sat doing homework. The nurse came in and gave some STD pills. We returned to the homework. The doctor peeked in to say the rape kit would be administered in another 20 minutes. We got back to the homework. The mother had to leave for a phone call from the relative watching the girl's siblings, and she asked me to estimate how long the kit would take. We got back to the homework. Then came the crisp knock and jostling in of two police officers. The young girl looked away and her mother nodded. They politely asked me to step outside with them. They didn't question my age or appearance or race or gender. They thanked me for coming and then dropped to a conspiratorial tone. About being sick of the rates of sexual assault in this community, and the under-reporting, and the need for me to tell them what I knew. Perhaps it was a good thing I didn't know what they already did: the rape by the boyfriend, the subsequent rape by another classmate, and the abandonment in an unknown apartment for the hours after. As I stared at the officers silently, I somehow convinced them I was withholding information. "Look, you are a college student, doing well. Your community works hard and isn't like this. You have to help her ... And her mother is a single mother that doesn't care, doesn't think this is a big deal." I muttered my legally mandated and protected confidentiality with the victim, and turned around, thinking I would return to more homework. But I was met with frantic eyes. The mother sat hugging her daughter, and singing softly. The assiduous student was shivering and panicked.

I finally broke the tense silence. I told them again that I was from RVA, I was there for them, and I was prohibited from telling anyone anything about what I heard or saw or learnt from them. I also told them the officers were very eager. I didn't tell them how they tried to pit my brownness and University of Chicago education against these women's blackness and assumed backwardness. The mother smiled at me. "But, did they get the video?" her daughter blurted out. Then she started crying. At which point, the mother got up and told me I should speak to her daughter, and that she would give us privacy.

For the rest of the night, between the rape kit, another police team, more medicines, and finally the discharge, I learnt about how the new boyfriend who promised to "do nothing, just hang" had taken her to a friend's empty apartment. How another classmate had shown up. How the boys had taken turns with her and recorded everything on their phone cameras. And how they had told her they would post it across the school if she told anyone. She had told the officers their names and to check their phones. But she didn't want to talk to the officers anymore. Given the neighborhood she lived in, and that she had a younger sister, she just wanted to be done with this and move on. Her mother had brought her to the hospital, and had even coaxed her into telling the cops who was responsible. But her mother didn't see the point in any further interaction, either.

She wanted to return to school work. I delayed her some, rattling off information, ensuring she knew her legal rights and possible avenues of support. But not trying to ensure she did what I thought I would have done. I also told her that feeling a range of emotions—numbness, calmness, fear, pain or nervousness—was normal. She shrugged. She was done. We returned to the homework.

A few hours later, just as we were all leaving post-discharge, an older nurse walked in and closed the door. "Look, you are like my daughter. And I'm telling you what I'd tell her. All men are after one thing. You need to protect yourself, OK? Don't give your mamma here so much heartache." Again, a shrug. I quickly began telling her again that it wasn't her fault, and she shrugged. Mother thanked me for everything and said she understood there was a long road ahead. As I provided her counseling resources, she noted, "I need to talk to my other daughter too, about just knowing what people are capable of ... I need to have these tough talks."

I share this particular story not because it's 'the' rape story of popular imagination. I share it because it exemplified for me the need to leave my own assumptions at home. Because it is one where the survivor was held tightly and guided by someone the survivor loves dearly, despite the pain and failure this person themselves felt.

Nights like these sowed the seeds for an initiative that a few friends and RVA volunteers launched the next year: Southside Sexual Assault and Violence Educators (Southside SAVE). Needless to say, we weren't the most sought-after club on campus. But through presentations in high schools, dorms and community meetings, our young initiative afforded us the space and confidence to speak with the community about the effects of sexual abuse. Many police officers, teachers, nurses, friends, sisters and others who respond to rape with positive intentions also slip into victim-blaming, guided by the pervasive societal norm in which rape is coupled with sex rather than being coupled with criminal code sections.

In the decade since, and now as a lawyer, I have witnessed repeatedly that the stories of healing after a sexual assault are all diverse. They are all difficult. They are all unlike what we see on TV. And they are all stories of survival. And the way a story unfolds is determined by the uniqueness— both constraints and strengths—of each individual and their support system or lack thereof.

These stories challenge our "civilized" society to speak about the real taboos: veiled patriarchy, which is not immediately palpable walking down the road, or into a club, or out of a job interview, or into a relationship, but that nevertheless continues reinforcing notions of masculinity and femininity, which in turn facilitate blaming female victims for what happens to them while often denying male victims that anything ever even happened. We continue accepting rape as the dark side of sex and attribute something uncontrollable, rather than criminal, to the abuser.

I hope it might lead you to understand how so many people you know are in fact silent, but resilient, survivors. I hope it compels you to go and talk to your son, daughter, friend, relative, about both these real dangers and the importance of speaking up for change.

Finally, I hope it encourages thinking about rape in the complicated, real way in which it actually exists: perpetrated by those who haven't been made to check their privilege, on those who lack some form of privilege, and in the context of a nation that is comfortable in the privilege of being relatively better and thus often resists self-evaluation.

My green RVA pin, loyally sticking to one of my weathered bags, is waiting for the day it inspires as much dialogue as it attracts confused eyeballs: *Imagine a World without Rape. What are you doing to Create that World?*

Resources

National

The Rape, Abuse and Incest National Network (RAINN). The nation's largest anti-sexual violence organization partners with more than 1,100 rape-treatment centers around the country. *rainn.org*
National sexual assault hotline: (800) 656-HOPE

MaleSurvivor. Offers support, treatment, research, education, advocacy and activism in the name of overcoming the sexual victimization of boys and men. *malesurvivor.org*

The National Sexual Violence Resource Center (NSVRC). Founded by the Pennsylvania Coalition Against Rape (PCAR), the resource hub collects and disseminates information on sexual violence including statistics, research, position statements, statutes, training curricula, prevention initiatives and program information. *nsvrc.org*
Toll-free hotline: (877) 739-3895

Survivors Network of Those Abused by Priests (SNAP). A support group of survivors with chapters located across the country. *snapnetwork.org*
Philadelphia chapter: (267) 992-9463

The Military Rape Crisis Center. Free crisis care, legal assistance and other services to both active-duty personnel and veterans. *militaryrapecrisiscenter.org*
(202) 540-9060

Pennsylvania

The Pennsylvania Coalition Against Rape (PCAR). A statewide network of 50 rape-crisis centers in all 67 counties in Pennsylvania. *pcar.org*
Toll-free hotline: (888) 772-7227

Philadelphia

Women Organized Against Rape (WOAR). The city's only rape-crisis center offers free counseling, specialized treatment and prevention education services to men, women and children. *woar.org*
24-hour hotline: (215) 985-3333

The Philadelphia Children's Alliance. Coordinates a multi-agency, interdisciplinary response to minimize further trauma to victims of child sexual abuse. *paphiladelphia.nationalchildrensalliance.org*
(215) 387-9500

The John J. Peters Institute. Provides outpatient assessment and treatment services to children and adult victims of sexual abuse. *jjp.org*
(215) 701-1560

ACKNOWLEDGMENTS

IT TOOK US YEARS to get to the point where we could be emotionally ready to get this project off the ground. This book—and our own personal stories in it—simply would not have been possible if we had not endured the healing process, which, as those affected by abuse know, is excruciatingly painful at times. But we are so grateful that we did. And not just for the sake of our marriage, which, of course, was the most important motivator for our healing. *The Survivors Project* is the most important work of journalism either of us has ever done. We are thankful to be in a position to give voice to others who have been silent for so long. We could not have done it alone.

We would like to thank those who supported this project in various forms.

First and foremost, we thank the contributors who wrote essays for this project. We hope this process was as cathartic for you as it was for us.

We thank *Philadelphia Weekly*, which has long been committed to helping victims of sexual violence. Thanks specifically to editor-in-chief Stephen H. Segal, chief operating officer John Gallo, and chairman and chief executive officer Anthony Clifton, who were outspoken in their support of this important project. It's not the easiest thing to discuss, we know.

We thank the advocacy groups, here in Philadelphia and around the country, that helped spread the word about the project and connected us to contributors: the Philadelphia Children's Alliance, Women Organized Against Rape (WOAR), the Pennsylvania Coalition Against Rape (PCAR), the Rape, Abuse and Incest National Network (RAINN) and MaleSurvivor. Thanks also to Dennille Schuler of Ceisler Media for helping us network with local stakeholders. The work you all do to help people reclaim their lives is truly awe-inspiring.

Thanks to family and friends who supported us during this project and especially during the difficult years that led us here: Natalie, Paul, Michael, Alexis and Caitlin Sachdev, our love for you is just too big for words; Patrick Hoffmann, who always knew the truth; Rose Oponski, you will always be a source of inspiration; Todd Hoffmann, who bridged a difficult gap; Denise and Danielle Evans, who took the next step; Michelle Higgins, Mark Stambaugh, Meridith Casino, Mike Tier, Chris Kane and Bill Morefield, you're the best friends anyone could ever ask for; Anastasia Barbalios, your contributions as Work Wife will always be cherished; Anthony Erace, whose eyes are always keen; and everyone else who had to endure our misery through all of this.

A special and heartfelt thanks to Mylisa Kesselman and Carrie Lee, our counselors at WOAR. You gave us the tools we needed to heal ourselves, and our marriage. For that, we are forever grateful.

And to Mia Raya Hoffmann: You've helped us heal in more ways than you could ever comprehend and have given us tremendous hope for the future. We can't wait to meet you.

Made in the USA
Charleston, SC
08 March 2013